Julie Deconinck, Philippe Humblé,
Arvi Sepp, Hélène Stengers (Eds.)

Towards Transcultural Awareness in Translation Pedagogy

Repräsentation – Transformation
representation – transformation
représentation – transformation

Translating across Cultures and Societies

herausgegeben von

Michaela Wolf
(Universität Graz)

This book series is designed to provide a forum for interdisciplinary approaches to the discussion of translation in its wider sense. Special emphasis is given to works which focus on the research of translation and interpreting in their role of (de-)constructing cultures and societies. Particularly welcome is the interaction with neighbouring disciplines (cultural studies, sociology, anthropology, gender studies, literary studies, comparative literature, historiography, etc.).
All texts are peer-reviewed.

Die Reihe ist ein Forum für interdisziplinäre Ansätze in der Diskussion kulturmittlerischer Phänomene im weitesten Sinn. Besonders willkommen sind Arbeiten, die das Übersetzen und Dolmetschen in ihrer Rolle als Beitrag zur (De-)Konstruktion von Kulturen und Gesellschaften untersuchen. Die interaktive Zusammenarbeit mit Nachbardisziplinen (Kulturwissenschaften, Soziologie, Anthropologie, Gender Studies, Allgemeine Literaturwissenschaft, Vergleichende Literaturwissenschaft, Geschichtswissenschaft, etc.) ist ausdrücklich erwünscht.
Alle Texte werden anonym begutachtet.

Band 12

LIT

Towards Transcultural Awareness in Translation Pedagogy

edited by

Julie Deconinck, Philippe Humblé,
Arvi Sepp, Hélène Stengers

LIT

Cover image: Philippe Humblé

Printed with the support of the Brussels Institute of Applied Linguistics (BIAL) at the Vrije Universiteit Brussel

Bibliographic information published by the Deutsche Nationalbibliothek
The Deutsche Nationalbibliothek lists this publication in the Deutsche Nationalbibliografie; detailed bibliographic data are available on the Internet at http://dnb.d-nb.de.

ISBN 978-3-643-90919-0 (pb)
ISBN 978-3-643-95919-5 (PDF)

A catalogue record for this book is available from the British Library

Zweigniederlassung Zürich 2017
Klosbachstr. 107
CH-8032 Zürich
Tel. +41 (0) 44-251 75 05
E-Mail: zuerich@lit-verlag.ch http://www.lit-verlag.ch

Distribution:

In the UK: Global Book Marketing, e-mail: mo@centralbooks.com
In North America: International Specialized Book Services, e-mail: orders@isbs.com
In Germany: LIT Verlag Fresnostr. 2, D-48159 Münster
Tel. +49 (0) 2 51-620 32 22, Fax +49 (0) 2 51-922 60 99, e-mail: vertrieb@lit-verlag.de

e-books are available at www.litwebshop.de

Contents

Julie Deconinck, Philippe Humblé, Arvi Sepp and Hélène Stengers
Introduction:
Towards Transcultural Awareness in Translation Pedagogy 1

THEORETICAL REFLECTIONS ON TRANSLATION PEDAGOGY AND TRANSCULTURALISM

José Lambert
The Position of Translation Training: Another Success Story? 13

Jan Walravens
Towards a Culture-based Paradigm for Translator Training 39

Kanavillil Rajagopalan
Translation as Bridge-building and Transculturation 53

Elżbieta Tabakowska
Grammar, 'Cultural Meaning' and Translation Pedagogy 65

TRANSCULTURALISM IN TRANSLATION TEACHING

Natalia Kaloh Vid and Vlasta Kučiš
Teaching Translation in the Context of Culture and Ideology 79

Natalia Naydenova
Teaching Translation in Banking and Finance:
Cross-cultural Aspects 99

Judith Woodsworth
Transposing Voices: Teaching Interculturalism in a
Literary Translation Course 115

Anna Vermeulen and Ana Ibáñez Moreno
Audio Description as a Tool to Enhance Intercultural Competence 133

THE ASSESSMENT OF TRANSCULTURAL COMPETENCE IN TRANSLATION

Catherine Way
Teaching and Assessing Intercultural Competence:
From Common Ground to Divergence 157

Geoffrey S Koby
Intercultural Errors and Translation Assessment: Two Small
German–English Case Studies 181

June Eyckmans
Cultural Competence in Translation Studies and its Assessment 209

Alexandra Rosiers
How Does a Study-Abroad Experience Contribute to the
Intercultural Competence of Student Translators? 231

List of Contributors 257

Subject Index 263

Name Index 269

Abbreviations and acronyms

3C	Cross-Cultural Competence
ACB	American Council of the Blind
AD	Audio Description
ADLAB	Audio Description: Lifelong Access for the Blind
AENOR	Asociación Española de Normalización y Certificación (Spanish Association for Standardization and Certification)
ARDELE	Audiodescripción como Recurso Didáctico en la Enseñanza de Lenguas Extranjeras (Audiodescription as Didactic Resource in the Teaching of Foreign Languages)
ATA	American Translators' Association
AVANTI	Avances en Traducción e Interpretación
BAI	Broadcast Authority of Ireland
CATS	Canadian Association for Translation Studies
CDA	Critical Discourse Analysis
CDI	Calibration of Dichotomous Items
CEFR	Common European Framework of Reference for Languages
CG	Control Group
CIC	Cultural and/or Intercultural Competence
CIOL	Chartered Institute of Linguists
CNPq	Conselho Nacional de Desenvolvimento Científico e Tecnológico (Brazilian National Council for Scientific and Technological Development)
CTTIC	Canadian Translators, Terminologists and Interpreters Council
CQS	Cultural Intelligence Scale
DTS	Descriptive Translation Studies
ECQA	European Certification and Qualification Association
ECTS	European Credit Transfer and Accumulation System
EG	Experimental Group
ELP	European Language Portfolio
EMT	European Master's in Translation
ESIT	École supérieure d'Interprètes et de Traducteurs (Higher School of Interpreters and Translators)

EST	European Society for Translation Studies
FLA	Foreign Language Acquisition
FLL	Foreign Language Learning
FLT	Foreign Language Teaching
IATIS	International Association for Translation and Intercultural Studies
ICC	Intercultural Communicative Competence
ICS	Intercultural Studies
IDRC	Interpretation, Decisions, Resources and Constraints
IFRS	International Financial Reporting Standards
IMS	Independent Media Support
ISO	International Standard Organization
ITU	International Telecommunication Union
LSP	Language for Specific Purposes
MIT	Massachusetts Institute of Technology
MPQ	Multicultural Personality Questionnaire
MPQSF	Multicultural Personality Questionnaire - Short Form
MT	Machine Translation
ONCE	Organización Nacional de Ciegos de España (Spanish National Organization of the Blind)
PACTE	Procès d'Adquisició de la Competència Traductora i Avaluació (Process for the Acquisition of Translation and Evaluation Competence)
SATI	South African Translators' Institute
SL	Source Language
SLA	Second Language Acquisition
ST	Source Text
TBLL	Task-Based Language Learning
TL	Target Language
TransCert	Trans-European Voluntary Certification for Translators
TrC	Translator Competence
TS	Translation Studies
TT	Target Text

Acknowledgements

First and foremost, the authors wish to thank the blind reviewers for their insightful comments and helpful suggestions. We are also very grateful for the guidance provided by Michaela Wolf, editor of the LIT book series Representation – Transformation. Finally, we wish to thank John Linnegar, Liz Potter and Anja van de Pol-Tegge for their minute attention to detail in editing and formatting this publication.

Julie Deconinck, Philippe Humblé, Arvi Sepp and Hélène Stengers

JULIE DECONINCK, PHILIPPE HUMBLÉ, ARVI SEPP AND HÉLÈNE STENGERS

Vrije Universiteit Brussel

Introduction: Towards Transcultural Awareness in Translation Pedagogy

The recent integration of translation degree programmes into European university curricula is boosting much-needed research in translation pedagogy. The four editors of this volume all teach translation at the Vrije Universiteit Brussel, Belgium, and in our teaching practice we have long subscribed to the notion that all translation, regardless of genre and context, is inherently and fundamentally about communicating between and across cultures. We take it as read that any translation course must first and foremost raise awareness among students that every text is permeated by culture, and that the appraisal of the cultural distance between sender and receiver is a necessary condition for any translational activity to be successful. However, even if such course aims sound fairly straightforward, we realize they may be achieved through a multitude of different teaching approaches and learning methods, many of which are un(der)reported at present. It is for this reason that we decided to invite a wide range of distinct and distinctive voices in Translation Studies to bring their theoretical insights and teaching experiences to bear on the topic at hand: how to tackle the cultural dimension in translation pedagogy.

We believe that the resulting volume showcases the diversity of theoretical perspectives in the field of Translation Studies, and testifies to the myriad of teaching opportunities prompted by the topic of translation and culture. Our contributors' theoretical assumptions are inspired by a variety of disciplines and paradigms, and the more practical contributions present a wide range of tried-and-tested learning activities, covering a multitude of languages, translation genres, and modes of instruction. Some contributions provide pedagogical ideas for a single translation workshop, others for an entire course module, yet others for the curriculum as a whole. Taken together, the variety of contributions shows that the integration of

Translation Studies into the world of academia has created both unprecedented opportunities and new tensions between theory and practice. What our authors do seem to have in common, though, is an unshakeable conviction that the construct of translator competence, however elusive it may be, cannot be disentangled from the construct of (inter/trans)cultural competence.

Before we proceed, however, we must address the thorny issue of terminology. The literature in this field has seen a proliferation of terms; e.g. 'cultural competence', 'cross-cultural awareness', 'intercultural communication', 'multiculturalism', to name but a few, alongside a variety of overlapping definitions. As referenced in both the contributions of Jan Walravens (this volume) and Judith Woodsworth (this volume), the term 'cross-cultural' seems to imply the carrying or bearing of meaning *across* something, such as the divide that could be seen to exist between languages or cultures. In this respect, David Katan (2009: 1) relates cross-cultural competence to being able to mediate between particular countries or cultures, whereas he considers intercultural competence a generic skill, required for any intercultural interaction, regardless of country or culture. As can be seen from a quick glance at the titles of the contributions gathered in this volume, many of our authors favour the term 'intercultural'; intercultural competence is generally associated with the ability to interact meaningfully with people from different cultural backgrounds through an awareness of one's own cultural frame and that of others, as well as the willingness and ability to mediate the difference.

Nevertheless, we decided to use 'transcultural awareness' rather than 'intercultural awareness' in our title, and we must therefore account for this decision. For one, the prefix 'trans-', meaning *beyond* as well as *across*, seems to us more flexible, versatile, and inclusive than its alternatives, features that seem rather fitting in an age of globalization and (super)diversity. Andreas Hepp (2015: 3), for instance, stresses that the concept of 'transcultural' is more abstract than that of 'intercultural', since it involves processes of communication that *transcend* specific cultures or societal groups rather than occurring between individual members of specific groups or cultures. In a similar vein, Sarah Boye (2016) states that the concept of the 'intercultural' implies a rather static and restricted definition of culture and communication, drawing on an image of people from clearly separated, well-defined cultures interacting with each other and overcoming this divide in an equally clearly separated and well-defined 'third space' (cf. Bhabha 1994; Kramsch 2009). The authors in this present volume start from the premise that through translation, cultural differences between dominant cultures are not reinforced but rather renegotiated and transformed. Therefore, as Boye (2016: 48) has it, this idea of 'renegotiation' of cultural identities is "much more clearly carried in the semantics of 'transcultural', implying as it does, the occurrence of transformation". More than 20 years ago, Meinert Meyer (1991, as cited in Eyckmans, this volume) also employed 'transcultural' in the term 'transcultural competence', which he saw as the third and final stage of cultural competence. After the initial 'monocultural' stage, involving a stereotyped and ethnocentric view of the foreign culture, learners reach the 'intercultural level', where they can explain the cultural differences between their own and the foreign culture. Ideally, they then reach the 'transcultural' level, where they can appraise intercultural differences and negotiate their meaning.

Negotiating cultural distance and/or mediating between cultural differences are images, even tropes that emerge repeatedly in the contributions gathered in this volume. Yet more fundamentally, perhaps, the question arises whether we can actually continue to take the idea of different and distant cultures for granted. As argued by Kanavillil Rajagopalan (this volume), against the backdrop of "a fast-shrinking world and ever-growing contact between peoples" (p. 58), a 'cross-pollination' of ideas, languages and cultures is occurring, leading in turn to cultural hybridity and heterogeneity – upending the notions that a culture is a distinct and bounded entity, and that translation always involves the bridging of an assumed divide between one's own culture and that of the other. In *Enlarging translation, empowering translators* (2007), Maria Tymoczko stresses that the activity of translation heightens transcultural awareness, which she equates with the ability to appreciate that cultures are open, heterogeneous, and characterized by generativity and performativity – much like languages (Tymoczko 2007: 235–236). In this light, the idea of a fixed, identifiable cultural distance between source and target audience is turned on its head, yet at the same time, in a world of ever-moving parts, the ability to negotiate and mediate this distance (or lack thereof) becomes all the more necessary, challenging, and potentially enriching. We may not be at the level of transcultural awareness yet, as proposed by Meyer (1991), but we hope to move towards it – hence the title of this collection.

The present volume is divided into three sections. Part I, entitled 'Theoretical reflections on translation pedagogy and transculturalism', provides a forum for a wide range of theoretical explorations. The four contributions each foreground – and frequently challenge – common assumptions in the field, testifying to the considerable scope of the subject at hand and providing food for thought in the process. In the first contribution, **José Lambert** addresses the recent integration of translation training programmes and its adjacent scholarly field of Translation Studies into the world of academia, arguing that the history of both translation training and Translation Studies, each flourishing in its own right, significantly predates the concept and model of a modern 'academic' discipline of translation. He grapples with the possible tensions that exist between translation training and Translation Studies, and underscores the diversity of paradigms and traditions that have existed in the field of Translation Studies ever since its inception. He concludes by pondering whether its academic integration will indeed lead to a closer integration of these various paradigms, giving rise to a much-warranted transdisciplinary approach, or to further fragmentation.

One such transdisciplinary approach is the one championed by **Jan Walravens,** who highlights the striking parallels that exist between the academic disciplines of Translation Studies and Intercultural Studies. He posits that translation is, quintessentially, a cross-cultural activity, as it requires meaning to be transferred from one place to another. As such, he here conceives of languages and cultures as separate, bounded entities, whose divides can only be effectively bridged by translators when they are schooled in intercultural competence. Walravens further argues that translators always take some kind of political stance, and that the subjective – and cultural – nature of translator choices should therefore be made more visible in the translation classroom through activities that stimulate reasoning and reflection. The parallels between Translation Studies and Intercultural Studies that thus emerge may lead to new paradigms for translation pedagogy. It is paramount that translation theory be informed by praxis, and vice versa; another gap that must be bridged if the discipline is to thrive further in academia.

Kanavillil Rajagopalan, by contrast, questions the very notions of translation as a bridge-building activity and of the translator as some kind of cultural broker, for he refuses to conceive of any given culture as "hermetically closed unto itself as a self-contained entity" (p. 54). Instead, he argues that the forces of globalization are leading to ever increasing contacts between cultures and languages, resulting in cross-pollination and hybridization, or, in other words, to the phenomenon of transculturation. This phenomenon is said to add a whole new dimension to translation theory, since it defies the idea of translating as bridge-building previously taken for granted. However, Rajagopalan is adamant that transculturation will not render the activity of translation obsolete. On the contrary, as globalization opens up new transnational and transcultural spaces, it will trigger a myriad of new communicative opportunities.

Finally in this section, **Elżbieta Tabakowska**'s contribution straddles theory and practice. Inspired by both cognitivist theory and ethnolinguistic research, she considers the close link between cognition and cultural encoding, and proposes that grammatical structures, since they are inextricably embedded in how we perceive and process the world, carry a cultural load. As such, she is loath to limit the discussion of culture in the translation classroom to that of cultural references. As repositories of culture, grammatical structures must be held up to the light too, and to this end she presents the reader with two case studies involving the translation of Polish grammatical structures into English: one showcased in a Polish literary text, the other in a shampoo advertisement.

In Part II of this volume, entitled 'Transculturalism in translation teaching', the contributors draw on their ample pedagogical experience and present us with learning activities they have undertaken in their own classrooms. As a case study, **Natalia Kaloh Vid** and **Vlasta Kučiš**' chapter outlines a learning activity in which Slovenian translation students at the University of Maribor were asked to focus on the ideological underpinnings and cultural specificities of advertising slogans in both English and German. The authors show how students, by using Critical Discourse Analysis (CDA) as a methodological tool, were enabled to critically reflect on the existing Slovenian translations of these adverts and to offer more appropriate solutions in the case of perceived inadequacies. The comparison of the 'hidden' ideological backgrounds of advertising slogans in the source and target cultures by students is shown to heighten their awareness of the ideological messages encrypted in the advertisements. Similarly to Walravens, the authors see ideology as a crucial cultural constraint, which must be unearthed and rendered visible in order to improve translational decision-making.

Natalia Naydenova focuses on the importance of cross-cultural awareness in a particular domain of specialized knowledge. In her contribution, she addresses the professional training of Russian students who wish to become translators in the highly competitive field of international business and finance. The author presents the outline of a translation module specifically designed for these students, and it is one that entails a major focus on cross-cultural training, placing particular emphasis on the difference between Russian and Anglo-Saxon culture in the business and finance environment. This difference is shown to extend far beyond specific terminology; it also informs stylistic and communicative conventions, to name but two. Naydenova offers the reader a set of tailor-made exercises that were developed for the pilot version of the module, arguing that the inclusion of this cross-cultural component is essential for her students if they wish to meet employers' expectations once they graduate and enter the job market.

Moving from highly specialized to literary translation, **Judith Woodsworth**'s contribution shows how on a French–English translation course at Concordia University (Montreal), a specific translation and writing exercise helps to improve both translation techniques and English writing skills. The assignment, which entails the interviewing of someone from a third culture and then writing a story in English about it, makes students keenly aware of the challenges and mechanisms of intercultural transfer, including the translation of orality. As such, it reveals to them that the translation process involves translating cultural realities rather than merely finding equivalents for words and linguistic structures. Woodsworth offers a step-by-step breakdown of the structure and aims of the story-telling assignment, and provides some glimpses of the positive student feedback she has received. Together, the students' texts reflect the cultural diversity of the Montreal university population, and celebrate the pluralism of Montreal as a multilingual city.

If cultural empathy is crucial to the translation process, then **Anna Vermeulen** and **Ana Ibáñez Moreno** present us with a task-based learning project likely to boost exactly that. The project requires Belgian L2 students of Spanish and translation to produce audio descriptions (AD) of Dutch-language Belgian films for (blind) Spanish target audiences. Through comparing the ADs of different learner groups in the classroom, this project offers a highly practical approach to raising awareness among students of how expression is informed by perception, and how perception is in its turn biased by culture. Furthermore, by appraising the possible impact of these various ADs on the target audience, students are actively engaged in the negotiation of cultural distance between sender and receiver. Post-project questionnaires suggest that students are indeed conscious of building up their intercultural communicative competence in the process.

In the third and final part of the present volume, entitled 'The assessment of transcultural competence in translation', authors delve into the sometimes vexing issue of assessment, an area where research has been scarce up to now. The first contribution in this section, however, is still very much informed by pedagogical concerns, and draws on both theoretical insights and practical experience. In this chapter, **Catherine Way** also argues that intercultural competence on the part of the translator should go beyond mere knowledge of cultural references. Instead, she explicitly champions the importance of cultural empathy, which she sees as key to breaking out of one's own – deeply embedded – cultural perspective, in turn allowing for the successful negotiation of the cultural distance between sender and receiver, deemed crucial in the translation process. Firmly rooted in her own pedagogical practice, Way presents a three-fold collaborative learning project that enables legal translation trainees to build cultural empathy, as well as allowing teachers to assess their learners' progress in this respect through the use of rubrics.

Geoffrey S Koby's contribution reports on the assessment of intercultural translation errors. To this end, he catalogues the errors due to culture-specific items that were produced in actual examination situations by two different sets of translators – undergraduate students of translation on the one hand, and candidates for the American Translator's Association (=ATA) certification examination on the other. Koby addresses the question as to whether different categories and frequencies of cultural translation errors were observed in the two sets of texts. Although cultural errors are mostly equated with cultural references in this contribution, i.e. they are frequently lexical and/or terminological in nature, the data obtained from this pilot study suggest that a lack of intercultural contextual knowledge is at the heart of these errors, and that the ATA requires finer-grained cultural error categories. The data also highlight the difficulty of identifying in advance culture-specific items that will prove challenging in any given text.

By contrast, **June Eyckmans** discusses current practices in translation assessment and proposes an assessment method for measuring cultural competence that does allow for the identification of 'culturally-laden' test items in advance. She emphasizes the potential of a norm-referenced assessment method for assessing – in a way that is both valid and reliable – cultural competence and translation competence as an integrated whole, for it is shown that these two constructs are impossible to tease apart. Test items that carry discriminatory power in such an approach are not limited to the lexical dimension; they can also be morphological, syntactic, even discoursal – if culture determines the way we see the world, it will permeate an entire text. Eyckmans reserves pride of place in her contribution for idiomatic language, and argues that phraseological knowledge – as a cultural deposit – must be included in any appraisal of cultural competence.

If future translators are to be aware of the socio-cultural, political and ideological underpinnings of their implied audience, as stated implicitly or explicitly by many authors in this volume, the final contribution presents us with an extracurricular approach to meeting this challenge. In order to incorporate the development of transcultural competence in a translator training programme, the strategy reported on in **Alexandra Rosiers**' contribution is to encourage, even require, translation students to take part in an Erasmus exchange. Using a socio-psychological approach to measure intercultural competence, Rosiers investigates the influence of an international sojourn on the development of 'multicultural effectiveness' among student translators at Ghent University, Belgium, who spent time abroad as part of a mandatory exchange programme. Findings reveal that the intercultural competence of these students had indeed increased as a result of living abroad, an improvement which could mostly be attributed to a significant increase in open-mindedness and flexibility. Future research should help to ascertain whether these findings can also be correlated with increased translation competence.

It goes without saying that the contributions together raise a multitude of new questions, proving that this volume is anything but the last word on the subject. Many lines of enquiry are still to be explored; as the theoretical underpinnings move and shift, new research questions are bound to arise, and new ideas for teaching and assessing transcultural awareness will continue to emerge. However, by broadening the conversation and opening up new research and pedagogical opportunities, we hope that this volume will provide Translation Studies scholars and practitioners with new theoretical insights and practical teaching inspiration.

Brussels, Belgium, September 2017

References

Bhabha, Homi K. 1994. *The location of culture*. London/New York: Routledge.
Boye, Sarah. 2016. *Intercultural communicative competence and short stays abroad: Perceptions of development*. Münster: Waxmann.
Hepp, Andreas. 2015. *Transcultural communication*. Chichester: Wiley-Blackwell.
Katan, David. 2009. Translation as intercultural communication. In Jeremy Munday (ed) *The Routledge companion to Translation Studies*. London/New York: Routledge, 74–92.
Kramsch, Claire. 2009. *The multilingual subject*. Oxford: Oxford University Press.
Meyer, Meinert. 1991. Developing transcultural competence: Case studies of advanced language learners. In Dieter Buttjes & Michael Byram (eds) *Mediating languages and cultures. Towards an intercultural theory of foreign language education*. Clevedon: Multilingual Matters, 136–158.
Tymoczko, Maria. 2007. *Enlarging translation, empowering translators*. Manchester: St Jerome.

Theoretical Reflections on Translation Pedagogy and Transculturalism

JOSÉ LAMBERT

University of Leuven/Federal University of Ceará

The Position of Translation Training: Another Success Story?

To the memory of Gideon Toury,
unforgettable scholar,
who realized that our destiny is
to construct worlds,
not to destroy them.

Abstract

Experts in translation matters know that the institutionalization of translation is much older than the institutionalization of Translation Studies (Gile 2012). The history of translation training also started (Pym 2011) long before the idea and the model of an academic discipline had been formulated (Holmes 1972). The integration of Translation Studies into the academic curricula deserves to be treated as a remarkable moment in the history of universities and in the history of the world of knowledge, but many translation scholars are unaware of the particularities of these developments. One of the paradoxes is that worldwide communication in the Age of Internationalization favours both further isolation and fragmentation and integration. What is the centre? Is the internet a sufficient barometer of the world of knowledge in Translation Studies or in other disciplines? Scholarly approaches to translation issues have been expecting their recognition for a few decades, based on very different traditions. Integration trends may have been obvious, but new fields of study do not depend only on academic worlds (Snell-Hornby 1988). Whatever the distinctions and definitions may tell us about the various provinces of Translation Studies and translation training, one cannot see how Toury's requirements in relation to Translation Studies (1980; 1985) would not also apply to contemporary translation training.

Keywords: academic curricula, translation training, internationalization, multinational business communities

1. Names and concepts: where and when?

Academic approaches focusing on cultural phenomena have often felt self-confident in their definitions, but definitions tend to be static, especially in their didactic dimensions. The problem is that cultures are dynamic, and hence a challenge for research. Until the 1970s, organized and collective research on translation issues were limited to a few areas that are now considered subareas of a new academic discipline. Since Even-Zohar (1976),[1] the added value of theoretical and methodological work on the position of translation phenomena, rather than on their definition alone, has become clear. At that moment, Even-Zohar was focusing on literary translation, but in fact his arguments apply to translation phenomena in general terms.

After the end of World War II, various scholarly, didactic and professional translation initiatives were established, first of all in view of a new market – the translation market for both interpreters and translators. At that time, translation theory was not the primary issue, but waves of theories would soon circulate. In recent decades, the scholarly world of translation has heavily increased in our globalizing world, and much more is needed than theory or practice, though nostalgia of the good old theory–practice dilemma has not really died out. The internet and a few institutions tend to recognize both translation and Translation Studies (TS) around the world as more or less unproblematic issues. But the real discovery of translation as an intellectual and an economic issue started decades ago, long before the advent of TS. Such origins may have been forgotten even by experts. At this time, it seems worthwhile to study whether

---

[1] Scholarly information on the birth of the discipline tends to be very erratic, notwithstanding the support that can now be found on the internet, especially as far as the period 1970–1990 is concerned (from Holmes, Popovič, Van den Broeck and Even-Zohar to Theo Hermans and Mary Snell-Hornby). Or, rather, it is the use of such information that is erratic. It is obvious that the historical information, which is not lacking nowadays, is hardly counter-checked by our younger scholars around the globe. Let us mention once again that the famous text by Even-Zohar was delivered at the Leuven Literature and Translation Symposium in 1976, where Holmes, Van den Broeck, Lefevere, Bassnett, Lambert and, above all, Toury and his master, Even-Zohar, planned the "foundation of the discipline". "It was a real group", said Gideon Toury in 2009, and the story has been written and analysed at least twice by Hermans (1985, 1999), among others, in English, and in accessible publications. Reducing those years in terms of *Translation theory*, or in terms of *theory and practice*, as has been done so often, confirms that in more recent times easy, simple and indirect information was used. Which people, groups or concepts have been in interaction, even after 1990 (and the creation of the internet), is grist to the mill for critical intellectuals.

and how translation training may have changed and may still need to change when being established in university and academic programmes after having developed worldwide in ad hoc higher-education networks. Often, a shift in positions implies shifts in definitions.

It has often been stressed that the translator's profession – including interpretation, which developed even earlier – is one of the oldest professions in the history of humankind, and that a scholarly *awareness of translation*[2] developed much later, in several historical movements. As has been illustrated in *The name and nature of Translation Studies* (Holmes 1972), the names that have been used in the languages of the world (de Swaan 2001) for referring to the translation phenomenon, even in modern academic terms, are probably less relevant than the cultural position and origin of the many translation theories and practices that have taken shape. At least one does not go without the other, as they say. And this will be the starting point in our cultural exploration of translation training.

"Theories" and "practices" were key words in the years when translation experts started formulating their first panoramic views, when new translation theories were booming. It may be assumed by now that the combination of both words refers to an approach that has been revised since translation was incorporated into academic programmes. True, many shifts and turns in translation matters are still very young.

In several of his historical texts – let us call them "positions" – Eugene Nida was not concerned when he juxtaposed "theory", "practice" and "science", which already implied that more was needed than theories for developing a science:

> Developments in linguistic theory have shed important light upon the theory and practice of translation, resulting in the recognition that translating is basically not a process of matching surface forms by rules of correspondence, but rather a more complex procedure involving analysis, transfer, and restructuring. Such linguistic procedures as transformation and componential analysis provide far more satisfactory bases for translation than have existed in the past. At the same time, the theory of translation is able

[2] This translation awareness (we suggest "translation culture") had developed in various societies long before the 20th century. The innovation in the "real group" around 1976–1980 and beyond (Toury really started his life's project around 1980, when Holmes began resigning) was their ambition to establish an academic discipline. But at the beginning of the 19th century similar ideas had circulated around the Humboldts! It has been made clear that *theory*, or *theory and practice*, were much too narrow for Holmes (1972) and for the academic world of translation.

> to provide linguistic science with new insights into structure and with improved methods for testing hypotheses. (Nida 1969: 483)

Nowadays, one may wonder whether at that moment in history the distinction was really visible between *translating* and *translation*; such an ambiguity would probably not survive in our contemporary situation, while the very idea of any *Science of Translation* has little chance of being preferred to *Translation Studies*. Do theories in a given discipline lead only to practices?

Vinay and Darbelnet (1959) claimed to provide a *méthode de traduction*, whereas Georges Mounin (1963) was convinced to have identified 'the theoretical problems of translation'. For two or three decades, an impressive number of new translation *theories* were circulating, and they were often linked to particular *practices*, not to the various areas of any discipline, which did not yet exist. Translation historiography, the sociology of translation phenomena, or machine translation (MT), perhaps localization, also require a certain use of theories. But in the mid-1970s the idea spread that:

- Theories were only a moment in the entire construction of a new discipline called, little by little, *Translation Studies* (Holmes 1972), which would go on to survive.
- Translation scholars (located within TS) claimed explicitly to go in search of a translation theory (Toury 1980); and many colleagues did not like this much, obviously because of other priorities.
- Research of a new kind – *Descriptive Translation Studies* (DTS) (Toury 1995) – was seen as essential to the elaboration of more open (functional) theories to replace/complete the former normative theories; no future without a theory, but more was needed. Normative theories were excluded as a basis for the explanation of translations within culture.

Whatever the theoretical discussions and developments may have been, old and new names, as well as old and new approaches, coexisted during the last decades of the 20th century. Various competing options survived together at the moment when the new discipline was institutionalized in the academic world, under various names, although the power of the new lingua franca – there is more than one particular lingua franca (Tak-hung Chan 2014) – has largely privileged the concept of TS. Are TS a model for the Anglophone world only? Most colleagues overlook the fact that translation training was institutionalized much earlier, at least since the 1930s; for example, at Heidelberg and at the École supérieure d'Interprètes et de Traducteurs (ESIT) in 1957, but at another level, that is, within the ad hoc network of translating training institutes (which have developed mainly since World War II). Even after World War II, universities kept their gates closed to translation. Not translation training, but rather TS, which had been planned within and for universities, was the basis for the new discipline at the end of the 20th century, especially since the recognition of PhD degrees in TS on several continents. It does not seem a coincidence that German promotors of *Skopostheorie* largely preferred *Wissenschaft* (*Übertragungswissenschaft*; *Übersetzungswissenschaft*) to *Forschung*, which Holmes would obviously have supported. Ďurišin published his book on comparative literature under the title *Vergleichende Literaturforschung* (1972).[3] Theories have been spreading in many disciplines since World War II; Warren and Wellek's *Theory of literature* (1948) produced a real shock in literary studies (as one would call it now); only later was the *science* idea underlying the belief in theories questioned. Not unlike Nida, Hans Vermeer and his many colleagues did not feel embarrassed by the science, in which practices or pragmatics (*übersetzen/übertragen*) were more central than *studies* (research). Such priorities were confirmed in the programmatic *Entwurf eines Curriculums für einen Studiengang Translatologie und Translatorik* (Ammann & Vermeer 1990), which can be identified as the translation training counterpart of Holmes 1972 – or, rather, of TS – but Holmes was not ignored by coincidence.

Indeed, a remarkable coincidence in the theoretical discussions since 1975 has been the formulation of the norms concept as a new key to translation matters. While the sociological origin of norms has been made explicit since the beginning of Toury's career (1975), and Levý happened to make use of the norms idea in the first half of the 1960s, which was probably due to Mukařovsky and his generation,[4] Vermeer started exploring norms as a way into translation matters during the 1980s. Neither Toury nor Vermeer, who were in contact with each other before 1990, concerned themselves with the academically well-known chicken-and-egg dilemma of *who was first*. They preferred concentrating on their own – quite relevant – priorities. Holmes did not really make use of norms, not even after 1976, although he took part in such discussions after the first formulation of

[3] The English title *Sources and systematics* sounds quite different. But how good was Ďurišin's English? We happened to notice how great fans of Skopos were fully unaware, unlike Vermeer, of the distance between (D)TS and Skopos (see Leal 2010).

[4] Of course, the concept of "norms" has had a long history in Sociology, including in former Czechoslovakia.

Toury's concepts. Toury and Even-Zohar had already exchanged concepts such as norms and (poly)systems a few years before the Leuven Symposium in 1976.

Translation training was not really central to the canonical programme worked out by Holmes. Was this by accident? Around 1990, the issue was rather how to plan the future of research on translation. Holmes was no longer there by 1990, and both Toury and Vermeer had produced their most innovative work between 1980 and 1990. One among the few public confrontations between Toury and Vermeer took place at Leuven in 1990, on the occasion of Vermeer's Centre for Translation Studies (CETRA) Chair Professorship, when an ambitious confrontation was planned around the norms issue as a crucial matter in the translation world.[5] The exploration of translation in culture and recent developments in research were explored along largely parallel lines by two very well-informed experts. The only strong disagreement in their attitudes referred to their concept of "the discipline", and not to *norms*: translation training was located in "the applied branch of Translation Studies" by Holmes and Toury, whereas it was the heart of the matter – the core business – for Vermeer. Without directly saying so, they had a very different discipline in view, some 20 years after Holmes' text and some ten years after Holmes had ended most of his scholarly activities. This was confirmed in Vermeer's and Toury's publications after 1990: their life projects kept them separated, notwithstanding the rich understanding between them.

It is probably – and largely – due to the (still) growing impact of English as the scholarly language par excellence as the lingua franca in the world of knowledge that many translation scholars happen to be unaware of the problematic scholarly status of TS, or even of its conceptual and terminological issues. Where do the key concepts come from? Would ignoring the backgrounds of their own discipline even be possible in literary studies, linguistics and social science?

However, let us not worry, for the time being, about terminology issues in languages other than English. The issue is not innocent at all, as has been explained in several publications about various linguae francae (Tak-hung Chan 2014). The wide and apparently unproblematic use of TS in almost any internet text where translation is at stake nowadays leaves the

[5] Owing to technical difficulties (in 1990), the tape recording is no longer available; records of important discussions from the Leuven Symposium and from the symposium at Castellón between Skopos and DTS scholars are also missing.

impression that this concept is unproblematic and requires no further clarification. But scholarly disciplines, particularly new ones, tend to require more *discipline* from their members. The monopoly position occupied by the English language is heavily indebted to cultural, economic and political power positions, in the case of TS and in many other disciplines.[6] Another vicious circle? Without translation, the lingua franca would probably not have spread across the globe (Tak-hung Chan 2014; Meylaerts & González Núñez, forthcoming).

Of course, TS was used first, and quite systematically, by Holmes in his key article (1972), and it has been used systematically on the internet. When many researchers dealing with translation issues ignore the conceptual background of their very young discipline, one can assume that TS is not yet a well-established academic discipline. The difficulty is not that no other models are allowed; in the tradition of academic scholarship, new approaches deserve their chance, and they may even be needed, but not in isolation. The establishment of equivalent, updated or competitive concepts – in English and other languages – ought to be encouraged as part of the growth of the discipline. This is exactly what Toury did for more than 30 years on the basis of Holmes' map, but on the basis of previous information, not in isolation. The lack of homogeneity or interaction in scholarly activities cannot be envisaged as progress as long as it reflects proliferation or eclectivity. Holmes himself took care with the issue, not unlike Ammann and Vermeer. Translatology, traductology as well as Skopos theories may very well cover activities that are scheduled within TS, but the interaction has not taken place, except perhaps in a few footnotes. The same applies to various so-called "non-Western" approaches. One of the obvious consequences of internationalization is that it reveals the necessity to adapt translation training as well as TS to translation markets, which is something very different from specific nations, or from East–West or North–South. Both TS and translation training have largely overlooked market principles, first of all in strictly economic terms. And while being heavily dependent on national education systems, both have underestimated basic international components in the language and translation markets, for example in the networks of linguae francae. But do both

[6] It has been stressed that 'the big nations' also tend to dominate translation theories or research (Susam-Sarajeva 2002); but Israeli, Canadian, Australian, Czech, Slovak, Dutch and Belgian scholars can easily demonstrate the opposite.

TS and translation training deal with translation? What's in a name, particularly when training translators? Such basic rules are particularly relevant whenever our discourse (terminology or concepts?) happens to be different from the language used on the street, that is whenever it is used in view of new definitions and goals (as the result of scholarship). It cannot be surprising at all that Holmes and quite a few of his colleagues intended to suggest a conceptual framework for translation *scholars*.

Neither Holmes nor his predecessors worried much about world markets, and their dialogue with colleagues was indeed inspired first of all by a given view on the Western world. Hence new generations have stronger reasons for planning systematic interaction with other scholarly groups. Concepts and terminology have much more than a symbolic status in scholarly matters, certainly when multilingualism and translation (and language) are at stake. Long before Holmes, many individual scholars (linguists, philosophers, writers and professional translators) had written heavy tomes on translation issues, but they did not claim the status of translation scholars because the discipline had no academic tradition at that stage. Ammann and Vermeer (1990) did not even aim at such an academic position, hence the ignorance/exclusion of Holmes (1972). Holmes himself was convinced that a new key concept was needed. It was no less clear why translation theory was rejected as the general name, not only in Holmes (1972), but also by several of his colleagues, especially Toury, who went on to be the key theoretician of TS for three decades. That same theoretician even suggested more specific names for his model that would stress how and why the new discipline was in conflict with the traditional theoretical views. He had a certain responsibility in the hesitation between target-oriented TS and DTS, which he introduced himself. Other scholars originated *The manipulation of literature*, which gave an external profile to a new group of scholars ("It was a real group", according to Toury himself in 2009) and which in the discourse of other groups quickly became *The manipulation school*. It is not unknown that "schools" identify scholars who are "different". One of the striking observations should have been that Holmes was no longer involved: Toury was going to show where the heritage was, but only insiders were going to notice. And heritage for whom, exactly? True, the picture was not simple. The Holmes programme was probably not incompatible with our contemporary world problems, but this is exactly where previous concepts and labels are in need of follow-up.

2. Success story?

In recent years, it has often been said and written that TS is one of the success stories of the contemporary university, whereas, according to the discourse of university presidents and authorities, contemporary academia seems to be anything but booming, except in the size of its student body. Let us recognize, however, that when authorities submit to rankings and to other (non-academic) competitions, they tend to submit universities to business criteria. Whether (this kind of) academia will survive will be known by the 22nd century.

Anyway, while the recognition of fully new diplomas has become extremely difficult worldwide, TS has become established in several steps and on every continent as a component of internationalization: first in translation training institutes outside of universities, at least in a few important countries and cities. After expansion (in Canada, Hong Kong, India, Italy, Spain, former Yugoslavia, Turkey, Russia, South Africa, India, China, Australia, Taiwan and New Zealand), a few dozen universities have recognized the new discipline at the highest level: as a PhD curriculum. The dissemination and institutionalization of TS can indeed be envisaged as exceptional to the extent that it has taken place on all continents, though not at all universities, and to the extent that several large (strategic?) countries – the so-called BRICS (Brazil, Russia, India, China and South Africa) are among them – have not hesitated to open their doors to TS. Particular political considerations seem to have been decisive in Spain (at the end of the Franco regime), in Russia and in the ex-Communist bloc (after the collapse of the Berlin wall), in South Africa (as part of the Mandela regime), in China (after Mao) and in Brazil (during and since the Lula years). The most impressive development, that is the intercontinental creation of PhD curricula, has obviously been influenced by the Bologna Declarations, which themselves first spread in and around Europe. More than 55 countries accepted cooperation through the Bologna agreements, well beyond European countries: it is indeed not simply a Western phenomenon any more. And there is no doubt about the most fundamental explanation – internationalization. It was like a must. And now? Is TS really welcome in academia beyond the borders of Europe? Is it really an added value? And why or where exactly?

A success story? Let us rather wonder for whom exactly: nothing is either good or bad, as Hamlet taught us; the problem is *for whom* things are good or bad. In quite a few situations, TS was also a short story. In countries eager to support TS, several newly established centres were closed a few years later, for example the University of Amsterdam, where Holmes formulated the academic concept, and several institutes in the United Kingdom, where globalization, hence translation, suddenly became the new future. It is not our responsibility to determine whether or where there are too many new institutes or programmes. But the silence about translation matters in a few countries has implications about those countries themselves, as well as about their higher education and training. Until the second half of the 1980s, translation happened to be a kind of province of Applied Linguistics or Comparative Literature/Literary Studies.

This was one of the leitmotifs in Snell-Hornby's texts until she was elected President of the European Society for Translation Studies (EST). At that time, TS was officially established as autonomous, and not only any longer in Europe: in Canada, the Canadian Association for Translation Studies (CATS) has been active since the 1980s, the International Association for Translation and Intercultural Studies (IATIS) extended the discipline in other continents and the EST itself followed the movement. Extensions within the various particular universities were another story. Many TS faculty members are on loan from neighbour departments (Comparative Literature, General Linguistics, French, Italian and Russian Studies); and it is often unclear who benefits from such borderline games, as local deans might confirm. Within the various international organizations, translation training and TS coexist, and their 'cohabitation' – as the French would call it – has not inspired many updates in their goals, certainly not in relation to Holmes (1972).

The professional people representing the new discipline, that is, translation professors, students and researchers, are convinced that history has changed: their chance of promotion has suddenly improved, while their neighbours from Linguistics and Literary Studies are often in serious trouble. External perspectives indicate, however, that the new status of Translation Studies has not really been supported by its immediate neighbours, neither within universities nor in the various research foundations (where networks of commissions decide about resources). What exactly the colleagues of those translation scholars happen to know about the new discipline might inspire some pessimism. And would the insiders, that is, the individual translation scholars, be so much better informed and/or in agreement about their exact goals? Many among them are newcomers, many among them have been attracted by a new area of study, or by their backgrounds as a translator (of literary masterpieces?). The younger generation often happens to identify with TS without knowing much about the origins and the name of the discipline. Moreover, the external image of the discipline within the various international societies is reflected in questions such as: "So, you are a translation theorist, aren't you?"; "But tell me, is this a good translation or not?"; "How do you tell your translation students to solve this particular problem?" To what extent are we ourselves responsible for this confusion?

Through the various countries and continents, the institutional views on TS, its goals and its future reflect heterogeneities, and quite some disharmony, in both internal and external terms, that is in translation departments and academic communities. The exact chronological origin of many institutes and programmes: in the 1950s, in the 1970s (as in Spain), around 1990 (in South Africa, in Eastern Europe) or after 2000, is as symptomatic as the new rhetoric borrowed from internet models. Fortunately, several excellent colleagues from Organization Studies (as well as from TS) have taught us that too much homogeneity may conceal a lack of creativity.

The ambiguity was that TS, as envisaged by Holmes and by Toury, was not the first nor the only institutionalization of scholarly activities related to translation. Translation training began much earlier, but given the traditions of the academic world, it has functioned in special education networks and, in many countries, outside the university. Other academic endeavours (in philosophy, linguistics, theology/biblical studies, MT or localization) have had an impact on the translation landscape, particularly between 1950 and 2000; and very rich translation cultures belong to the history of culture since (or before) Julius Caesar, without having had any link until very recently with the development of the institutionalized 'Western model'. How can so many different cultural experiences currently cohabit within the so-called "globalizing world of knowledge"? Making use of English and the name TS does not necessarily mean that the same discourse is used. Within the so-called "Western world", such questions apply first of all to translation training. The difference in many situations on the different continents is that the "Western tradition" of both translation training and TS is often requested as a model. But which model? In particular, in publications from North America, the recommendation is to go East or South. But how far exactly? What is then overlooked in most cases is that there has been and still is a rich East in translation culture and in TS in the eastern part of Europe (and not only Jakobson, Levý, Popovič) which heavily inspired Holmes, Van den Broeck and others.

3. Name vs nature and vice versa

Both historical and conceptual developments explain how a given field of scholarship has taken shape – or better still: how and why given positions have changed. In fact, our considerations about diachronic perspectives need to be supported by synchronic verifications from our present century, and the whole world is involved: geographical parameters such as East and West or North and South tend to be static, and they tend to ignore the mobility of communication. De-territorialization? Sometimes, yes; sometimes not at all.

In our case it might be delicate to trust the internet too much as a barometer of our observations (in which language?), unless our questions and the answers obtained happen to provide clear results. The first problem is that the internet did not even function during the years when the first formulations of TS were born. On the other hand, the same internet has had an obvious influence on the public and on insiders' information about TS. Whoever wants to keep up with scholarly or even everyday matters nowadays tends to watch their computer screen. Again: in which language? It is not true that language does not matter from the moment we use the tongue of, for example Voltaire or Trump. Networks of electronic information allow for fast and very intercultural observations on academic matters such as TS.

Let us first check the extent to which the historical information taken into consideration in the previous paragraphs stimulates our world of knowledge. Based on the contemporary information available in English, there is no doubt about the success of TS as a concept: any first contact with the internet registers TS as:

- the title of (more than one) journal(s);
- the title, or partial title, of quite a large number of books;
- even as the title of 'popular TS books' (goodreads, classics, bestsellers?);
- scholarly societies;
- book series.

And, little by little, the reader moves into the encyclopaedic and academic definition of the concept, as in Wikipedia:

> Translation studies is an academic interdiscipline dealing with the systematic study of the theory, description and application of translation, interpreting, and localization. As an interdiscipline, Translation Studies borrows much from the various fields of study that support translation. These include comparative literature, computer science, history, linguistics, philology, philosophy, semiotics, and terminology … The term 'translation studies' was coined by the Amsterdam-based American scholar James S Holmes in his paper "The name and nature of translation studies", which is considered a foundational statement for the discipline. In English, writers occasionally use the term 'translatology' (and less commonly 'traductology') to refer to translation studies, and the corresponding French term for the discipline is usually *traductologie* (as in the Société Française de Traductologie). In the United States there is a preference for the term Translation and Interpreting Studies (as in the American Translation and Interpreting Studies Association), although European tradition includes interpreting within translation studies (as in the European Society for Translation Studies). (Wikipedia "Translation studies", n.d.)

We have good reasons, again, to avoid approaching conceptual information in terms of right or wrong, as in the good old definitions and dictionaries. But the genealogy of the concept recognizes Holmes' key concept as well as his key text, including the competing terminology (translatology), especially in other languages. What may have happened since Holmes (1972)? What's in a name such as TS that is not provided by other names?

So far, internet documentation confirms a manifest degree of institutionalization of the academic discipline, even as an "interdiscipline", which refers to insiders' opinions. Such institutionalization probably reflects a globalized world map in which international academic discourse is dominated by English. A Western discipline? Yes, and no. TS is not even homogeneous in English and, in scholarly worlds where English has no monopoly, it may have different priorities (as in Belgium, the Czech Republic, France, India, Portugal, Russia and Ukraine). The problem is that a genealogy of concepts that refers to Holmes as the father indicates particular interference with more recent concepts. A few examples from the websites of universities illustrate this point:

> Turn your love of languages into a marketable profession … (University of Illinois Urbana-Champaign: <http://www.translation.illinois.edu/>).

> The programme balances Translation Studies theory with practical translation work; you will develop both academic and professional skills, pre-

paring you for the translation profession or PhD research in the field. (University of Glasgow: <http://www.mastersportal.eu/studies/32622/translation-studies-translation-professional-practice.html>).

The Division of Literatures, Cultures, and Languages, in cooperation with East Asian Languages and Cultures and the English Department, teaches undergraduates to develop and apply their foreign language knowledge to the production and analysis of translations. The minor is designed to give students majoring in a variety of fields the tools to consider the practical and theoretical issues brought up by translation as an aesthetic, cultural, and ethical practice. (Stanford University: <https://majors.stanford.edu/translation-studies>).

You have insight in the objectives, traditions, and methods in Translation Studies, especially from a linguistics perspective. You are able to analyse concrete translation problems from a theoretical linguistic perspective in a given department. (Department of Comparative Literature and Linguistics, Radboud Universiteit Nijmegen: <http://www.studie-gids.science.ru.nl/2015/science/course/37693/>).

Since the 1980s, translation as practice and as theory has become central to Comparative Literature. Traditionally, this was not the case: the discipline, founded largely in the United States by post-war European émigrés, devoted itself almost exclusively to the European languages and demanded that all texts be read in the original language. But as the canon has expanded to include many non-European literatures, including various creole and hybrid literatures and oratures, scholars have acknowledged the necessity of using translations in research as well as in teaching. Whereas it used to be the case that most major African literary works could be read in either French or English, such is not the case of writers such as Ngũgĩ wa Thiong'o, whose African languages also require translation. Along with the practical turn to translation in Comparative Literature has come, not surprisingly, the critical and theoretical assessment of translation in the context of globalization, multiculturalism, cultural hybridity, post-colonial theory, and an emphasis on interdisciplinarity. With its interest in crossing the borders between languages, cultures, and national literatures, Comparative Literature is implicitly committed to performing and to assessing theoretically the function and value of 'translation' in the widest sense of the term. (Department of Comparative Literature and Translation Studies, Washington University, St Louis: <https://complit.artsci.wustl.edu/graduate/core-course-requirements-phd>).

The Certificate in Translation Studies adds an attractive dimension to Comparative Literature PhD degrees and to all foreign language and English PhD degrees. Translation is a fascinating and challenging field of study

> for both graduate and undergraduate students, as our well-subscribed offerings have shown. Growing in theoretical, methodological, and cultural sophistication, translation studies is emerging as a significant and useful aspect of Comparative Literature and of the humanities in general. Thus, it follows that the Certificate represents an important supplement to the training of our students as they enter the job market. ('Entering the job market', Washington University, St Louis: <https://complit.artsci.wustl.edu/graduate/translation_studies>).

> This programme enhances practical skills in translation and provides an intellectual and philosophical perspective on the activity of translation. (MSc in TS, University of Edinburgh: <http://www.ed.ac.uk/literatures-languages-cultures/translation-studies>).

No one expects all these institutions to promote their programmes with the same terminology, but it is striking that part of the attraction is recommended by reference to neighbouring disciplines, languages in particular. On the other hand, translation itself is identified in either/or terms (profession vs PhD), and the link is not clear at all between what was formulated in 1972 and "Translation Studies". Would there be alternative curricula? In the case of PhD research, dealing with language and translation, it may not be sufficient to make use of the same words in the same language. Students, staff members, academic authorities and even everyday society wonder about the profile behind TS.

The silence about the conflict between translation training and TS is most strange. The intellectual ambitions of the curricula are never lacking in the various advertisements, but one of the key questions for outsiders, that is the potential audience, is this: Does TS provide its students with competences as translators, interpreters and/or localizers, besides the expected academic background?

The consequence is that our (new) academic community has strong grounds for *keeping self-critical* and for wondering also about the everyday world outside of academia where TS was first welcome, also under different labels, until this very day. All the more since TS is heavily indebted to non-academic societies and their worries about internationalization. Not unlike businesses – and universities, for the past few years – translation scholars may also have strong reasons for distinguishing between *internal and external relations* with regard to their resources and priorities (<https://complit.artsci.wustl.edu/graduate/translationstudies>).

It seems that their recent progress in academic terms has struck them with some blindness from the moment they need insights beyond the borders of their own discipline, as might be deduced from the recent fascination with *the turns of TS* and from the recent bibliography on interdisciplinarity (Gambier & Van Doorslaer 2016): in our internal discussions, we tend to overlook several revolutions at the world level that have had an impact on translation. Would the world of translation be independent from communication issues? Or from political and economic shifts (internationalization; the nature of communities)? Is it so certain that the approach to translation requires connections to neighbour disciplines?

A new, international publication, *Teaching translation* (Venuti 2017), provides us with a rich illustration of the varieties and complexities discussed so far. As suggested by the title, the book represents at least substantial components of what is being called "translation training", and in quite a few countries (before and since Holmes, who is often quoted). When reading, however, that "translation studies now consists of a recognizable body of knowledge that is codified as a curriculum" (ibid.: 1–2), one imagines that we focus on the success story/stories that are the object of study in many publications (Gambier & Van Doorslaer 2016), and that they are almost always in English. But almost every chapter in the book initiates us into workshops of various kinds that also confirm the introduction, where TS appears to be "in the making", as Schlegel would have put it. How to combine this officially recognized heterogeneity of TS in the United States with that of other countries – for example, Canada, Spain and the United Kingdom (and also French Culture rather than French TS?) – is more than quite a challenge: since the discussions focus on everyday academic work, the compatibility between countries that have such different institutional traditions in matters of languages and academia seems like wishful thinking. Would TS in Canada be a mere province of the US tradition? It would be worthwhile to analyse the canonized, less canonized and missing concepts (theory, practice, norms, equivalence, translatability, comparative literature, world literature) comparatively in very different bodies of knowledge, for example *The meta-language of translation* (Gambier & Van Doorslaer 2009). By definition, new programmatic publications, including "The name and nature of Translation Studies" (1972), reflect both traditional and future-oriented views. The fact remains that, after some 50 years, TS has indeed generated research, concepts, cultural insights that deserve to be studied from the moment its name is used. And it is equally certain that interaction and confrontations will be the result, sooner or later. A more specific question is already how translation training, which has strong Canadian and intercontinental roots, will read as *teaching translation.*

At any rate, the institutionalization of TS is on its way, in a range of styles, and it is obviously part of both nationalization and internationalization. It could also be part of politics and economics, including when it resists concepts such as norms, as sociologists have often demonstrated.

4. Back to the beginning: The chicken and the egg

Some of the ambiguities and heterogeneities described so far are narrowly linked to the pre-academic and extra-academic past of translation training. Other ambiguities are linked to the intra-academic development of TS (e.g. MT, computer linguistics and corpus linguistics). Although Holmes, Toury and several colleagues from the Leuven 1976 days had promoted integration via international scholarly organizations, the results were not too spectacular: changes in academic institutions were visible at the top rather than at the bottom.

As the promotional texts listed above illustrate, many translation scholars, and certainly many colleagues in TT, have a limited view on the state of the art. One wonders how, exactly, staff members or even full curricula fit into the academic discipline without this historical awareness.

At the beginning of the 19th century in Germany, the Humboldt generation imagined translation curricula as part of the 19th-century university – almost during the days when Goethe imagined his World Literature. And this was also an event in the history of *translation culture.* Was it also the result of an imperialistic worldview? Well, that's another story. Several colleagues have been worried that translation cultures are possibly expressions of imperialism: language policies, translation policies, translation curricula, how could they *not* reflect any particular worldviews, especially when academia and its world of knowledge function within universities based in nation-states?

It is not unknown that the systematic training of interpreters (oral translators) was a requirement for political power throughout the ages: the training of "translators" (as we call them when referring to the written intercultural transposition of texts) was no 20th-century discovery. Throughout the ages, across languages and countries/continents, various translation traditions have developed, quite often under the influence of particular schools, and hardly ever under the impact of individual intellectuals (philosophers, writers, translators): let us connect them to "translation cultures". Not only France (the *Belles Infidèles*), but also Germany (*World Literature*), Turkey (Atatürk) and Brazil (*Anthropophagy*) had their own particular traditions in the linguistic (verbal) integration of neighbouring cultures. In modern times, it has become increasingly accepted among insiders that there is "no language policy without a translation policy" (Meylaerts & González Núñez, forthcoming). Since, as Even-Zohar has argued, no culture is in non-contact, research about translation is supposed to clarify the history of world maps through the ages and include the norm systems underlying translation training.

In one of his many panoramic articles on translation training, Pym (2009) has demonstrated how many different perspectives have oriented training thus far. Contemporary translation scholars tend to locate scholarly discourse on translation phenomena in the decades after World War II – or even in the Age of the Internet – which implies an enormous generalization in terms of geography and culture. But Pym's historical and intercontinental explorations do not confirm that World War II was the real breakthrough, except for the first institutionalizing waves of translation training. We may even wonder to what extent the first generation of academic theoreticians (Nida, Mounin, Steiner, and later Vinay & Darbelnet) have had an institutional impact on Linguistics, though they have prepared the way for translation as an academic field. It is due to them that translation generated an image among a certain generation of colleagues. Until the parallelism between communication (process, message, reception) and translation had been discovered (first by Jakobson and then in the 1970s), there was no convincing argument for introducing translation as a concern for (inter)cultural research in various disciplines (e.g. in Law or Anthropology).

The necessity of any concept of *translation culture* was hardly a scholarly problem before the so-called 'globalization' phenomenon, which TS discovered at a late stage (Lambert 2007; Lambert & Gheorghiu 2014). Given their international academic responsibilities, colleagues from all disciplines had to make use of several languages, and translators/colleagues happened to be one of the solutions – but only as a service (as part of the secretary's office?). Even in academia, translation continues to be treated as a grey market (not quite a black market): colleagues who partly rewrite our English texts do not need any payment, right? Not unlike many journalists or website editors, a large group of academics are convinced that they produce their own texts in more or less average English (*No, I don't translate at all!*), while dialoguing mainly with English publications and before begging for some free assistance from an excellent colleague. Where would this kind of translation be visible at all, except to the eye of English native speakers? Translation scholars have known (for a few years now) that such utterances simply confirm cultural unawareness of translation phenomena.

One symptomatic discussion about translation training and TS is that of Chesterman (2009), in "The name and nature of Translator Studies", where the Holmes heritage is subjected to revision on (at least) one particular point, and where it is shown how (almost?) any subareas from the Holmes map could now be worked out into more elaborate research fields. A number of recent research tendencies in Translation Studies focus explicitly on the translator in some way, rather than on translations as texts. These trends might be grouped under the term 'Translator Studies'. The article argues that this new focus is inadequately represented in Holmes' classic map. Evidence of the recent trends is found especially in translation sociology, but also in translation history and in research into the translator's decision-making processes. A broad outline of Translator Studies would cover sociology, culture and cognition, all looking at the translator's agency, in different ways (ibid.: 13).

Focusing on the translator is one of the expected explorations within the discipline, but it reminds us of a well-known dilemma from medical studies: from the moment any medical doctor specializes in a therapy, he runs the risk of losing a "large spectrum strategy". The problem will be this: which option is more efficient? Looking for the translator behind any translation phenomenon tends to be a self-evident movement in any investigation of translation (many sociologists happen to miss it in DTS projects). In our contemporary world of networking in multinational environments, the search for the individual translator might become delicate, since quite a few business-oriented translation cultures support collectives rather than individuals (Piekkari 2016). This dilemma may lead to the conclusion that the study of translation cultures ought to be part of both DTS and translation training. Again, *the one does not go without the other.* There is no need to reiterate that, so far, macroscopic questions about translation cultures are not very visible in translation training curricula. Do our teachers assume that translation is forever? In the discussions about *Translation today*, Newmark wondered why translation would suddenly change after so many centuries (see his many interventions in Anderman & Rogers 2003).

Besides translator-focused research*, indirect translation* (relay translation) offers a strategic research field that can be made acceptable to translation training only on the basis of descriptive research and within larger panoramic views (i.e. within a larger spectrum). First of all, part of the terminological hesitation depends on the distinction between a target-oriented view and a more process-oriented approach, which is rather indebted to interpreting operations (*relay interpreting*), hence to translator- or translation training-focused points of view. It is symptomatic that even a well-informed scholar from Organization Studies, Piekkari (2016), borrows a normative attitude from particular translation scholars, notwithstanding the very systematic use of indirect communication processes in business communication. Just like many areas in TS, the recognition of indirect translation has developed on the basis of literary research before being acknowledged as an immense research area that includes texts ranging from literary classics to travel stories and medical handbooks. The dominant option in translation training can be made flexible only through descriptive arguments, based on a more open attitude towards the discipline. Separate worlds?

Almost two centuries after the Humboldts, Ammann and Vermeer (1990) claimed no position for translation training within the traditional university. Institutes such as Heidelberg, Germersheim, as well as those in other countries, happened to have particular (and ambiguous) links with universities – and ambiguous ones at that, thanks to frequent antagonism. Has *integration* really taken place? Even after the Bologna agreements in 1998 – that is, after the reforms between higher education and universities in many countries – the antagonism between training and research has not fully disappeared.

True, access into the academic world was probably the most fundamental revolution for both TS and translation training. I still separate one from the other because their development until the end of the 1980s (and perhaps even until today) has been so different. Nevertheless, more than one integration movement has taken place in more recent years. It is not by chance that one or both (?) *wings* have been generally connected to Applied Linguistics, or that translation scholars are often treated as linguists when they encounter historians or philosophers. And what are they called in the various research foundations around the globe when decisions are made about nominations, about distributing funds and about rankings? The growing administrative autonomy of TS, especially since the recognition of the PhD degree in the discipline, has generated fully new situations: the identity of internal as well as external neighbours has changed.

As a key to communities, translation has been involved in revolutions on a worldwide scale (see Ong 1982; Castells 2000 [1996]): for example, without translation, communities such as the European Union (EU) would not be able to function. But what kind of academic structures/research traditions take this into consideration when focusing on globalization? There is not much hope that Wikipedia or the recent election of an American president will soon become a canonical topic in (D)TS, but the hypothesis is that without certain patterns from a new translation culture (multilateral distribution, indirect translation, simultaneous or consecutive interpreting), our contemporary world would look somewhat different. It will be the task of translation training rather than (D)TS to update their skills, at least if the dream of being involved in the permanent flow of worldwide communication is not to be affected by eclecticism. Insights from Organization Studies, economics or political science will be very welcome.

As *interdisciplines* gain currency, it should be pointed out that their origin is in DTS, although they are too often reduced to wishful thinking. How do they function in everyday life? Together with TS, translation training has entered the academic world, where both have their own responsibilities. Yet how will they cohabit after spending their first decades as separate traditions? As a result of the "integration" of a few continents in the Age of Globalization (Gentzler 2008; Marais 2014; Tak-hung Chan 2014) and despite the existence of electronic worlds of knowledge, new integration movements still struggle against protectionist and somewhat nationalistic ideologies. Updating academic programmes in the Age of Globalization involves much more than updating translation or language maps.

5. And politics?

It is well known that contemporary universities are open to business-oriented priorities regarding their web presence, social networking and subsequent use of rankings. Business-oriented options were partly responsible for the creation of translation training institutes. It is only recently that TS has accepted the idea that the market concept is to be taken seriously, not only for the study of business-focused research, but as a stimulating idea for any approach to (communication and) translation matters. This has been the case not just in the Western world of the 20th or the 21st century, but also in previous ages and as a general assumption. The paradox is that within DTS there is nothing more neglected than the business world; questions such as language policy and multilingualism are considered regarding various kinds of institutionalization. But multinational business communities are systematically overlooked within TS, which is made all the more evident through the few isolated initiatives in this direction (Gouadec 1990; Janssens et al. 2004; Brunelière 2016; Piekkari 2016). Or, rather, except for those with a background in Organization Studies?

Let us reformulate the point that translation training began with the programmatic ambition of dealing with business matters and preparing competent translators for their new jobs (Vinay & Darbelnet 1959). MT had similar ambitions and therefore it won strong the support from international companies. The result has been that several new areas have been explored and that several companies have benefitted from new training approaches. The final difficulty seems to have been that translation activities have continued to be treated as a service. It is in an interdisciplinary spirit that Organization Studies has discovered language and translation issues, although not as a service, but at decision-making and management levels. It is not too clear how a few particular innovative centres (except, e.g., Gouadec's) have abandoned service-oriented concepts; they have shown, at least, that the individual translator is an insufficient basis for doing so.

To what extent Sociology may join the effort will become clear at a later stage. Neither translation training nor DTS has really been kept informed of the exploration of language and organization/management issues in other disciplines. An additional handicap is the traditional external image of translation training-oriented education. Individual scholars based in TS hardly ever succeed in penetrating business networks or multinational enterprises: they are simply not welcome. After all, what could language experts tell managers about communication? Could such handicaps be avoided by working alongside teams from Organization Studies, Economics or Psychology? Institutional power was not a founding pillar of TS: perhaps the academic world would not even have accepted it. Our so-called "world of knowledge" still feels confident in traditional frameworks.

How could translation training institutes penetrate and investigate the particular translation markets they were aiming at without taking concepts such as translation culture and the translation market seriously? More will be needed than (normative) translation theories. And from the moment the need for research is recognized, academic expertise from more than one discipline will be required.

References

Ammann, Margret & Vermeer, Hans J. 1990. *Entwurf eines Curriculums für einen Studiengang Translatologie und Translatorik.* Heidelberg: Institut für Übersetzen und Dolmetschen der Universität Heidelberg.

Anderman, Gunilla & Rogers, Margaret (eds). 2003. *Translation today: Trends and perspectives.* Clevedon: Multilingual Matters.

Brunelière, Jean-François Mathieu. 2016. *Glocalisation d'une multinationale: Enjeux de la traduction dans la communication en ligne. Autour de la Peugeot 2008 au Brésil.* Florianópolis: UFSC/PGET [unpublished PhD thesis].

Castells, Manuel. 2000 [1996]. *The rise of the network society.* Malden/Oxford/ Carlton: Blackwell.

Chesterman, Andrew. 2009. The name and nature of Translator Studies. *Hermes: Journal of Language and Communication Studies* 42: 13–22.

de Swaan, Abram. 2001. *Words of the world: The global language system.* Cambridge: Polity Press and Blackwell.

Ďurišin, Dionýz. 1974. *Sources and Systematics of Comparative Literature.* Trans. Peter Tkác. Bratislava: U Komenského.

Even-Zohar, Itamar. 1976. The position of translated literature within the literary polysystem. In James S Holmes et al. (eds) *Literature and translation: New perspectives in literary studies.* Leuven: Acco, 117–127.

Gambier, Yves & Van Doorslaer, Luc (eds). 2009. *The meta-language of translation.* Amsterdam/Philadelphia: John Benjamins.

Gambier, Yves & Van Doorslaer, Luc (eds). 2010–2014. *Handbook of Translation Studies.* Amsterdam/Philadelphia: John Benjamins.

Gambier, Yves & Van Doorslaer, Luc (eds). 2016. *Border crossings: Translation Studies and other disciplines.* Amsterdam/Philadelphia: John Benjamins.

Gentzler, Edwin. 2008. *Translation and identities in the Americas. New directions in translation theory.* London/New York: Routledge.

Gile, Daniel. 2012. The institutionalization of Translation Studies. In Yves Gambier & Luc Van Doorslaer (eds) *Handbook of Translation Studies* (Vol 3). Amsterdam/Philadelphia: John Benjamins, 73–80.

Gouadec, Daniel. 1990. *Le traducteur, la traduction et l'entreprise.* Paris: Afnor.

Hermans, Theo (ed). 1985. *The manipulation of literature. Studies in literary translation.* London: Croom Helm.

Hermans, Theo. 1999. *Translation in systems. Descriptive and system-oriented approaches.* Manchester: St Jerome.

Holmes, James S. 1972. The name and nature of Translation Studies. In Raymond van den Broeck (ed) *Translated!* Amsterdam/Atlanta: Rodopi, 67–80.

House, Juliane. 2003. English as a lingua franca. *Journal of Sociolinguistics* 7(4): 556–578.

Janssens, Maddy, Lambert, José & Steyaerts, Chris. 2004. Developing language strategies for international companies: The contribution of Translation Studies. *Journal for World Business* 39: 414–430.

Lambert, José. 2007. Translation and globalization. In Armin Frank et al. (eds) *Übersetzung – translation – traduction. Ein Internationales Handbuch zur Übersetzungsforschung. An international encyclopaedia of Translation Studies. Encyclopédie internationale de la recherche sur la traduction* (Vol 2). Berlin/New York: Walter de Gruyter, 1680–1700.

Lambert, José & Gheorghiu, Catalina (eds). 2014. *UNIVERSE-cities as problematic global villages. Continuities and shifts in our academic worlds.* Tubarão: UFSC/PGET and CopiArt.

Leal, Alice. 2010. Being a CETRA student: A critical account of the 2009 Summer School. *Scientia Traductionis* 7: 190–206.

Levý, Jiřý. 1969. *Die literarische Übersetzung. Theorie einer Kunstgattung.* (transl. Walter Schamschula). Frankfurt am Main: Athenäum.

Marais, Kobus. 2014. *Translation theory and development studies: A complexity theory approach.* London/New York: Routledge.

Meylaerts, Reine & González Núñez, Gabriel. Forthcoming. No language policy without translation policy: A comparison of Flanders and Wales. *Language Problems and Language Planning.*

Mounin, Georges. 1963. *Les problèmes théoriques de la traduction.* Paris: Gallimard.

Nida, Eugene A. 1969. Science of translation. *Language* 45: 483–498.

Ong, Walter. 1982. *Orality and literacy. The technologizing of the world.* London/New York: Routledge.

Piekkari, Rebecca. 2016. Translations and translators in the field of International Business. *Interdisciplinary Guest Lecture.* CETRA Chair Antwerp, 29 August.

Pym, Anthony. 2009. <http://usuaris.tinet.cat/apym/on-line/training/2009_translator_training.pdf> (ac cessed 18 September 2017).

Pym, Anthony. 2011. Training translators. In Kirsten Malmkjær & Kevin Windle (eds) *The Oxford handbook of Translation Studies.* Oxford: Oxford University Press, 475–489.

Sapiro, Gisèle (ed). 2008. *Translatio. Le marché de la traduction en France à l'heure de la mondialisation.* Paris: CNRS.

Snell-Hornby, Mary. 1988. *Translation Studies. An integrated approach.* Amsterdam/Philadelphia: John Benjamins.

Susam-Sarajeva, Sebnem. 2002. A multilingual and international Translation Studies? In Theo Hermans (ed) *Cross-cultural transgressions. Research models in Translation Studies. Historical and ideological issues* (Vol 2). Manchester: St Jerome, 193–207.

Tak-hung Chan, Leo. 2014. Under the shadow of three linguae francae: Repositioning translation in South-East Asia. *Asia Pacific Translation and Intercultural Studies* 1: 2–27.

Toury, Gideon. 1980. *In search of a theory of translation.* Tel Aviv: Porter Institute for Poetics and Semiotics.

Toury, Gideon. 1995. *Descriptive Translation Studies and beyond.* Amsterdam/Philadelphia: John Benjamins.

Venuti, Lawrence. 2017. Introduction. In Lawrence Venuti (ed). *Teaching translation. Programs, courses, pedagogies.* London/New York: Routledge, 1–14.

Vinay, Jean-Paul & Darbelnet, Jean. 1959. *Stylistique comparée du français et de l'anglais: méthode de traduction.* Paris: Didier.

Wellek, René & Warren, Austin. 1948. *Theory of Literature.* New York: Harcourt, Brace, and Co.

Wikipedia. *Translation Studies.* <https://en.wikipedia.org/wiki/Translation_studies> (accessed 18 September 2017).

JAN WALRAVENS

Université Libre de Bruxelles

Towards a Culture-based Paradigm for Translator Training

Abstract

Translation is, quintessentially, a cross-cultural activity. It takes place on the borderlines between cultures and attempts to transcend the divide that separates two (or more) peoples, communities or individuals. Intercultural models implicitly convey a wish to translate, that is, to "carry" meaning from one place to another. Recent insights into Translation Studies suggest that translation is never noncommittal: translators always engage in some kind of political discourse, leading to their "unavoidable visibility". Perhaps the role of the "visible translator" should be made more explicit in translation training programmes. In doing so, parallels with Intercultural Studies emerge, which may lead to new paradigms for translation pedagogies.

Keywords: Translation Studies, Intercultural Studies, theory, praxis, translator training

1. Culture-based translation discourse

It does not take a giant leap of the imagination to see that translation is, quintessentially, a cross-cultural activity. Translation always attempts to cross the divide that separates two (or more) peoples, groups, opinions, policies or individuals. The ultimate goal is always to get some kind of meaning or message across.

This observation may seem almost trite, especially in the light of past and present research in the fields of both Translation Studies (TS) and Intercultural Studies (ICS). However, it does merit our full attention and academic scrutiny in view of the massive amount of research that is being carried out in these fields and – perhaps more importantly – the various and rapid turns both disciplines are taking. The intrinsically multidisciplinary stance of these domains should also make us wonder whether they do not increasingly overlap from a methodological and theoretical perspective. In this chapter, I offer an illustration of how the (early) development of ICS as an academic discipline was a calque of the emergence of TS (Walravens 1997: 173). Snell-Hornby (1988: 35–36) presents a brief survey of the foundations of TS; by simply replacing "Translation Studies" or "translation" in her text with "ICS" or "intercultural capability" a faithful description is maintained, revealing seemingly parallel disciplines. When two academic disciplines share common interests and appear to develop along similar lines, a *status quaestionis* seems to be in order.

Before going to the heart of the matter, however, it may be useful to make a few preliminary comments in order to avoid possible terminological confusion, which often exists – also in academic circles. First, when we use the term "Translation Studies" it should be, by and large, interpreted as Snell-Hornby defined it back in 1988:

> Translation studies [is] an integrated and independent discipline that covers all kinds of translation … In this view, translation draws on many disciplines, but is not equal to the sum total of their overlapping areas… As a discipline in its own right, translation studies needs to develop its own methods based … on the complexities of translation. (1988: 35)

Eighteen years later, she complemented this view, saying that

> [translation] discourse must, in the final analysis, be culture-based, reflecting … "different perceptions of the world". Given such a discourse, and given our plurality of languages, approaches and cultures, there is every reason for optimism that Translation Studies will continue to develop into a success story of the 21st century. (Snell-Hornby 2006: 175)

In addition to her wish for a separate identity for TS in 1988, two decades later the author added a clear and explicit desire to fully embrace the plurality of today's world.

Secondly, the terms "cross-cultural" and "intercultural" are often used intermittently. I propose to adopt the distinction that Brislin makes:

> One approach to "cross-cultural research" is to carry out parallel studies, that is, studies of similar concepts in different cultures. … "Intercultural research" refers to studies of people from different cultures coming into contact and interacting frequently, often in face-to-face relationships. (1993: vii)

Brislin's distinction between "cross" and "inter" clearly puts ICS on the same playing field as TS. Translation as a praxis is indeed much more a matter of contact and interaction than a question of parallel studies (although the latter is not to be excluded, of course). Let us also note that Brislin, like Snell-Hornby, explicitly refers to the complex plurality of today's world (a lucid, albeit slightly obvious, prediction in the 1990s).

2. Translation-based intercultural discourse

Now that terminological clarity has been established and that we have highlighted the importance that the two disciplines which concern us attach to multiple world views, we can further develop the basic premise of this chapter: there seems to be a close methodological link between TS and ICS. It therefore stands to reason that pedagogical approaches in both fields will find some common ground. Our starting point is to consider intercultural theory and praxis as a basic metaphor of translation (see Gannon & Pillai 2010 for a rationale behind using metaphors as an analytical tool in ICS).

Intercultural models, as well as projects in the field (e.g. in education or development aid), implicitly convey a wish to translate, that is, to carry something (meanings, messages, intentions, ideologies) from one place to another – therefore appealing to the very etymology of the word "translate": the past participle *translatus* of the Latin verb *transferre*. In many cases, of course, what is actually transferred can easily transcend the level of texts (or spoken messages, in the case of interpreting) to include money (e.g. to support a non-governmental organization), technical devices (e.g. water pumps for desert villages) or technological equipment (e.g. laptops for a local school – in some instances, pencils may perhaps also qualify as "technology"). But even within such pragmatic contexts, we maintain that our basic metaphor of translation remains valid. Grossberg (2000: 24–25) addresses the tension that exists between theory and praxis and contends that the academic's intellectual

> commitment has to be balanced by an equally strong commitment to maintaining a sense of passion and political involvement … Some people have suggested that the true "spirit" … of cultural studies is located outside the academy.

Leistyna (2005: 2) takes the debate a step further by pointing to the necessary but difficult link between, for instance, the scholar at the Massachusetts Institute of Technology (MIT) and the relief worker in Somalia:

> Unfortunately, in many forms of human mobilization, theory is disconnected from practice, denying that practices are always undergirded by particular theoretical perspectives and assumptions.

The two preceding quotations clearly echo the eternal debate in TS about where the exact location of the discipline should be: solidly anchored in academia, or running free in the fields of practice? Or to put things differently: Can a praxis ever aspire to dwell within the theoretical walls of academia? In any event, intercultural endeavours, be they solely theoretical or entirely practical, will always transcend – directly or indirectly – the boundaries of the printed page because of the passion and the commitment with which they were undertaken.

3. An example of *discomfort* in "culture as translation"

In order to illustrate the insights quoted above, I would like to offer a short example of how intercultural work (both theoretical and practical) can indeed be seen as a form of translation. The source used is a book authored by Michael Berry et al. (2008): *"That's not me". Learning to cope with sensitive cultural issues*. We refer to this work rather extensively because we think it adequately illustrates the common ground that exists between translation and intercultural discourse. In addition, we see how the eternal gap between theory and praxis can be bridged. In *"That's not me"*, two main cases are presented. The first results from an (exchange) teaching experience at Johannes Kepler University in Linz, Austria (Berry et al. 2008: 15):

> The Austrian example presents trauma associated with the consequences of "Anschluss" and WWII. … In intercultural contexts, reference to the Austrian association with Nazi Germany often triggers intercultural discomfort, placing Austrian students on the defensive when they assume that exchange students are "loaded" with a negative view of Austria's role during the Second World War.

Secondly, the insights from a ten-year experience with American and French exchange students at the Turku School of Economics, Finland are discussed. The heart of their intercultural communication problem can perhaps best be summarised as follows (Berry et al. 2008: 44):

> This intercultural communication process often contributes to the Finnish students' discomfort with talking about silence. Discomfort and reticence conjoin to further hide from those uncomfortable with silence … the positive cultural dimensions of Finnish comfort with quietness.

Berry et al. (2008: 45) further explains that part of the problem resides in accurately understanding and translating the Finnish words "*hiljainen*" and "*hiljaisuus*" into English (silent/quiet/shy) or French (*silencieux/tranquille/timide*). The translated terms are used interchangeably by the Finns. In addition, some (but not all) students explicitly associate "silent" with nature and "quiet" with social contexts. In other words, the Finns make no explicit distinction between "silent" and "shy". This is essentially a problem of translation that may indeed lead to cultural misunderstanding: a foreigner referring to the Finns as "shy people" may simply be "misinterpreting" their comfort with silence.

It would be beyond the scope of this contribution to dwell on the details of the studies mentioned. I will therefore concentrate on the methodological path that the researchers and teachers involved chose to take. In both case studies, the intercultural issues that learners had to deal with can best be described as a feeling of discomfort: "war-related trauma" for the Austrians, and 'discomfort with quietude by foreign guests' for the Finns. In order to address and come to terms with this lack of comfort, a movement (or "translation") is proposed from "poverty points" towards "rich points":

> When reference is made to silence and shyness in the Finnish case and the Anschluss/WWII in the Austrian case, this can initially lead to the discovery of intercultural poverty points. These negative misinterpretations can result when one conceives of and evaluates another's cultural ways through one's own cultural prism of living and communicating, and conversely when one is influenced by … external standards of … identity. … Discovery of intercultural rich points comes via helping one another to better understand what is taken for granted in the cultural "logic" of the other's culture. (Berry et al. 2008: 11–12)

In both the Austrian and the Finnish cases, students are made aware (through multiple verbal and written exchanges with the visiting foreign students) that feelings of cultural discomfort are often self-imposed because identity is "an invisible mishmash of internal and external perceptions of oneself and others" (Berry et al. 2008: 12).

We have called attention to the work by Berry and his colleagues because we see their approach as "prototypical". Similar basic strategies, however, can be recognized in other work done in ICS (for instance, Trompenaars 1999; Pinto 2000; Lewis 2006 – to name only these three). Most, if not all, researchers establish their own theoretical framework (creating "categories", "classifications" or "dimensions") from which they proceed to propose – implicitly or explicitly – a method for dealing with cultural difference (mainly based on, or illustrated by, a series of cases and examples). Always, some kind of translation is being performed: a cultural item or issue that is not easily understood across the border is transferred to a "third space" – I use the term here as it was coined by Bhabha (1994) and further explored by Berry et al. (2008) – where it is reflected upon and "processed" through an underlying model or theory. Ideally, the result of that procedure or analysis is an elucidation that will lead to improved communication across cultures. After all, both in ICS and TS, the ultimate goal is to eliminate the feeling of "discomfort" that results from limited (or non-existent) understanding between two (or among several) parties.

4. From praxis to theory, and back

Now that the logic behind our basic premise (i.e. "intercultural work *is* translation") has been illustrated, I wish to turn our attention to recent developments in TS and examine how the obvious links between the two disciplines may lead to new avenues for translation pedagogy.

In his paper "Translation Studies. A didactic approach", Wilss (2004: 10) warns that a highly abstract or theoretical approach to translation (as often pursued in academia) might lead to (or even reinforce) a genuine split between practitioners and academics. According to him, "translation teaching must … be directed towards the day-to-day purposes of translation work …".

The stance taken by Wilss allows us to address and come to terms with a view that persists to this day in the minds of many, that is, that theorising about translation is the exclusive domain of academia and that teaching translation skills should be the sole terrain of specialized translator training programmes. The origin of this view is intimately linked to the emergence, in the 1980s, of Descriptive Translation Studies (DTS). Hermans (1985) introduced scholars to the "manipulation of literature" as a way of studying translation primarily as a societal and historical phenomenon. Toury (1980) and Even-Zohar (1979) helped us to read and understand translations as the result of interacting and often conflicting polysystems. Most of the scholars exploring this type of research worked at universities and, as conscientious academics, their main goal was to describe "translational phenomena", without voicing opinions about the quality of the translations studied. Hence, they were wary of normative and practical considerations or questions such as what constitutes a *good* translation or how we can translate *better*.

In the last decade of the 20th century, several studies attempted to "transcend" empirical research. A prime sampling of work conducted in this vein is offered in *Beyond Descriptive Translation Studies* (2008), edited by Pym, Shlesinger and Simeoni. Laviosa's contribution to this book is a clear example of the

> transition from theoretical and descriptive study to translator training ... Teachers of translation are independently drawing on the insights of corpus-based Descriptive Translation Studies and would seem to be aiming, in the long term, to formulate bridging rules that postulate what translator trainees should be doing if they adhere to the patterns of translational behaviour unveiled by descriptive scholars. (2008: 119)

Obviously, this approach does not fully bridge the gap between theory and praxis, but it certainly opens up the potential for fruitful debates between "professors" and "teachers", between theoreticians and practitioners. Interestingly, a corollary of the same debate exists in ICS. Frame advocates

> the need to deconstruct the limits which have traditionally been used to structure the field of intercultural communication, but which now appear as artificial constraints which prevent scholars from getting to grips with the complexity of the social activity on which they work. ... On the epistemological level, this underlines the potential of culture-interactional research within communication science, reinforcing the importance of the study of communication processes in the former, while providing the latter with key insights into the influence of culture(s) on these processes, through theoretical models ... (2014: 39–40)

Frame clearly wishes to establish a link between theoretical models of intercultural communication and intercultural communication "in the field", which should mutually inspire and benefit both stances. A prime form of "working in the field" is, of course, teaching.

5. Inside the translation classroom

From what precedes, it is safe to say that work done in the classroom today is examined with keen interest by academics. This important shift from "pure" academics to day-to-day praxis seems to be paralleled by novel approaches within translator training. In her book *Multiple voices in the translation classroom,* González Davies (2004) proposes a dynamic pedagogical model for the translation classroom based largely on active student participation and critical reflection. She highlights differences between language learning and translation competence, suggesting (albeit indirectly) possible links between both:

> Most other subject categories taught as undergraduate degrees have been learnt at school with textbooks … This is not the case with translation. … Its closest relative could be Language Learning. (González Davies 2004: 11)

González Davies' book offers a long and varied list of "activities and tasks" that all seem to support one main goal: moving the students "outside the classroom". This means that they should be ready to work as true professionals (fully capable of managing constraints such as time, money and deadlines). But professional know-how also implies a thorough understanding of "subjectivity". This is what she has to say about this major, but often underrated, "aptitude":

> As to the translator's subjectivity, it is directly related to intrapersonal and emotional intelligence: knowing one's strong and weak points and using one's personal … background to advantage. Motivation and the willingness to be flexible and open-minded will certainly influence professional success as well. All of this will be reflected in each student's learning, translating and translator styles, which will be different, ranging between risk-taking or prudent … (ibid.: 217)

Indeed, political choices, however well informed they may be, will always be rooted in subjective preferences (at least to some degree). As such, (political) choices always involve some risk-taking: the outcome is never guaranteed. With this type of thinking about translation (training), the notion of subjectivity becomes less problematic than one might at first glance surmise. As a matter of fact, the work done, for instance, by Baker (2006) and Cronin (2006), shows that translation is always political (in one way or another), and hence subjective. The way this can be done is illustrated in *Translation in undergraduate degree programmes* (Malmkjær 2004). Malmkjær offers a rich variety of practical proposals that allow translators' voices to be heard more clearly in the classroom, but her book seems to be lacking a strong and encompassing methodological framework. Gile's (2009) *Basic concepts and models for interpreter and translator training* proposes to offer just that. Chapter 10 of Gile's book (entitled "Integrating more theory into training") is especially worthy of our attention: it proposes the IDRC framework (interpretation, decisions, resources and constraints). The framework starts from the premise that translation is a form of "action" on a text which leads to the 'production' of another text. Production necessarily operates under "constraints" (insufficient linguistic or extra-linguistic knowledge, lack of time) but fortunately also with the help of "resources" (lexicon, grammar, ample extra-linguistic knowledge). The author then goes on to present a user-friendly model (ibid.: 248–249) that will lead to a target text on the basis of 'interpretation' and 'decisions' (i.e. the translator's "actions"). We are offered a list of theoretical angles (Skopos theory, DTS, domestication vs foreignization, cognitive approaches and translation universals) on which translators can base their actions (preferably in a spirit of "complementarity"). Finally, IDRC is described as a tool that can be used effectively in the classroom (ibid.: 257): it (albeit gently) "forces" students to explain their translation actions within the framework of specific theories.

6. Praxis first?

The attempt to integrate the position of the practitioner of translation with that of the theoretician is certainly much to Gile's credit. Yet, in the eyes of some academics, the practitioner is still an obedient second who is (ideally) inspired by one or other (or several) theoretical model(s). Perhaps we can take things a step further. Let us be bold and pretend, for a minute, that "theory of translation" does not exist. And let us ask our translator what inspires their translational choices. It is more than likely that they will say that "putting across (intercultural) meaning" (or any synonymous variant of that phrase) will be their prime concern. Having freed our translator from the (daunting) weight of "theory", we can put their methodological reflections into the context of pragmatic concerns. It is important to note that letting the translator speak "freely" does *not exclude* the potentially rich input of theoretical reflections or models. The wealth and complexity of the translator's comments on their own work will, of course, be fuelled by their own general background and the type of training they will have received up to a given point. This approach may be especially meaningful to translators with little experience who are invited to communicate their translation strategies in a clear and coordinated fashion: the benefits in translator training contexts are obvious.

7. A framework for "practical reflection"

In previous publications, a user-friendly and flexible 'heuristic' framework was described that allows the translator to put their very own reflections into an easily readable frame (Walravens 1994; 2010). Two detailed examples of how the same frame can be used as a context for translator strategy can be found in academic articles referring to my own experience translating for the theatre in Flanders (Walravens 1999; 2002). A succinct summary of the underlying principles of my approach should therefore suffice here. Directly addressing the translator with any given task at hand, the following steps are proposed (in a suggested but not stringent order):

1. Express (implicitly for yourself *and* explicitly for anyone who wants to hear your voice) the (intended) goals of the target text; this can be done, for instance, in a written log or an electronic blog – ready for any interested party to consult.
2. Establish (for yourself, but accessible to all parties potentially interested or concerned) a database with useful and relevant background information (historical, social, economic, geographical and cultural) that will support and justify the translation choices eventually made.
3. Identify a series of (potential) links between steps one and two, so that a "network" appears that will allow you to "connect the dots" between both steps.
4. Write up a tentative translation that is based on the preceding steps and submit it to a reader whom you ask to test the result within the framework of your pre-stated goals (or skip this step and launch your translation, knowing that it is based on grounds that *you* are ready to defend).

8. Conclusion

In this chapter, I propose that translators – from the initial stages of their training onwards – should be made fully aware that they are cultural mediators and that mediating between cultures requires careful consideration. Translating is about making choices, and choices are never "noncommittal". By allowing and enabling (young) translators to be clear and transparent about their own decision-making processes, we invest them with responsibility for their own endeavours. The openness that is therefore created between translator and reader (student and teacher) also allows the latter to comment on (and, perhaps, enjoy) the translated work with thorough insight and increased understanding. And the former will be all the better positioned to defend their choices and to gauge possible criticism. In the process, teachers may also learn from students.

I hope to offer a modest contribution to paradigms for translator-training programmes that allow translators, including beginners, to step into the light. Not for their own glory, but with an eye to further intercultural understanding through translations based on reason and reflection – within specifically (pre)defined contexts. I wish to create a *comfort zone* that provides transparency for the two main parties addressed in this chapter, that is, students in translator training programmes and those who have to judge their work. Perhaps the proposal described in this chapter will allow translators and their readers to voice balanced and informed comments on both the procedure and the product of translation. The question for research should no longer be "Is this a *good* translation?" but rather "*Why* is this translation *the way it is*?"

This question opens up the possibility for all readers of translated texts to understand better the translation process *and* to acquire deeper intercultural understanding. If the be all and end all of intercultural contact is indeed a matter of translation, then a clear understanding of the "why?" of translation choices may guide us effectively when we are faced with intercultural challenges.

References

Baker, Mona. 2006. *Translation and conflict. A narrative account.* London/New York: Routledge.

Berry, Michael, Carbaugh, Donald, Innreiter-Moser, Caecilia, Nurmikari-Berry, Marjatta & Oetsch, Walter. 2008. *"That's not me". Learning to cope with sensitive cultural issues.* Leobersdorf: Digitaldruck.

Bhabha, Homi K. 1994. *The location of culture.* London/New York: Routledge.

Brislin, Richard. 1993. *Understanding culture's influence on behaviour.* Orlando: Harcourt Brace.

Cronin, Michael. 2006. *Translation and identity.* London/New York: Routledge.

Even-Zohar, Itamar. 1979. Polysystem theory. *Poetics Today* 1(1–2): 287–310.

Frame, Alex. 2014. On cultures and interactions: Theorizing the complexity of intercultural encounters. In Saila Poutiainen (ed) *Theoretical turbulence in intercultural communication studies.* Newcastle upon Tyne: Cambridge Scholars Publishing, 29–44.

Gannon, Martin & Pillai, Rajnandini. 2010. *Understanding global cultures*. London: Sage Publications.
Gile, Daniel. 2009. *Basic concepts and models for interpreter and translator training*. Amsterdam/Philadelphia: John Benjamins.
González Davies, Maria. 2004. *Multiple voices in the translation classroom*. Amsterdam/Philadelphia: John Benjamins.
Grossberg, Lawrence. 2000. The sins of cultural studies. In Jan Baetens & José Lambert (eds) *The future of cultural studies. Essays in honour of Joris Vlasselaers*. Leuven: Leuven University Press, 23–34.
Hermans, Theo (ed). 1985. *The manipulation of literature*. London: Croom Helm.
Laviosa, Sara. 2008. Description in the translation classroom. Universals as a case in point. In Anthony Pym, Miriam Shlesinger & Daniel Simeoni (eds) *Beyond Descriptive Translation Studies. Investigations in homage to Gideon Toury*. Amsterdam/Philadelphia: John Benjamins, 119–132.
Leistyna, Pepi. 2005. *Cultural studies. From theory to action*. Oxford: Blackwell.
Lewis, Richard. 2006. *When cultures collide. Leading across cultures*. Boston/London: Nicholas Brealey International.
Malmkjær, Kirsten (ed). 2004. *Translation in undergraduate degree programmes*. Amsterdam/Philadelphia: John Benjamins.
Pinto, David. 2000. *Intercultural communication. A three-step method for dealing with difference*. Leuven/Apeldoorn: Garant.
Pym, Anthony, Shlesinger, Miriam & Simeoni, Daniel (eds). 2008. *Beyond Descriptive Translation Studies. Investigations in homage to Gideon Toury*. Amsterdam/Philadelphia: John Benjamins.
Snell-Hornby, Mary. 1988. *Translation studies. An integrated approach*. Amsterdam/Philadelphia: John Benjamins.
Snell-Hornby, Mary. 2006. *The turns of Translation Studies*. Amsterdam/Philadelphia: John Benjamins.
Toury, Gideon. 1980. *In search of a theory of translation*. Tel Aviv: Porter Institute.
Trompenaars, Fons. 1999. *Riding the waves of culture*. London: Nicholas Brealey.
Walravens, Jan. 1994. Translation into Flemish (?): A heuristic approach. *Meta* 39(1): 122–131.
Walravens, Jan. 1997. Cross-cultural capability: From 'skill' to 'science' (?) Parallels with Translation Studies. In David Killick & Margaret Parry (eds) *Cross-cultural capability. The why, the way & the means*. Leeds: LMU, 168–174.
Walravens, Jan. 1999. De (zachte) dwang van de (literaire) tekst of de illusie van de vrijheid. Een voorbeeld. *IDIOMA* 11: 99–108.
Walravens, Jan. 2002. Loving in translated worlds: From New Orleans to Antwerp. Or: how to translate sexual innuendo in T Williams' A streetcar named desire. *Language and Intercultural Communication* 2(2): 111–119.
Walravens, Jan. 2010. Een theoretisch vertaalmodel dat *werkt*. In Chris Van de Poel & Winibert Segers (eds) *Tolk- en vertaalcompetentie. Onderwijs- en toetsvormen*. Leuven: Acco, 137–147.

Wilss, Wolfram. 2004. Translation Studies. A didactic approach. In Kirsten Malmkjær (ed) *Translation in undergraduate degree programmes.* Amsterdam/Philadelphia: John Benjamins, 9–15.

KANAVILLIL RAJAGOPALAN

State University at Campinas

Translation as Bridge-building and Transculturation

Abstract

The phenomenon of transculturation adds a whole new dimension to translation theory since it calls for a fundamental rethink of the hitherto largely unproblematic idea of looking at translation as an essentially bridge-building activity and the translator as some sort of a culture broker. Some people might hasten to conclude from this that the days of the professional translator are numbered and that translation itself is destined to become, with the passage of time, mostly an outmoded and thoroughly dispensable activity. I claim in this chapter that such pessimistic scholars err in jumping to precipitous conclusions on the strength of a barebones analysis of facts on the ground. This is so because, although many facts on the ground may be changing faster than imagination can catch up with them, what one cannot simply ignore is that tensions of all sorts still persist and, by virtue of these, the continued need for new ways of building bridges across newly opened chasms is bound to remain. The real challenge, therefore, is to make educated guesses about what awaits the professional translator at the end of the road, as globalization forges ahead the way it currently does, making new transnational, transcultural environments ever closer to reality and liberating new kaleidoscopic possibilities of communication and transcultural interaction.

Keywords: transculturation, globalization, professional translation, role of translation

1. Introduction

The word 'translation' inevitably suggests the idea of prising meaning off from where it is originally embedded in order to plant it in a context which is in some sense alien, and in very many cases even 'hostile'. At least that is the word's default meaning, as can be easily verified from the fact that, in the last half a century or so, the majority of translation theorists have either positioned themselves against the received wisdom contained in this definition or have sought to vindicate its fundamental truth by adding some conditional clauses and cautionary 'ifs' and 'buts'. Therefore, Venuti (1995) can contemplate translation as an arena where forces intent upon subjugation and forces equally bent on resisting them are battling it out. However, it seems to be the case that, from Venuti's point of view, what is really at stake is on whose turf this process of 'transplanting' is to be carried out and who ultimately is to bear the costs of the operation.

Silverstein (2003: 76) makes an important point when he argues that an ideological focus on *denotational textuality* – coherent language-as-used to represent states-of-affairs involving things-in-universes-of-reference – provides the benchmark as well as starting point for millennia of wishful as well as wistful theorising about 'translation' and its various (im)possibilities.

But then, this should surprise no one who takes note of the fact that the traditional view of translation is very much ensconced in a conceptual frame of things where a whole host of other assumptions in relation to meaning. For instance: "its full presence within the language where it is originally 'encrypted'", "its putative independence relative to immediate context", "its fundamental translatability", "the idea of perfect, 100% translatability across languages (albeit, as a point of reference, unattainable in practice, but not in principle)", "the total unnecessity of translating the *meaning* of a word within the confines of the same language" (as strange as this might strike someone at first blush, this is but a straightforward corollary of the idea of perfect translatability across languages" – of which the widely attested perception that so-called 'interlingual translation' is translation only by default), and so forth.

Also present in that conceptual frame is the idea of cultures as distinct entities, in much the same manner as individual languages are believed to be, each hermetically closed unto itself as a self-contained entity, subject to its own laws and regulations. What one seldom pauses to take note of is the fact that, as translation theorists widened the scope of their attention from the narrowly linguistic to the broadly socio-cultural, many of them in fact still opted for, often unbeknown to themselves, moving along the selfsame well-trodden path and keeping intact most of the theoretical baggage and working assumptions they had accumulated all along. That is to say, most of the time they were proceeding on the smug assumptions that the work they had so far done in concentrating on the 'purely' linguistic was all right in its essentials; it needed only to be supplemented by looking at additional factors from the broader context of culture.

In other words, there can be little doubt that the word 'translation' continues to call forth its traditionally consecrated sense of simply transporting or transplanting meaning by virtue of the fact that any attempt to rethink it or use it in any unconventional manner would imply having to revise a firmly established worldview in its entirety. That established view casts its long shadow even as we occasionally have a go at revisiting the scene and suggest alternative views.

2. Anthropology and translation

In their book *Translating cultures: Perspectives on translation and anthropology*, Rubel and Rosman (2003) claim right at the outset that, from a historical point of view, it is only relatively recently that the word 'translation' came to be used, especially in the Western world, in the strict sense of transfer of meaning between two distinct *languages*: "In its broadest sense", they point out, "translation means cross-cultural understanding." (1) But then they hasten to add:

> The central aim of the anthropological enterprise has been to understand and comprehend a culture other than one's own. This inevitably involves either the translation of words, ideas and meanings from one culture to another, or the translation to a set of analytical concepts. Translation is central to 'writing about culture'. (ibid.)

So, there is a profound sense in which the discipline of anthropology and the practice of translation share a common goal: namely, that of fostering intercultural understanding. And, in an even more profound sense, it seems correct to venture that translation was first an anthropological and, only secondarily, a linguistic matter.

Furthermore, if Rubel and Rosman are right in their claim, there is no way one can hope to achieve a full understanding of what a given culture is all about, except through a proper appreciation of the role of translation and of the untiring efforts of countless translators in the very emergence and subsequent florescence of that specific culture. Translation and culture are, one might say, mutually imbricated in each other. Álvarez and Vidal (1996: 2–3) fully endorse this position and put it even more straightforwardly by noting that "[t]ranslation is *culture bound* and exhorting translators always to be sensitive to "the importance of the cultural milieu of each language".

Arguing along the same lines, Carbonell (1996: 81), in a paper entitled "The exotic space of cultural translation", asserts that "any approach to a given culture always involves a process of translation". As I pointed out in a review of the book in which that paper was published (Rajagopalan 1999: 376), "[p]resumably, the author seems to imply 'any culture *other than one's own*' – an inference authorised by his mention of the anthropological and ethnographic fields as the 'handiest examples' and also by his claim that it may be equally true in respect of 'any case of cultural contact'".

I recall having made a point of inserting that caveat because, as it happens, one usually proceeds on the assumption that one is always 'fully at home' in one's own culture and, therefore, is in no need of translation or any other means of mediation. One's own culture, so the argument would run, obviates the need for translation in the strict sense or, at the very least, mitigates it (a view perfectly in consonance with our earlier claim that so-called 'interlingual translation' is translation only by default). A culture other than one's own, on the other hand, would increase the need for translation.

Partly corroborating such a claim, Tymoczko (2012: 5929) regards the idea that "[t]ranslation involves negotiating fundamental linguistic and cultural anisomorphisms and asymmetries" as one of the "theoretical principles currently accepted in translation studies". Undergirding all such theoretical claims is the unstated assumption that cultural differences invariably require some sort of translation in order to be overcome, while at the same time placing restraints on efforts to smooth over all sticking points in a fully satisfactory manner.

No doubt this position (i.e. the view that translation fundamentally involves intermediation between what, by implication, turn out to be two clearly demarcated cultural domains) is also subject to possible contestation, especially if we take into account claims such as the one made by Deleuze and Guattari (1986: 232) to the effect that more and more people are today being forced to "live in a language that is not their own". They therefore become "a nomad and an immigrant and a gypsy in relation to [their] own language". What Deleuze and Guattari are referring to is the situation that millions of people in the world, uprooted and displaced from their 'original' cultural milieus for one reason or another, are forced to inhabit languages that they cannot call their own.

This phenomenon, a mostly post-colonial by-product, adds a whole new dimension to the problem of translation in an already shrinking world and its constantly intermixing of cultures. Incidentally, this often involves, at least in the beginning, some form of post-colonial contestation and battle for who gets to control the reins, but it goes far beyond it.

3. Culture and translation

When it comes to translating a text from one language to another (i.e. interlingually), everyone agrees that there is an inevitable slip between the cup and the lip. What makes the ideal of a 'perfect transfer of meaning' from the source text (ST) to the target text (TT) a tantalizing impossibility has to do, according to some scholars, with the socio-political climate prevailing at the time the translation work is carried out. In other words, translation per se might be an activity taking place or being carried out within the strict confines of the languages in question, but its destiny is in the hands of *extra*-linguistic factors. Therefore, Robinson (1997: 3) claims: "Equivalence is a social fiction controlled by fleeting target-cultural norms." What makes equivalence a fiction, then, is the fact that it is controlled by factors that are themselves uncontrollable.

The idea that all translation invariably involves some amount of violence is underscored by Venuti (1995: 18) when he argues: "Translation is the forcible replacement of the linguistic and cultural difference of the foreign text with a text that will be intelligible to the target-language reader."

And he goes on to remind us that what he calls the deliberate 'foreignizing' of the TT is always already at work "resist[ing] the hegemony of transparent discourse" (ibid.) and this takes place from within, by deterritorializing the target language itself, questioning its major cultural status by using it as a vehicle for ideas and discursive techniques which remain minor in it, which it excludes (ibid.: 305).

Recalling Schleiermacher's 1813 lecture *Ueber die verschiedenen Methoden des Uebersezens* ("On the different methods of translating"), in which he made the powerful plea that translation be viewed as an important practice in the Prussian nationalist movement, Venuti concludes that Schleiermacher's point was that foreignizing translation might help enrich the German language without at the same time threatening its essential native 'genius'. For Venuti, however, such a gesture, for all its sincerity and good intentions, "rest[s] on a chauvinistic condescension toward foreign cultures" (ibid.: 99).

Venuti is right only to the extent that the identities of language, cultures and so forth are held to be discrete and clearly demarcated from one another if "the unbridgeable gaps between cultures" exist (306). This view has been shown to be largely a hangover from an essentially 19th-century zeitgeist (see Hutton 1999). Once we recognize that we live in a world still coming to terms with the impact of globalization and the eroding of concepts and categories that a bygone world order and its accompanying worldview had put in place, the picture before us changes in ways in which it becomes difficult to sustain Venuti's bold thesis.

In a paper titled "Willingness to communicate and cross-cultural adaptation: L2 communication and acculturative stress as transaction", Gallagher (2013: 53) begins by noting that [w]ith the ever-expanding movement of individuals to all corners of the globe for the purposes of business, entertainment, education, economic opportunity, and political asylum, the need to understand and facilitate intercultural contact grows more important every day.

Gallagher hits the nail on the head when he recognizes the utmost importance of globalization and its direct impact on much of our day-to-day reality. What he nevertheless stops short of recognizing, it seems to me, is that, along with growing cross-cultural contact, globalization also gives rise to a 'cross-pollination' of ideas and cultures and, even more pertinently for our present purposes, their languages.

What a post-Venuti view of translation must necessarily take into account is the undeniable fact that his prized notions of 'foreignization and domestication' as the two equally viable alternatives for the translator to choose from, as well as those supposedly hard-and-fast categories of 'native' vs 'foreign' on which his whole thesis rests, have mostly become fuzzy in our age of a fast-shrinking world and ever-growing contact between peoples and what used to be, until recently, their distinct and distinctive cultures. The much-celebrated post-colonial 'difference' has been shown to be a carry-over from the colonial heritage; it has mostly given way to total 'indifference' and recognition of mutual 'interdependence' (Ramanathan & Pennycook 2007). Any contemporary view of translation will risk stillbirth if it fights shy of these radical ongoing changes in our conceptual apparatus.

The following is a case in point that should hint at what we are up against. A language such as English, which has long lost its status as the property of any one nation, or any one culture, has all but eliminated any vestigial distinctions between native and non-native users. So much so that there are some scholars who have even started stressing the need for postulating 'nativized foreign language' as a new category (Prćić 2014).

Some additional support for the case sketched in the foregoing paragraph may be found in the writings of scholars such as Simon; in the final chapter entitled "Revising the boundaries of culture and translation" of her book *Gender in translation: Cultural identity and the politics of transmission*, Simon (1996) takes inspiration from Spivak (1992) and Bhabha (1994), arguing for the theorizing of translation within the broader context of cultural studies: "After all," she says, "the globalization of culture means that we all live in 'translated' worlds, that the spaces of knowledge we inhabit assemble ideas and styles of multiple origins, that transnational communications and frequent migrations make every cultural site a crossroads and a meeting place" (1996: 134).

4. Dilemmas of globalization

Nevertheless, invoking globalization as a watershed and a game changer does not solve all our problems either. For there remains the highly contested issue of whether globalization succeeds in bringing about the much-vaunted 'universal culture', as many early enthusiasts were led to believe. In this light, right at the outset of their editorial introduction to *Translation: Theory and practice: A historical reader*, Weissbort and Eysteinsson argue that "the notion of a global culture in a single language is not a promising prospect; indeed, it is, perhaps fortunately, virtually impossible. Vital cultural expressions always involve both the local and the global; the problem of translation is inherent in them, and also in their dispersion and historical delivery" (2006: 1).

They do this immediately after admitting that "[t]ranslation is still of the utmost importance in the affairs of a world that has gone through the rapid technological development called modernization, which furthermore has enhanced international relations to the point where people feel they can legitimately talk of 'globalization'" (ibid.: 2).

Weissbort and Eysteinsson are right in their contention that the global cannot be contemplated in isolation; its spread always takes place in tandem with the local. Indeed, one is but the flipside of the other. But their argument about globalization and single languages unable to hang together is somewhat flawed by the fact that so-called 'single' languages are but figments of our imagination, aided and abetted by political conveniences of particular historical moments. Talk of single language in their pristine purity, inoculated against 'contamination' by outside influences, does not square with the undeniable fact that not many languages have ever existed under such circumstances. Rather, language contact and the resultant hybridization, whether incipient or advanced, have always taken place, and so has translation, whether in an informal, haphazard fashion or as a more formalized practice. Translation theory should take into account the effects of language contact that results from it or is, on the contrary, occasioned by it.

However, those who get carried away by all the hype about globalization and all the win-win benefits it is supposed to bring about often overlook the fact that what is typically passed off as globalization is nothing but a set of values traditionally promoted by the hegemonic powers, only this time ingeniously pasteurized and camouflaged as universal. As a result, those same old iniquities and conflicts of values and mores are still there, except that they have been swept under the carpet. There is, after all, some truth to the frequently heard murmurs in the corridors that globalization is often a euphemism for 'MacDonaldization' or 'Coca-Colonization'.

5. Transculturation

The full impact and ultimate consequences of globalization on national and regional cultures around the world were anticipated by the Cuban anthropologist, Ortiz (1995), when he coined the term 'transculturation' as early as 1947, long before the term 'globalization' itself had become common currency. The term refers to the merging of what were traditionally considered distinct cultures, each closed unto itself and mostly impervious to outside influences, thanks to their built-in mechanisms of resistance and also to what has come to be referred to as the 'cultural discontinuity hypothesis' that emerged primarily from the early work of anthropologists such as Malinowski and Boas, according to which there was a yawning, unbridgeable gap between some cultures.

Having recently recovered from the trauma of being reviled and condemned for their forerunners' callous practice of pillaging the treasures of bygone civilisations under the guise of scientific expeditions, the anthropologists of the early 20th century were all too anxious to shy away from being seen as 'meddling with' the culture of the people under their investigation. Some of them even went so far as to treat the culture of the 'natives' as sacrosanct and off-limits for them – except by way of studying it, and that too from a safe distance – so as not to 'contaminate' it through their very physical presence. For these early anthropologists of the new generation, who claimed for themselves the status of being heirs to a genuinely 'scientific turn', their field of enquiry had no place for advocacy of any kind, not even by way of rooting for their stated cause. Hastrup and Elsass (1990: 306) argue that the rationale for advocacy is never ethnographic and that advocacy is incompatible with anthropology as scholarship: "[W]hat is required of the anthropologist as scholar … is to raise the context awareness of the people themselves so that they may eventually become better equipped to plead their own cause."

In many ways, modern linguistics bears a strong imprint of its having evolved out of anthropology, especially in the United States (Errington 2008). It also bears traces of ethnocentrism that characterized the discipline that was its early source of inspiration and the home turf of some of its early practitioners. Therefore, referring to the European colonial practice of power and exploitation in Asia and Africa, Cooper (2005: 4) says that many of those nefarious practices were meant to "project outward [European] ways of understanding the world, [and, furthermore], to demarcate colonizer from colonized, civilized from primitive, core from periphery".

Today, anthropology has transcended those early mistakes and has become a most vibrant discipline, under the aegis of which ground-breaking research is being undertaken. However, globalization has presented hitherto unimaginable challenges, forcing anthropology to re-evaluate some of its foundational principles – indeed, to the point of there being more and more scholars raising serious doubts about its continued existence, at least in its traditional mould and, no doubt, just as many not yet ready to admit defeat (Camaroff 2010; Kohl & Jebens 2013). Even more poignantly, the concept of transculturation throwing a spanner in the works makes it imperative to rethink many of our taken-for-granted assumptions about culture and a host of kindred phenomena, including language.

6. Conclusion

To recapitulate, transculturation is the hallmark of a globalized world, where hitherto divergent and often conflicting cultural elements have slowly but steadily caved in under the forces of contact and mutual influence. These cultural elements included distinctive norms of communication and characteristic social etiquettes, expected behaviours, gestures, etc, elements that once helped distinguish distinct individual cultures and keep them apart.

Does the unabated advance of transculturation obviate the need for translation in future? This question naturally crops up, especially if one remains wedded to the idea that translation is at best and at its plainest interlingual translation. It arises, too, if we also agree that globalization is chipping away at a number of – what we until recently thought were – cut-and-dried, hence non-negotiable identities, among which is that of individual languages, each with its contours firmly and securely delineated. Anyone who hastens to jump to the conclusion that the days of translation are numbered ought to take a deep breath and examine the whole issue more carefully.

In a more profound sense than the one in which it is usually understood, translation antedates the days when individual languages were distinguished from one another and given a 'local habitation and a name'. In a wider sense, translation is present in every conceivable interaction by means of language. Saussure's much-celebrated 'twin talking heads' is only conceivable by subtracting from the picture the role of the translator, the one who mediates between the two talking heads and makes it possible for the two to understand each other. In fact, it is only when we have provisionally or tactically effaced the intermediary function of translation that, like Saussure, we are able to postulate the existence of a language that the speakers have in common that we gain the impression that what one person speaks is readily and unproblematically understood by the listener and vice versa.

Translation will have a role to play as long as there is a need to communicate using language in the process. The future that awaits the translator may well be egregiously different from what we have thus far assumed it to be, but, as of now, there is no conceivable way in which the work of the translator can be made redundant.

Acknowledgements

I wish to thank the Conselho Nacional de Desenvolvimento Científico e Tecnológico (Brazilian National Council for Scientific and Technological Development)

(CNPq), a funding agency under Brazil's Ministry of Science and Technology, for financing my research (Grant no 301589/2009-7).

References

Álvarez, Román & Vidal, María Carmen-África (eds). 1996. *Translation, power, subversion.* Clevedon, Philadelphia/Adelaide: Multilingual Matters.

Camaroff, John. 2010. The end of anthropology, again: On the future of an in/discipline. *American Anthropologist* 112(4): 524–538.

Carbonell, Ovidio. 1996. The exotic space of cultural translation. In Román Álvarez & María Carmen-África Vidal (eds) *Translation, power, subversion.* Clevedon, Philadelphia/Adelaide: Multilingual Matters, 78–84.

Cooper, Frederick. 2005. *Colonialism in question: Theory, knowledge, history.* Berkeley, CA: University of California Press.

Deleuze, Gilles & Guattari, Félix. 1986. *Kafka: Toward a minor literature* (transl. Dana Polan). Minneapolis: University of Minnesota Press.

Errington, Joseph. 2008. *Linguistics in a colonial world: A story of language, meaning, and power.* Malden, MA: Blackwell Publishing.

Gallagher, Hugh. 2013. Willingness to communicate and cross-cultural adaptation: L2 communication and acculturative stress as transaction. *Applied Linguistics* 34: 53–73.

Hastrup, Kirsten & Elsass, Peter. 1990. Anthropological advocacy: A contradiction in terms? *Current Anthropology* 31(3): 301–311.

Hutton, Christopher. 1999. *Linguistics and the Third Reich: Mother-tongue fascism, race and the science of language.* London/New York: Routledge.

Kohl, Karl-Heinz & Jebens, Hoger (eds). 2013. *The end of anthropology?* London: Sean Kingston Publishing.

Ortiz, Fernando. 1995. *Cuban counterpoint: Tobacco and sugar.* Durham, NC: Duke University Press.

Prćić, Tvrtko. 2014. English as the nativized foreign language and its impact on Serbian. *English Today* 30: 13–20.

Rajagopalan, Kanavillil. 1999. Review of *Translation, power, subversion* by Román Álvarez and María Carmen-África Vidal (eds). *Babel* 45(4): 374–377.

Ramanathan, Vaidehi & Pennycook, Alastair. 2007. Talking across time: Postcolonial challenges to language, history, and difference. *Journal of Contemporary Thought* 25: 25–53.

Robinson, Douglas. 1997. *The translator's turn.* Baltimore: Johns Hopkins University Press.

Rubel, Paula G & Rosman, Abraham (eds). 2003. *Translating cultures. Perspectives on translation and anthropology.* Oxford/New York: Berg.

Silverstein, Michael. 2003. Translation, transduction, transformation: skating "Glossando" on thin semiotic ice. In Paula G Rubel & Abraham Rosman (eds)

Translating cultures. Perspectives on translation and anthropology. Oxford/New York: Berg, 75–108.

Simon, Sherry. 1996. *Gender in translation: Cultural identity and the politics of transmission*. London/New York: Routledge.

Tymoczko, Maria. 2012. Translation theory. In Carol A Chapelle (ed) *The encyclopaedia of applied linguistics*. New York: Wiley, 5928–5937.

Venuti, Lawrence. 1995. *The translator's invisibility*. London/New York: Routledge.

Weissbort, Daniel & Eysteinsson, Astradur (eds). 2006. *Translation: Theory and practice: A historical reader*. New York: Oxford University Press.

Elżbieta Tabakowska

Jagiellonian University of Kraków

Grammar, 'Cultural Meaning' and Translation Pedagogy

Abstract

In agreement with modern principles of translation pedagogy, translation competence must include a knowledge of grammar in the broad sense, that is, not only in terms of formal and semantic properties, but also in terms of the cultural load carried by units of language. In agreement with cognitivist theory, the author argues that it is not only lexical items (realia) or idioms and set expressions that have cultural meaning; grammatical structures also do. Culture-sensitive aspects of grammar, which is the subject-matter of ethnolinguistics, have to be made manifest to translators, albeit not within the traditional framework of the grammar translation method. To substantiate this claim, the author presents two case studies: an extract from a Polish novel in which the writer employs the cultural meaning of the reflexive pronoun *się* in order to bring into relief the relationship between the characters, and a commercial media advertisement.

Keywords: cognitivist theory, ethnolinguistics, cross-cultural competence, Polish grammar, translation teaching

1. Translation, culture and cognition

The expanding field of Translation Studies (TS) means accepting the fact that translation is ubiquitous, that it is a crucial process of the human mind and a crucial element of human life. In the words of the author of the introduction to a recent anthology on translation,

> translation proves a relevant factor for culture and cognition and … this relationship can help understanding translation itself: hence, the concepts of translation, cognition and culture are strongly and deeply interwoven. (Hanenberg 2015: 4)

As a result, the role of translation has repeatedly been defined as that of a mediator between cultures.

Most scholars accept various modern versions of Von Humboldt's claim, summarized as the statement that "the culture of one language differs from cultures of other languages, as every nation has its own repertoire of thoughts expressed in everyday communication" (Osadnik 2008: 159, my translation). Translation, therefore, cannot be limited to the transposition of words, phrases and sentences, but it has to take into consideration the "treasure, which is the culture of a given nation" (ibid.). Yet, frequently, scholars limit their discussions to what is known as 'cultural realia'. They categorize such culture-specific elements and compile more or less comprehensive lists, including items pertaining to geography, ethnography, art, ethnicity, politics and society.[1] Following such classifications, strategies and procedures for translating cultural realia are proposed as guidelines for aspiring translators. However, the corpora thus obtained could be enriched by including the results of research done in the field of lexical semantics within the framework of prototype theory, for example.[2] The idea that the structure of the lexical categories in a natural language is prototypical, with some of the category members being 'better' than others and prototypical effects being culture-sensitive, is relevant to both the theory and the practice of translation. To recall a classic example, the fact that the common category 'bird' is represented by a sparrow in some cultures and by a humming bird in others might obviously influence the process of 'intercultural mediation'.

The subfield of linguistics that has become known as 'ethnolinguistics' opens up new and promising vistas in its own right. Aiming to construct what they define as a 'linguistic picture of the world', the proponents of ethnolinguistic research on (lexical) semantics describe the close links that exist between cognition and cultural encoding. For instance, inspired by the work of Wierzbicka, the group of Polish scholars led by Bartmiński, a prominent linguist, has produced analyses of the culturally most heavily loaded Polish nouns, such as *los* (fate), *dom* (house/home) or *ojczyzna* (homeland), which will certainly be of great use to those teaching and doing translation from or into Polish (cf. Bartmiński 2009/2003). For instance, in a well-known Polish poem the author talks about "fear in a man's black glove" chasing "the citizen of a small country" (Lipska 1986/2003).

[1] For a recent survey, see Wróblewski (2015).
[2] Introduced and discussed in Lakoff (1987).

Although appropriate as a translation, the phrase lacks the original implication of ominous security-service surveillance (the agents used to wear black leather gloves).

Idioms and set expressions constitute yet another topic frequently dealt with in work on the translation, culture and cognition triad. The problem of culture-sensitive diversification is well known, and relevant translation procedures are well covered in the literature.[3] Other culture-specific linguistic expressions, such as those discussed under the rubric of intertextuality or, more generally, 'cultural references', attract the attention of both language and translation teachers.[4] Useful as they are for translation pedagogy, studies on various kinds of 'cultural realia' tend to leave out some important aspects of cultural diversification that go beyond lexical items or set expressions and involve formal structure and grammar. Whereas it is recognized that "cultural differences are reflected in language", the relation between grammar and culture is often limited to such obvious categories as "the category of grammatical gender, number, verbal aspect, etc" (Osadnik 2008: 168, my translation). The 'etc' is hardly ever developed into a fully-fledged discussion, and the translators' inability to deal with culturally loaded grammar is added to a long list of their failures.

2. Cross-cultural competence (3C) or translation competence

Translation pedagogy cannot be effective unless it is based upon a maximally precise description of translation competence. But such a 'precise description' is extremely difficult to produce, as exemplified by the outcome of two years of hard work by an international group of experts recruited in 2009 by the European Commission. A solid basis for university programmes, the expert 'list of competences' produced by Gambier's 2008 Master's in Translation (EMT) expert group (http://ec.europa.eu/dgs/translation/programmes/emt/key_documents/emt_competences_translators_en.pdf) is still not considered ideal, nor is it generally approved by those concerned.

Referred to as cross-cultural competence (3C), in translation pedagogy 'intercultural competence' is generally defined as a complex of 'sub-com-

[3] See, for example, the relevant section in Baker (1992) or language-specific studies dealing with particular language pairs (e.g. Gottlieb 1997).

[4] For a discussion and further reading, see, for example, Olshanskaya (2011).

petences', such as language competence (high language proficiency), textual competence (knowledge of text types and rules of text composition) and sociolinguistic competence (knowledge of differing discursive practices). Obviously, these competences overlap, and the '3C' is taught nowadays in relation to cultural aspects of language structure and cultural contexts of language use. However, syllabi show limitations similar to those found in the theoretical discussions. The established interdependence between cognition, culture and translation is often limited to such entities as cultural realia or idioms and set expressions, while close ties between culture and grammar are rarely brought to the fore. In the neighbouring discipline of Cultural Studies, the situation is not much better: 'cultural competence' is said to include "studies about the target culture ranging from everyday life to social and political institutions", and it is carefully kept apart from 'linguistic competence' (Pietrzak 2009: 325).

Authors of syllabi and curricula often oscillate between two approaches: they either write of 'translation *training*' or of 'translation *teaching*'. The choice reflects their underlying philosophy: translation considered as a craft involves attaining the level of expertise achievable by training, and subsequent practice is accomplished by following instructions, which are first given and then implemented. On the other hand, translation considered as an art can be taught only through building up translation competence. Therefore, we are back to square one, facing the necessity to make the notorious 'craft-or-art' choice. Perhaps it is easier to choose when moot points are sorted out as a set of binary opposition. First, there is the opposition between the individual and the collective. While culture is a system of "products of human cognition" (Balicki 2009: 389) that constitute the common property shared by members of a community, an individual member of a culture imposes upon this general grid their own personal experience and identity. 'The collective' – preserved in collective memory – becomes embodied in language as a conventionalised repertoire of means of expression and communication. 'The individual' involves a creative interpretation of individual experience, grounded in and restricted by 'the collective'. The opposition may therefore be seen as that between the interpretative and the intersubjective (cf. ibid.: 392–393).

The second crucial opposition in this respect is that between 'the said' and 'the unsaid', that is, between explicit information that "transmits some new knowledge and gives names to elements of a foreign reality" as opposed to 'background knowledge', which includes "encyclopaedic information, logical reasoning and language proficiency, and pragmatic competences" (Tokarz 2008: 8; my translation).

It is these two oppositions that seem to underlie most arguments for teaching (rather than training) translation. I contend that building up translation competence involves sensitization to the interplay of the oppositions that were listed above. As I have said, I concentrate on culturally loaded grammatical structures. In the next section, I examine two grammatical phenomena as an illustration of an aspect of translation teaching that is not readily noticed and acknowledged.

3. Case studies: *się*[5] and *dla*

As mentioned above, in Cognitive Linguistics the 'cultural turn' has promoted research on culture-sensitive ways in which people's interpretation of reality becomes encoded in their language(s). If, as is claimed by the proponents of ethnosyntax (e.g. Wierzbicka 1979; Enfield 2002), the grammar of a natural language is permeated with the culture of the given linguistic community, then acknowledging this cultural load is as significant for theorists of language as it is for translation scholars.

The first case study presented below involves an extract from the prize-winning novel by the contemporary Polish writer Jerzy Pilch, titled *Pod Mocnym Aniołem* (2001), translated as *The Mighty Angel* (2010). The choice of a literary text was motivated by two reasons. First, following the proponents of the cultural turn, I support the claim that there is no fundamental qualitative difference between 'literature' and 'non-literature'. All texts use language in order to communicate, and in both 'the collective' merges with 'the individual'; but what is considered as 'literature' differs from 'non-literature' in that the former is a manifestation of a more creative and more conscious use of linguistic devices (Balcerzan 2013). The devices are available to all users of the given language, although authors of texts defined as literary show higher levels of consciousness and more inventiveness. This in turn results in a higher density of phenomena that can be selected as teaching points. Hence the second reason: the practical usefulness of 'literature' for the translation teacher. The case study focuses on the Polish lexeme *się* which is, historically, a reflexive pronoun, unmarked for gender

---

[5] A more comprehensive analysis of this item, in the context of untranslatability, was presented in Tabakowska (2002).

and number, corresponding to English reflexive pronouns *myself, yourself/selves, him/her/itself, themselves.* Apart from the prototypical uses in reflexive forms, as in

(1) *Janek się myje dwa razy dziennie*
Janek *się* washes twice a day
'Janek washes twice a day',

it is used in what descriptive grammars describe as *passive diathesis*, which involves demotion of the semantic role of the Agent by raising the role of the Patient. Therefore

(2) *Te schorzenia łatwo się leczą*
These diseases easily *się* cure
'These diseases are easily cured',

where the Patient becomes the grammatical subject, or

(3) *Ryby nie je się nożem*
Fish–Acc not eat–3 pers Sg *się* with a knife
'One does not eat fish with a knife',

or

(4) *Ochłodziło się*
Became cold–3 pers Sg *się*,
'It became cold',

where the impersonal form of the verb erases the Agent completely.

The above technical description needs not, of course, to make up part of a translator's education. What matters, however, is that forms exemplified by (2), (3) and (4) are among the most heavily culturally loaded grammatical constructions specific to the Slavic languages, particularly to Polish. Therefore (2) implies a pragmatic context in which the speaker demotes the Agent for some communicative purpose, although this Agent can still be recognized and identified, either by the speaker or by the receiver, using their background knowledge. In (2) above the collective Agent is identified as 'doctors', or, metonymically, as 'hospitals', 'medicine', etc. In (3), which is generic in meaning, the Agent is, as the prominent Polish linguist Klemensiewicz (1982) aptly puts it, "a generalised human being" restricted by social and cultural norms. Finally, (4) implies the impossibility of the Agent's recognition or identification.

Characteristically, structures exemplified by (4) occur in expressions referring to natural phenomena. The underlying 'background knowledge' is that such phenomena are governed by mysterious potent forces that cannot be known and which are usually menacing for human beings. This 'non-rationalist ethnophilosophy' is considered a characteristic feature of Slavic culture (cf. e.g. Wierzbicka 1979). In this light, a Polish theorist of translation posits:

> Whatever is subject to changeability and under-specification in Polish cultural mentality is replaced [in translation], as far as possible, with specificity, unequivocality and a coherent way of looking at the world. (Tokarz 2009: 20, my translation)

It seems natural that talking about unknowable agents should require impersonal structures, therefore implying that things 'happen by themselves'. As opposed to this metaphysical way of thinking, 'rational' cultures, such as those in English-speaking societies, have not developed parallel constructions or grammaticalized analogous concepts.

The above reasoning, perhaps more useful to translators, need not constitute an element of their education either. What is more directly relevant, however, is that in actual texts authors can use the construction consciously and creatively, imposing upon the receiver of the message an interpretation which is crucially informed by the cultural component, or the 'non-rationalist ethnophilosophical' thinking in this instance. The case discussed below provides just one example of this.

The Mighty Angel is a shocking study of addiction. The main character, who is the narrator and an alter ego of the author, records the history of his attempts to free himself from alcoholism. In a hospital ward, one of the other delirious patients writes a letter describing the practices of his, as he calls them, 'she-therapists':

> … the absolute, all-encompassing obsession of first-person narration. I, I, I. God forbid you should use the impersonal form. God forbid you should say 'a person' … God forbid the plural. (Pilch 2010: 105-6)

In the original, 'the impersonal form' is the notorious *się*, which the author of the letter uses further down in his account:

(5) … *no i zaczęło się.*

['Well began *się*.']

– Co się zaczęło? – wypytują … terapeucice, akcentując zwrotny zaimek 'się'.

['What *się* began? – ask the she-therapists, stressing the reflexive pronoun *się*.']

Co 'się' zaczęło?

['What began *się*?']

– Picie się zaczęło, zaczęło się pić – mówi Janek, a one (…) wykrzykują:

['Drinking began *się*, began *się* to drink – says Janek, and they shout:']

– Się piło! Się piło! Ale kto pił? Siępiło pił? … Kto pił?

['*Się* drank! *Się* drank! But who drank? *Się* – drank drank? Who drank?']

(…) Zamiast 'człowiek' trzeba mówić 'ja', … nie 'się-piło' ale 'ja piłem'.

['Instead of 'man' [one] should say 'I', (…) not '*się* drank', but 'I drank'.']

Being ashamed of one's alcohol addiction is probably a general feeling shared by most addicts. But presumably the verbal means that may be used in communication to cover this shame are not available to all of them. Pilch's Janek uses the 'ethnophilosophy' behind the form *się* in order to completely demote the Agent, or to remove himself from the scene; like a rain shower or a thunderstorm, drinking just happens to him, a forceful action performed by a mysterious power that remains beyond his control. In this way Janek tries to avoid remorse and responsibility, to which his 'she-therapists' react by trying to force him to use 'I' and therefore regain control.

The English translation was produced by Bill Johnston, a renowned translator of Polish literature into English. Insightful as it is, though, it still fails to do full justice to the passage quoted in (5).

(6) 'So then things started.'

'What things started?', ask the she-therapists (…), stressing the generic noun 'things'. 'Exactly which 'things' began?'

'The drinking started, the drinking began, says Janek, and they … exclaim:'

'The drinking began! The drinking started! But who was doing the drinking? Was the drinking started drinking? … Who was drinking?' (2010: 127-8)

Here the element of 'ethnophilosophy', the speaker's lack of control over activities performed by mysterious and potent forces, has been lost.

The second case study is of a different nature: it involves what might be described as 'cultural neutralization'.

In the era of globalization, whose influence upon various aspects of translation as a general human activity has been much discussed, interlingual translation has been observed to level out cultural differences and to reflect 'the globalized culture'. One of the many examples of such globalization is given in (7) below: The advertisements now regularly seen on billboards and television screens involve a change which results in a culture-loaded structure historically alien to Polish society:

(7) *Kwiaty* ***dla*** *twojego ogrodu, szampon* ***dla*** *twoich włosów*, etc.
['Flowers for your garden, shampoo for your hair …']

The preposition *dla* ('for'), as different from *do* ('towards'), the usual and traditional choice for expressions as those in (7), becomes an exponent of the cultural meaning of partnership and equal footing: one's garden or hair are conceptualized as recipients of valuable gifts, which they can value and appreciate.

Texts exemplified by examples (5)–(7) above illustrate the point made earlier in this chapter: grammatical structures are thick with cultural meaning, and aspiring translators should be made sensitive to this. Therefore, teachers of translation should build up the contextual dimension of translators' intercultural competence.

4. Translation teaching (as different from training)

From what was said above, it might seem that what is advocated here is the good old (and, in language teaching, totally discredited) 'grammar-translation' method. As language teachers of older generations might still remember, in its classical version the method was based on the belief that the best way to understand the words and structures of a foreign language is by translating them into one's native tongue. And since well-known and admired literary texts were believed to be the best paragons of proficient language use, the main teaching technique was interlingual translation, and the teaching materials used consisted of excerpts from prominent works of literature.

However, the 'new' version of the method, which I propose here as an element of translation pedagogy, means rejecting most of the 'old' tenets, for its assumptions are very different. Linguistic messages are inherently subjective; they come as particular effects of particular choices, made out of the linguistic repertoire available and conditioned by particular communicative purposes. Their meanings are created by the interpretations made by those who receive them, and therefore every reading of a text, translation proper included, is its translation. Translation proper, therefore, is not a mere reproduction of the original, but a creative production of what the translator believes to be the original meaning. Therefore, what is inevitably involved is imagination – a faculty of the human mind often referred to, implicitly or explicitly, in modern discussions of the translation process (cf. e.g. Abrantes 2015). Interest in imagination and memory has certainly been fostered by the turn towards cognitivism – in literature, in linguistics and in TS. One of the basic cognitive processes, namely, imagining things, implies the use of the individual's perception, experience and knowledge to create new images, to enrich them with detail and to recreate and recall them at will. Individual representations formed in the translator's mind are relative to what is defined as the translator's 'background knowledge', that is, they combine the reflection of culture with individual conceptualization. The latter is composed of cultural representations that belong to source and/or target cultures, since it is 'culture that furnishes the material for imagination' (Roth, quoted in Abrantes 2015: 58).

In the process of translation 'a culturally shaped mind mediates between what is read in a language and what is rendered in a different language' (Abrantes 2015: 61–62). The 'tacit influence of [native] culture' furnishes mental images that are originally set in a culture foreign to the translator. The foreign context can be misunderstood and mistranslated. Alternatively, the element of the foreign culture may have no counterpart in the culture of the TL, and what looks like mistranslation proves to be an instance of untranslatability – which is indeed the case in examples (5) and (6) above. Whether the 'lack-of-control-over-mysterious-forces' element would be better rendered by, for instance, amplification, is a subject for classroom discussion. The purpose of such a 'dynamic translation activity' is precisely to problematize and find justifications for alternative solutions rather than present an ideal one. In this sense, teaching translation ultimately becomes an exercise in imagination.

For that purpose, literary texts seem to provide the ideal teaching material – the only assumption of the old 'grammar-translation' method which would still be considered valid, even though in a changed context, as the higher level of creativity and larger concentration of devices traditionally defined as 'literary' throw the issues to be discussed into relief. This would, of course, be true in relation to 'cultural realia' as defined above. But it is important to remember that it is also in grammatical systems that particular ways of perception and conceptualization, as well as particular systems of values, feelings and emotions, are embedded.

References

Abrantes, Ana Margarida. 2015. Translation and imagination. In Peter Hanenberg (ed) *A new visibility: On culture, translation and cognition*. Lisbon: Universidade Católica Editora. 48–64.

Baker, Mona. 1992. *In other words. A course book on translation*. London/New York: Routledge.

Balcerzan, Edward. 2013. *Literackość*. Toruń: Wydawnictwo Naukowe Uniwersytetu Mikołaja Kopernika.

Balicki, Bogdan. 2009. "Kultura" – pojęcie problematotwórcze czy problematyczne? Kilka uwag z konstruktywistycznego punktu widzenia. In Balicki, Bogdan, Ryż Bartosz & Szczerbuk Emil (eds) *Kultura w nauce o literaturze*. Wrocław: Oficyna Wydawnicza ATUT, 385–393.

Bartmiński, Jerzy. 2009. *Aspects of cognitive ethnolinguistics* (trans. A Głaz). London/Oakville: Equinox.

Enfield, NJ (ed). 2002. *Ethnosyntax. Explorations in grammar and culture*. Oxford: OUP.

Gottlieb, Henrik. 1997. Quality revisited: The rendering of English idioms in Danish television subtitles vs printed translation. In Anne Trosborg (ed) *Text typology and translation*. Amsterdam/Philadelphia: John Benjamins, 309–338.

Hanenberg, Peter (ed). 2015. *A new visibility: On culture, translation and cognition*, Lisbon: Universidade Católica Editora.

Klemensiewicz, Zenon. 1982. *Składnia, stylistyka, pedagogika językowa*. Warszawa: PWN.

Lakoff, George. 1987. *Women, fire and dangerous things*. Chicago: Chicago University Press.

Olshanskaya, Natalia. 2011. De-coding intertextuality in classic and postmodern Russian narratives. *Translation and Interpreting Studies* 6(1): 87–102.

Osadnik, Wacław M. 2008. Przekład jako poszukiwanie ekwiwalencji kulturowej (o angielskim tłumaczeniu Wojnypolsko-ruskiej pod flagą biało-czerwoną Doroty Masłowskiej). In Piotr Fast, Przemyslaw Janikowski & Agata Olszta (eds) *Odmienność kulturowa w przekładzie. Studia o przekładzie 25*. Katowice/Częstochowa: Wydawnictwo Naukowe „Śląsk' i Wydawnictwo Wyższej Szkoły Lingwistycznej, 157–189.

Pietrzak, Paulina. 2009. Translation competence. In Łukasz Bogucki, Stanislaw Goźdź-Roszkowski & Piotr Stalmaszczyk (eds) *Ways to translation*. Łódź: Łódź University Press, 317–338.

Tabakowska, Elżbieta. 2002. Tłumaczenie gramatyki czy przekład kultury? In Władysław Chłopicki (ed) *Język trzeciego tysiąclecia II*. Kraków: Tertium, 71–80.

Tokarz, Bożena. 2009. Bariery kulturowe w przekładzie. In Piotr Fast, Przemysław Janikowski & Agata Olszta (eds) *Odmienność kulturowa w przekładzie. Studia o przekładzie 25*. Katowice/Częstochowa: Wydawnictwo Naukowe „Śląsk' i Wydawnictwo Wyższejv Szkoły Lingwistycznej, 7–24.

Wierzbicka, Anna. 1979. Ethno-syntax and the philosophy of grammar. *Studies in Language* 3(3): 313–383.

Wróblewski, Janusz. 2015. Cultural barriers in translation. In Łukasz Bogucki, Stanisław Goźdź-Roszkowski & Piotr Stalmaszczyk (eds) *Ways to translation*. Łódź: Łódź University Press, 109–143.

Sources of the examples

Lipska, Ewa. 1986/2003. Obywatel małego kraju. In Ewa Lipska *Sekwens*. Warszawa: Świat Książki, 8–17.

Lipska, Ewa. 1996. The citizen of a small country (trans. Regina Grol). In Regina Grol (ed) *Ambers aglow. An anthology of contemporary Polish women's poetry*. Austin, Texas: Host Publications, 231–232.

Pilch, Jerzy. 2001. *Pod mocnym aniołem*. Warszawa: Świat Książki.

Pilch, Jerzy. 2010. *The mighty angel* (trans. Bill Johnston). Kindle edition.

Transculturalism in Translation Teaching

NATALIA KALOH VID AND VLASTA KUČIŠ

University of Maribor

Teaching Translation in the Context of Culture and Ideology

Abstract

In contemporary Translation Studies, translation is defined as a transnational and intercultural communication activity. Therefore, one of the primary tasks of translators is to mediate not only between languages but also between cultures. As ideology is one a crucial cultural constraint, it is essential to teach students that the selection of translation strategies is always either implicitly or explicitly affected by the translator's ideology. The main aim of this chapter is to illustrate the importance of introducing Critical Discourse Analysis (CDA) as an adequate tool for ideological analysis in the translation classroom. The theoretical framework is based on Vermeer's Skopos theory and Van Dijk's Critical Discourse Analysis. By understanding how social relations of power are exercised and negotiated in and through discourses, future translators will be able to operate better at different levels during text (re)production and translation of a message. This contribution outlines a course in which the students were presented with advertising slogans in English and German. Both the authors of this contribution and the students concentrated on the ways in which information was structured as well as on 'unpacking' ideologically influenced constraints and cultural influences. As a next step, the students were asked to use the discourse analysis tools they had been acquiring to analyse Slovenian translations of the same advertisements and to offer their own suggestions in cases where they were not satisfied with the official translation.

Keywords: ideology, Critical Discourse Analysis, Skopos theory, advertisements

1. Introduction

The question of ideological influence on translation has always been a part of Translation Studies (TS). Fawcett (1998: 107) reminds us how "through the centuries, individuals and institutions have applied their particular beliefs to the production of certain effects in translations". He also claims that "an 'ideological' approach to translation can be found in some of the earliest examples of translation known to us" (1998: 106). Appreciating the significance of language as a carrier of not merely messages but also culture and culturally important components is essential to a proper understanding of the ideological approach to the study of translation.

The prevalence of cultural translation in modern Translation Studies (Snell-Hornby 1987; Nord 1991; Venuti 1992; Bassnett & Lefevere 1998; Bachmann-Medick 2006; Vermeer 2007) corroborates the idea that translation is both a linguistic activity and – even primarily – a culture-transferring pursuit. Therefore, translators must be not only bilingual – that is a given – but effectively bicultural too. As Nida (2001: 82) points out: "For truly successful translating, biculturalism is even more important than bilingualism, since words only have meanings in terms of the cultures in which they function." The main challenge, according to Heringer (2007), is that cultural differences make the development of an empathetic understanding of other cultures difficult. It is not only language, script, history, religion, customs, traditions, conventions and norms, but also subjective attitudes that can be disturbing factors. This process of 'understanding' a different culture automatically includes appreciating the importance of ideology as a crucial aspect that underlies any culture and therefore each translation. In her discussion of the ideological aspects of translations Schäffner (2003: 23) notes:

> Ideological aspects can […] be determined within a text itself, both at the lexical level (reflected, for example, in the deliberate choice or avoidance of a particular word […] and the grammatical level (for example, use of passive structures to avoid an expression of agency). Ideological aspects can be more or less obvious in texts, depending on the topic of a text, its genre and its communicative purposes.

This contribution focuses on our introducing ideological analysis as one of the important constraints in the translation of advertising slogans while working with the MA students from the Department of Translation Studies at the Faculty of Arts, University of Maribor, Slovenia As such, we wish to highlight the importance of ideological analysis through Critical Discourse Analysis as a contemporary didactic tool in the training programmes of future professional translators who should be well aware of their own importance as intercultural communication mediators. Although translation undoubtedly requires adequate linguistic knowledge, culture is no less important. Students often experience major difficulties when encountering culture-bound elements and 'get lost' when they are required to demonstrate that they are familiar with target cultural background. As a result, we are often confronted with the problem of culturally dysfunctional translation (Tymoczko 2006; Prunč 2008).

It seemed logical to look at advertising slogans in this light, as advertising is socially constructed through the discourse of clients, advertising practitioners, and consumers. This makes the advertising process ripe for discourse-analytic exploration (Hackley 2000: 44). Advertising is generally believed to be of critical importance to the success of companies and, although advertisements are ephemeral in that each one is short-lived, their effects are longstanding and cumulative: they leave traces of themselves behind, which combine to form a body of messages about the culture that produced them (Goddard 1998: 3).

A translated advertisement should reflect the ideology of the place where it is produced. It should also reflect the ideology of the time when it is produced. Consumers should recognize themselves in the advertisement. If they do not, they will assume that the advertisements are not directed at them and they may not trust the brand. Nord believes that "[a]lmost any decision in translation is consciously or unconsciously guided by ideological criteria" (2003: 111). Lefevere's view of any translation as a "rewriting of an original text and all rewritings, whatever their intention, reflect a certain ideology and poetics and as such manipulate literature to function in a given way" (1992: 13–26) also applies to the philosophy of advertising translation in the sense that advertising materials sometimes have to be rewritten in order to adapt to the ideology and culture of the milieu at which they are targeted.

The translation of advertising slogans is not so very different from other types of translation. However, in order for advertisements to reach a large audience, translating them requires particular skills, including creativity, trans-creation, in-depth cultural adaptation and localisation, discourse analysis, semiotics, pragmatics and cross-cultural communication, which always includes ideological aspects.

2. Ideology

Before we continue our discussion of the relations between ideology, language and translation, it seems necessary to clarify what ideology means and how it functions in society. The field of what has become commonly known as the 'theory of ideology' and its influences in various spheres is both diverse and expansive. The term 'ideology' has always been accompanied by its political connotation and defined as an instrument for legitimizing the power of a dominant social group or class. Hamilton states that ideology is a system of collectively held normative, and reputedly factual ideas and beliefs and attitudes advocating a particular pattern of social relationships and arrangements, and/or aimed at justifying a particular pattern of conduct, which its proponent seeks to promote, realize, pursue or maintain (1987: 39).

Lefevere describes ideology as the "conceptual grid that consists of opinions and attitudes deemed acceptable in a certain society at a certain time and through which readers and translators approach texts", and argues that "translation is governed above all by patronage, which consists of ideological, economic and status components" (quoted in Baker 1998: 137).

Following Lefevere's ideas about the influence of ideology on translation, Calzada Pérez suggests that Translation Studies digs into ideological phenomena for a variety of reasons (2003). One of the most important reasons is the fact that all language use is, as CDA claims, ideological. This means that translation itself as "an operation carried out on language use" is always influenced by ideology (ibid.: 2). Behind all choices made by a translator is a voluntary act that reveals the translator's socio-political and cultural surrounding. Prunč, who introduced the term 'translation culture', shares the same perspective and argues that the social construct of a translation culture is configured by a set of socially controlled translation relevant norms, rules, conventions, expectations, values and habitualised patterns of behaviour (2008: 24–25).

Applying these definitions to our study, we believe that ideology represents the opinions and attitudes of people in given societies and that these opinions and attitudes inform the production and consumption of advertisements. As such, the ideology of a given society affects the way translators translate advertisements in that society. We therefore find it essential to teach our students that the selection of any translation strategy is always either implicitly or explicitly affected by the translator's ideology. And that is in turn constrained by the norms of the society and its authoritative bodies, such as publishers, institutions, clients and governments. If an advertising campaign does not comply with the ideological constraints of the milieu that it targets, then the adverts may even be banned and, consequently, the products or services will not be sold in that region.

3. Theoretical background

We used the translation of advertisements as texts bound up in convention-and-culture to develop our learning method. We based it on the functionalist translation theories of Skopos and on CDA.

We believe Vermeer's Skopos theory, or the theory of purpose, is crucial to understanding a transcultural advertisement because, from the perspective of this theory, translation is "a process of intercultural communication and the end product is a text which is capable of functioning appropriately in specific situations and context of use" (Schäffner 1998: 3). Reiß and Vermeer (1991: 96) suggest that "*Die Dominante aller Translation ist deren Zweck*", that is, texts are always created for a certain purpose, and translation is therefore always purpose-made. According to Nord (2003: 2), only a translation that achieves the intended purpose may be called functional, and each translator of advertisements should therefore be aware of the specific purpose and function of the text in the target setting because "all translation decisions depend on the presupposition the translator has about the target consumer's interpretation of the message" (Valdés in Munday 2004: 205). The task of the translator is then not to translate an advertisement as closely as possible, but rather to achieve the same – or an even better – effect in the target setting.

The analysis carried out in class was also based on CDA, which exposes "the ideological forces that underlie communicative exchanges" (Calzada Pérez 2003: 2), and provides the assumption that ideologies are largely acquired and changed through discourse. The social–cognitive nature of ideologies as forms of social cognitions is always shared by social groups. CDA advocates that all language use, including translation, should be interpreted under the influence of various ideologies, which means that translation is always a site for ideological encounters. Van Dijk defines ideology as "basic systems of shared social representations that may control more specific group beliefs" (1996: 7). Álvarez and Vidal suggest that translation can become a form of control used by a 'superior' culture to create an image of the original, particularly for those who have no access to the reality of the original (1996: 3–4). They call attention to the abuse of power that translation can enable because all translation implies manipulation, whether conscious or not, of the original. If translators transform themselves from an invisible medium into a main participant in the process of a text's creation, then they automatically interpret texts by setting them against their general knowledge (about other texts, statements, discourses, conventions), and this knowledge is necessarily shaped by their social position and therefore it is ideological:

> Translators […] let their knowledge govern their behaviour, and that knowledge is ideological. It is controlled by ideological norms. If you want to become a translator you must submit to the translator's submissive role, submit to being possessed by what ideological norms inform you. (Calzada Pérez 2003: 7)

4. Context of the course and methodology

The research was conducted at the Department of Translation Studies, University of Maribor, Slovenia. We included 30 students (n = 30) of the first and the second years of the MA programme of Translating and Interpreting. All of them were native speakers of Slovenian. The participants were both male and female, aged between 22 and 25 years. Through working with the MA students from our department, we discovered that the use of ideologically based analyses of translations as a didactic instrument contributes to the quality of translation and a better understanding of the translated text's Skopos. It also provides a better insight into the connections between the use of language and the exercise of power, cultural values, and standard systems of the source and target cultures. CDA also develops critical thinking skills. We believe that learning to recognize connections between the use of language and the exercise of power is certainly useful. If students learn to uncover the ideological forces that underlie most forms of contemporary communicative exchanges, to negotiate the complex and mixed messages of the media, to identify racist language or any other ideological slant in a newspaper or magazine article, or to detect racial or sexual bias in advertisements or business reports, they will be able to mediate between cultures more effectively.

The instrument used in the study was Van Dijk's method of ideological textual analysis, which, in contrast to strictly linguistically oriented analyses (Fairclough & Wodak 1997), has developed a socio-cognitive analysis of discourse, oriented both to the lexicosyntactic features of texts and to cultural and social resources and contexts (which are even more important). On the basis of this categorization, Van Dijk lists structures and strategies of text and talk that are typically ideologically relevant, depending on topic, context, speech act and communicative goals:

- Strategies describing positive action are: emphasis, assertion, hyperbole, detailed description, prominent position; headlining, summarizing; narrative illustration, topicalization; attribution to personality; explicit; direct; argumentative support and impression management.

- Strategies describing negative action are divided into: de-emphasis; denial; understatement; de-topicalization; low, non-prominent position; marginalization; vague, overall description; attribution to context; implicit; indirect; no storytelling; no argumentative support and no impression management.

Of course, in most cases only positive strategies may be applied to the analysis of advertisements. However, the students used Van Dijk's instrument effectively because it provides the combination of both linguistic and functional methods.

Following CDA theory, and in the light of Van Dijk's (1988) framework as a basis for data analysis, the content of all the texts we used was individually examined at a micro level of analysis. The analysis therefore included revealing a generalized conception of foreground/background mechanisms that dealt with the following items:

- Lexicalization: It focuses on the use of biased words, concepts or ideologically laden terms.
- Dominant syntactic choices or grammatical metaphors are a powerful ideological tool that consists of various strategies as a response to possible interlingual translation problems such as passivization, nominalization, modalization and addition or omission.

During the translation the students were allowed to use various cultural and learners' dictionaries from English–German to Slovenian and from English–German to English–German. Students' personal notes and observations were recorded in a methodological diary. It was explained to the students that they would be uncovering potentially hidden meanings, deciphering linguistic structures, 'reading between the lines', unveiling the subliminal and, finally, that they would be asked to apply the textual analysis while translating. As we focused on the ideological background of advertisements, students were asked to think about religious, social, moral and ethical norms in Slovenian society. The issue of the restrictions imposed on the advertisements of certain products (such as spirits and tobacco) was not considered as we chose advertisements only of products that can be advertised in Slovenia without limitations.

The course, in other words, was not strictly 'academic' or theoretical, since the students were offered concrete ways of interpreting contemporary culture and its signs. The important distinguishing feature of advertising discourse is its function, since this is always to persuade people to buy a particular product. The course comprised both English and German source (ST) and target texts (TT). Students share the same first language (L1), Slovenian, on which we based translation practice.

First, we presented the most significant features of discourse analysis and explained how the students would benefit from it. To explain our choice of material, we provided a short overview of studies on powerful ideological forces within consumer culture (Wernick 1991; Hackley 2000; Ewen 2001). The purpose of the theoretical part was to illustrate how advertising practitioners use the embedded cultural knowledge they have acquired as consumers in the development of their own advertising; it also illustrates how discourses and narratives within cultural and social life become an encoded component of the ideological structures of advertising.

Secondly, we ran a survey among the students on the ideological values that dominate Slovenian society. The students stated that the most important values for Slovenians are: family and traditional family values (30%), a desire for perfection (18%), a hard-working mentality (12%), conservatism and the lack of an adventurous spirit (14.3%), healthy lifestyle (15.7%), materialism (8%), and stability and prestige (12%).

Thirdly, the students were given advertising slogans that had already been translated into Slovenian, which we analysed together in the classroom. We concentrated on how information is structured, how it 'unpacked' ideologically influenced constraints and cultural influences, and ways in which the creators of texts seek to determine their readers' viewpoints. The analysis performed by the students focused on linguistic signs (words). Iconic signs (visual representations), which are also very likely to be found in advertisements, and some other non-representational signs, such as graphics, were excluded from this part of analysis. It should also be noted that the students were asked to analyse only ideologically influenced lexical and semantic choices, not the general structure of advertising slogans. The students analysed 65 English advertising slogans: 25 for cars, ten for supermarkets and shops, 13 for cosmetic products and 17 for food and drink items.

In a second stage, we concentrated on the following questions that the students were later asked to respond to briefly in writing:

- Which linguistic elements of the text may be described as ideological – that is, racial, ethnic, social or sexual assumptions expressed on the level of both lexicon and syntax?
- Are they translatable?
- In which way should we modify the ST to transfer the ideological message?
- Is this ideological message suitable for our culture?
- Should it be conveyed at all?

Before discussing the results of the analysis, we isolated the most important ideologically influenced strategies used in Slovenian translations and used them to summarize the results:

- Use of polite instead of familiar addressing form (ti/vi).
- Use of familiar instead of polite addressing form (ti/vi).
- Over-emphasizing the product's quality.
- Retaining linguistic items referring to stability and prestige.
- Deletions, sometimes as a result of the conservatism of Slovenian customers.
- Influence of English and German on Slovenian.

5. Results and discussion

In what follows, we present the results of the students' analyses.

Strategies	**25 car advertisements**
Use of a polite instead of a familiar addressing form (*ti/vi*)	18
Use of a familiar instead of a polite addressing form (*ti/vi*)	None
Over-emphasizing of the product's qualities	15
Retaining linguistic terms applied to stability and prestige	25
Deletions	1
Influence of English and German on Slovenian	None

Table 1: The result of the analysis of 25 car advertisements

The results presented in Table 1 demonstrate that the most frequently used strategies are the use of a polite addressing form, retaining ideologically influenced elements of stability and prestige, and an emphasis on the product's quality, which earns the highest number of occurrences. Stability and prestige as primary social values of contemporary Slovenian society were carefully retained in all of the 25 car advertisements. In the students' opinion, this strategy made a product appear more reliable.

The use of a polite addressing form may be attributed to the translators' wish to achieve more effective communication by conforming to target social conventions, as the advertised products are expensive and potential customers should be respected. If they were addressed differently, the clients would probably feel ill at ease. The polite form appeared in the next examples, for instance:

1. Example: Citroën – 'Just imagine what Citroën can do for you' – '*Niti predstavljate si ne, kaj vse lahko Citroën stori* ***za vas***' ('You cannot even imagine what Citroën can do for you' – polite form of address).
2. Example: Opel – '*Wir bauen Ihr Auto*' was translated as '*Delamo* ***vaš avto***' ('We produce your car' – polite form of address)
3. Example: Pirelli – '*Die Beine Ihres Autos.*' '*Noge* ***vašega avtomobila***'. ('The legs of your car' – polite form of address)

In several cases, the quality of the product was further emphasized by adaptations and additions. The students concluded that Slovenian customers are more traditional and may not trust foreign products. Therefore, they need to be convinced over and above those in the original country of production.

4. Example: Peugeot – in the Slovenian translation, the slogan 'The drive of your life' was modified to '*Užitek v dovršenosti*', which literally means 'Enjoyment in <u>perfection</u>'.

In the only case of deletion, the deleted word was the adjective 'passionate' in the next example:

5. Example: Lexus – 'The passionate pursuit to perfection' was shortened in the Slovenian translation as '*Stremljenje k popolnosti*' ('Pursuit to perfection'). Although it is difficult to speculate, the students suggested that this may have happened for ideological, even censorial, reasons. In their opinion, Slovenian customers may have found this reference too explicit and even 'inappropriate'. Nevertheless, this was only a suggestion as we did not use any other surveys on the evaluation of a set of values in Slovenian society other than those of the students.

Strategies	**15 food and drink advertisements**
Use of polite instead of familiar addressing form (*ti/vi*)	**7**
Use of familiar instead of polite addressing form (*ti/vi*)	**5**
Emphasizing of the product's quality	**7**
Retaining the terms applied to stability and prestige	**None**
Deletions	**None**
Influence of English or German on Slovenian translation	**3**

Table 2: The result of the analysis of 15 food and drink advertisements

The results presented in Table 2 demonstrate that the most frequently used strategies when translating food and drink advertising slogans include the use of the familiar addressing form and an emphasis on the product's quality. A familiar addressing form was used in the Slovenian slogans for Orbit, Snickers, Wrigley's Airwaves**,** Red Bull and Coca-Cola.

The students came to the conclusion that the products were more likely to be consumed by younger people, who would prefer a more intimate form of address so as to identify with the product more easily. The case of the slogan for Snickers was particularly interesting because the students discovered two strategies: the use of a familiar instead of a polite form of address (*ti/vi*) and the use of a foreign word in the translation. They also noticed that the Slovenian translator introduced rhyme, a common and effective strategy in advertising slogans.

6. Example: The slogan for Snickers 'You are not yourself when you are hungry' was very successfully modified to *'Lačen si ful drugačen'* ('Hungry, you are fully different'). The use of the loan word *'ful'*, transferred from German once again, confirmed the influence of foreign languages on Slovenian.
7. Example: The same strategy of using a familiar instead of a polite form of address occurred in the translation of the following slogans: for Orbit – 'Eat. Drink. Chew. Orbit' – *'Jej. Pij. Žveči orbit.'*; for Red bull – 'Red bull gives you wings' – *'Red bull ti da krila'* and for Merci – 'Merci for being you' – *'Merci, hvala ker si'*.

8. Example: Actimel – the quality of the product is over-emphasized in an advertising slogan. The English variation is 'The little bottle with a lot inside' and the German '*Die kleine Flasche, die's in sich hat*'. Both slogans do not overly emphasize the quality of the product, while the Slovenian translation '*Majhna flaška z veliko dobrega*' means 'A little bottle with a lot of good'. The students did not agree with this translation, as in their opinion it was not appropriate to interfere with the slogan. Their suggestion was a more literal translation '*Majhna flaška z veliko vsebino*' ('A little bottle with a lot inside'). The influence of German on Slovenian is also evident as the word '*flaška*', which is derived from the German '*Flasche*', was used in the Slovenian translation, while there is an alternative in Slovenian, which is '*steklenica*', with the diminutive form 'stekleníčka'.
9. Example: Nestea – the same emphasis was noticed in the translation of this slogan, which in English is 'The start of something different' and in German '*Erleb mal was Neues*'. In the Slovenian slogan, which is otherwise a literal translation of the English one, the word 'different' was modified through the use of the extra word '*povsem*' ('totally'). Therefore, the slogan is '*Začetek nečesa povsem drugačnega*' ('The start of something entirely different'). The students also noticed that the Slovenian slogan followed the English, which uses the word 'different' and not the original German, which uses the word '*Neues*' (new). They agreed that this choice may have been ideologically influenced, as Slovenians are more conservative and do not like taking risks. 'Something different' sounds less 'risky' than 'something new'. However, the students agreed that it would be better to follow the German translation and use '*novega*' (new) instead of '*drugačnega*' ('different') in the Slovenian translation.

The influence of English is evident in the following example:

10. Example: Pepsi – the English word 'life' is orthographically changed but otherwise retained in the Slovenian slogan, 'Live for Now', which in Slovenian reads '*Lajf je moj*' ('Life is mine'). In the students' opinion, the word 'life' is familiar to the younger generation and there is no reason to omit it.

Strategies	**Ten technical devices**
Use of polite instead of familiar forms of address *(ti/vi)*)	7
Use of familiar instead of polite form of address (*ti/vi*)	2
Emphasizing of the product's quality	8
Retaining the terms applied to stability and prestige	None
Deletions	None
Influence of English or German on Slovenian translation	2

Table 3: The result of the analysis of ten advertisements for technical devices

The findings here are very similar to those for the car company slogans. The strategies of deletion and the influence of English or German were not observed. The most frequently used strategies when translating slogans for different types of technical device include using polite instead of familiar forms of address, retaining ideologically influenced elements of stability and prestige and emphasizing the product's quality, which marks the highest number of occurrences in the translated slogans.

11. Example: Philips – over-emphasis on the product's quality occurs in this slogan, which in English is 'Sense and simplicity' and in Slovenian '*Dovršeno in preprosto.*' ('<u>Accomplished</u> and simple')

The use of the polite form of addressing appeared, for instance, in the following example.

12. Example: Kodak – the slogan '*Kodak macht aus* ***Ihren Bildern*** *mehr.*' was translated as 'Kodak naredi iz **vaših slik** več.' (Kodak makes more **of your pictures** – a polite form of address)

Strategies	Ten shops
Use of polite instead of familiar form of address (*ti/vi*)	4
Use of familiar instead of polite form of address (*ti/vi*)	1
Emphasizing of the product's quality	5
Retaining the terms applied to stability and prestige	5
Deletions	None
Influence of English or German on Slovenian translation	3

Table 4: The result of the analysis of ten advertisements for shops

As may be observed in Table 4, the most frequently used strategies when translating the advertising slogans for different shops include the use of polite instead of familiar forms of address and an emphasis on the product's quality, which earned the highest number of occurrences.

The students also noticed the almost complete absence of the imperative, common in English advertisements, and concluded that Slovenians did not like to be told what to do or, in this case, what to buy. In the students' opinion, this may be a consequence of the mentality of a small nation. Students claimed that, historically, Slovenia had always been a part of other countries or kingdoms. As a result, although Slovenia has been independent for more than 20 years, Slovenians may still interpret the use of an imperative as a threat that somebody wishes to take control of them. It should be clarified at this point that these are students' assumptions and spontaneous ideas which were recorded during the procedure. The focus of the research was not on the issues of the Slovenian national psychology. This is the reason why we are not providing any theoretical foundation for these assumptions.

13. Example: Hervis – the use of the imperative occurred in only one example combined with a familiar instead of polite addressing form (*ti/vi*), in this advertisement, which reads 'Get movin'' and is translated into '*Zmigaj se*'.

Strategies	**13 cosmetic products**
Use of a polite instead of a familiar form of address (*ti/vi*)	4
Use of a familiar instead of a polite form of address (*ti/vi*)	2
Emphasizing of the product's quality	4
Retaining the terms applied to stability and prestige	7
Deletions	None
Influence of English or German on Slovenian translation	7

Table 5: The result of the analysis of advertisements for 13 cosmetic products

Table 5 shows that in the case of cosmetics advertisements, the most frequently used strategies were also the use of familiar instead of polite forms of address, especially in advertisements for men, as well as emphasizing the product's quality. The polite form of address is almost always used in advertisements for cosmetic products that address women, such as L'Oréal, Always and Schwarzkopf.

14. Example: Schwarzkopf – the slogan 'Professional haircare *for you'* was translated '*Profesionalna nega* **las za vas**.' (Professional hair care ***for you*** – a polite form of address. In the Slovenian version, rhyme is also introduced which cannot be adequately transferred into English)
15. Example: Always – the slogan 'Always trocken. Always sauber. Und mit Sicherheit ein gutes Gefühl. Spricht die Sprache Ihres Körpers.' reads in Slovenian as 'Always suho. Always čisto. In vedno dober občutek. Govori jezik **vašega telesa**.' (Always dry. Always clean. And always a good feeling. It speaks the language of **your body –** a polite form of address)

The only exceptions are slogans for Essence and Garnier cosmetic products, which are targeted at a younger generation.

16. Example: Garnier – in the translation of this slogan 'Garnier, take care, the familiar form of address '*ti*' was used, as evidenced in the verbal form 'Garnier, ***misli*** *nase*.' (Garnier, think about yourself – a familiar form of address)

The use of words such as 'need', 'worth', 'comfortable' and 'professional' is significant. All of these concepts were carefully translated into Slovenian as they imply an important ideological message, meaning these companies offer women the tools necessary to be attractive. This adheres to a common myth that women of all ages should work hard to maintain their beauty and present themselves as objects of men's sexual desire.

17. Example: Rexona – quality is over-emphasized in this slogan, which in English reads: 'It won't let you down' and in Slovenian: '*Nikoli vas ne bo razočarala.*' ('It will **never** disappoint you')

6. Conclusion

The aim of the method was to analyse students' knowledge of source and target cultures, the partners' expectations in the transfer of information, and the Skopos (purpose) of the translation. We wanted to investigate whether the students were able to recognize the special functions of textual structures in the communicative process. We suggest that by understanding how social relations of power are exercised and negotiated in and through discourses, future translators will be able to operate better at different levels during text (re)production and message translation, above and beyond the language level, that is, also at the communicational, social, empathetic and cultural level.

We decided to use advertising slogans because the practical benefits of the translation of this material should not be overlooked as the globalization of economies and trade intensification compel companies to communicate with consumers of various languages and cultures. There will be a growing need for communication and therefore for translation. An understanding of the ideological and functional processes behind the re-creation of advertising slogans in the TL will enable students to comprehend the needs of the global market better. We strongly believe that this is essential for any translator who wishes to enter the translation field of advertisements and commercials; as consumer needs are endless, this field can be highly profitable.

The objectives of our project were twofold: we sought to analyse the various linguistic components of each advertising slogan and to identify the ways in which it transfers cultural and ideological aspects of the source culture. While analysing the examples, students became highly adept at 'unpacking' the ideological content of any given advertisement and then at considering how that content depended upon the shared values of a particular interpretive community (such as a nation, a culture or a sub-culture) in order to achieve its aims. In the second and third stages, the students were asked to analyse the translations of slogans into Slovenian and then to offer their own translations, if necessary. Our task was to consider the ways in which advertisements use carefully chosen 'signifiers' to appeal to their 'implied' readers in the context of 'think global, act local'.

As we worked our way through numerous slogans we became increasingly mindful that, for our cultural translation students, advertisements provided ideal lenses through which to observe the formation of personal, social and cultural identities, especially as influenced by corporate media. We soon found ourselves discussing the role and importance of a translator as not merely a cultural but also an ideological mediator. We wanted to make it clear that translation is actually constructed in a specific socio-cultural context, not in a vacuum without any ideological impact. We also wanted to emphasize that it would be naive to think that translators are absolutely independent and their choices and strategies are not influenced by different socio-cultural norms informed by ideology. Translation always serves as a medium for transmitting ideological norms in a subtle, invisible way. A comparison of the 'hidden' ideological backgrounds of advertising slogans in the source and target cultures revealed the ideological messages encrypted in the advertisements, which any translator should be well aware of. Our experience confirmed that dominant strategies of translating cultural references are neither fixed nor permanent. The strategies and decision-making implied when dealing with ideological backgrounds are dynamic and may change depending on the background knowledge and age of a translator.

References

Álvarez, Román & Vidal, María Carmen-África. 1996. *Translation, power, subversion.* Clevedon/Philadelphia/Adelaide: Multilingual Matters.

Bachmann-Medick, Doris. 2006. *Cultural turns. Neuorientierung in den Kulturwissenschaften.* Reinbek bei Hamburg: Rowohlt.

Baker, Mona (ed). 1998. *Routledge encyclopaedia of Translation Studies.* London/New York: Routledge.

Bassnett, Susan & Lefevere, André (eds). 1998. *Constructing cultures: Essays on literary translation.* Clevedon/Philadelphia/Toronto: Multilingual Matters.

Calzada Pérez, María. 2003. Introduction. In María Calzada Pérez (ed) *Apropos of ideology. Translation Studies on Ideology – Ideologies in Translation Studies.* Manchester: St Jerome, 1–23.

Ewen, Stuart. 2001. *Captains of consciousness: Advertising and the social roots of the consumer culture* (25th anniversary edition). New York: Basic Books.

Fairclough, Norman & Wodak, Ruth. 1997. Critical Discourse Analysis. In Teun A Van Dijk (ed) *Discourse as social interaction.* Thousand Oaks, USA: Sage Publications, 258–284.

Fawcett, Paul. 1998. Ideology and translation. In Mona Baker (ed) *Routledge encyclopaedia of Translation Studies.* London/New York: Routledge, 106–111.

Goddard, Angela. 1998. *The language of advertising written texts.* London/New York: Routledge.

Hackley, Chris. 2000. Silent running: Tacit, discursive and psychological aspects of management in a top UK advertising agency. *British Journal of Management* 11(3): 239–254.

Hamilton, Malcolm B. 1987. The elements of the concept of ideology. *Political Studies* 35: 18–38.

Heringer, Jürgen. 2007. *Interkulturelle Kommunikation.* Tübingen/Basel: Francke.

Lefevere, André. 1992. *Translation, rewriting and the manipulation of literary fame.* London/New York: Routledge.

Munday, Jeremy. 2004. Some challenges to translation theory. Key debates in the translation of advertising material. *The Translator* 10(2): 199–220.

Nida, Eugene. 2001. *Language and culture-contexts in translating.* Shanghai: Shanghai Foreign Language Education Press.

Nord, Christiane. 1991. *Text analysis in translation: Theory, methodology and didactic application of a model for translation-oriented text analysis.* Amsterdam/Atlanta: Rodopi.

Nord, Christiane. 2003. Function and loyalty in Bible translation. In María Calzada Pérez (ed) *Apropos of ideology. Translation Studies on Ideology – Ideologies in Translation Studies.* Manchester: St Jerome, 89–112.

Calzada Pérez, María. 2003. Introduction. In María Calzada Pérez (ed) *Apropos of ideology. Translation Studies on Ideology – Ideologies in Translation Studies.* Manchester: St Jerome, 1–23.

Prunč, Erich. 2008. Zur Konstruktion von Translationskulturen. In Larisa Schippel (ed) *Translationskultur – ein innovatives und produktives Konzept.* Berlin: Frank & Timme, 19–41.

Reiß, Katharina & Vermeer, Hans J. 1991. *Grundlegung einer allgemeinen Translationstheorie.* 2. Auflage. Tübingen: Niemeyer.

Schäffner, Christina. 1998. Skopos theory. In Mona Baker (ed) *Routledge encyclopaedia of Translation Studies.* London/New York: Routledge, 235–238.

Schäffner, Christina. 2003. Third ways and new centers: Ideological unity or difference? In María Calzada Pérez (ed) *Apropos of ideology. Translation Studies on Ideology – Ideologies in Translation Studies.* Manchester: St Jerome, 23–43.

Snell-Hornby, Mary. 1987. Translation as a cross-cultural event: Midnight's children – Mittternachtskinder. *Indian Journal of Applied Linguistics* 2: 91–105.

Tymoczko, Maria. 2006. *Enlarging translation. Empowering translators.* Manchester: St Jerome.

Van Dijk, Teun A. 1988. *News as discourse.* Hillside, NJ: Erlbaum.

Van Dijk, Teun A. 1996. Discourse, opinions and ideologies. In Christine Schäffner & Helen Kelly-Holmes (eds) *Discourse and ideologies.* Philadelphia: Multilingual Matters, 7–37.

Venuti, Lawrence. 1992. *Rethinking translation: Discourse, subjectivity, ideology.* London/New York: Routledge.

Vermeer, Hans J. 2007. *Ausgewählte Vorträge zur Translation und andere Themen. Selected papers on translation and other subjects.* Berlin: Frank & Timme.

Wernick, Andrew. 1991. *Promotional culture: Advertising, ideology and symbolic expression.* London: Sage.

NATALIA NAYDENOVA

Peoples' Friendship University of Russia

Teaching Translation in Banking and Finance: Cross-cultural Aspects

Abstract

Bridging the gap between educational outcomes and employers' expectations is key to boosting the competitiveness of translation programme graduates in the labour market. To cater for this challenge, translation pedagogy needs to become more focused on specific domains of knowledge and place a special emphasis on cross-cultural awareness. This chapter is based on a case study of a course in translation for specific purposes developed for third-year students in the Translation Bachelor Programme (Russian–English) at the Peoples' Friendship University of Russia. It presents the structure, content and outcomes of a course that was designed for the banking and finance module and has a major focus on cross-cultural training.

Keywords: translation for specific purposes, financial translation, linguistic competence, cross-cultural awareness

1. Introduction

Since the "cultural turn" in Translation Studies (TS) dating back to the 1980s (Lefevere & Bassnett 1990), translation is no longer regarded as a primarily linguistic process, but as a culturally contexted activity. Translation as cross-cultural mediation implies re-creation rather than recovery of meaning (Sun 2007: 243). It is fundamentally an interpretative operation, which involves creative acts of meaning-making between languages and cultures. As a mediator, the translator is a participant in both cultures, and is engaged in performing and analysing interpretations both within and across cultural framings (Liddicoat 2016: 362). According to Hua (2016: 18), cross-cultural communication is concerned with

> how people from different cultural backgrounds interact with each other and negotiate cultural or linguistic differences which may be perceived or

> made relevant through interactions, as well as what impact such interactions have on group relations and on individuals' identities, attitudes and behaviors.

Teaching translation in the contemporary globalised and highly competitive business environment poses new challenges. A solid command of source (SL) and target (TL) languages and a knowledge of translation techniques become insufficient for those translators who want to work in a certain industry where linguistic communication is closely connected to professional practices and where cross-cultural encounters have become the norm. Dudley-Evans and St John (1998: 4–5) believe that language for specific purposes (LSP) requires its own teaching techniques. They define its major characteristics, which include focusing on the language (grammar, lexis and register), skills, discourse and genres appropriate to these activities. In our view, this set of characteristics pertaining to linguistic competence should be complemented by cross-cultural awareness: a translator specializing in a specific domain selects the appropriate translation strategy not only on the basis of language-related constraints, but also on the basis of culture.

Bargiela-Chiappini (2004) notes that international business discourse is both culturally situated and context-dependent. Knowing a language in order to communicate efficiently in a professional setting implies mastering three different concepts, all of them necessary to producing an adequate translation. The three elements to be considered are: (1) using the appropriate business-related concepts; (2) using the corresponding specific terminology in the target language, and (3) applying relevant communicative techniques (Palmer-Silveira 2013: 9–10). This triad should be considered from a cross-cultural perspective. As Lauring (2011: 234) points out,

> most authors in intercultural business communication argue that culture determines how individuals encode messages, what mediums they choose for transmitting them, and the way messages are interpreted.

The emphasis on cross-cultural awareness is essential in training translators, since they will be actors of an intercultural dialogue (see Grosman 1994; Kiraly 2015). However, it is difficult, if not almost impossible, to separate cross-cultural competence from other competences. For example, successful translation requires an ability to perform cross-linguistic comparisons, involving mediation between two language systems, and cross-cultural comparisons, presupposing an awareness of cultural conventions (Tomozeiu, Koskinen & D'Arcangelo 2016: 257). Therefore, the enhancement of the learners' cross-cultural competence involves linguistic and extralinguistic factors. Purely linguistic phenomena are constituted by the lexical and syntactic differences between the SLs and TLs as well as by stylistic aspects. Extralinguistic components comprise knowledge of culture-specific concepts and behavioural patterns that enables the translator to grasp key differences between two cultures.

This chapter deals with the professional training of students who wish to become translators in a certain domain of specialized knowledge: international business and finance. The designed course was piloted with a group of third-year students in the Translation and Interpreting BA Programme at the Peoples' Friendship University of Russia who chose the "Banking and Finance" module. The course is divided into 18 topics covering the main areas of finance:

basic concepts of economics	risk management
market	retail banking
money and monetary policy	corporate banking
accounting	investment banking
International Financial Reporting Standards (IFRS)	international trade
audit	trade finance
corporate finance	marketing
financial management	mergers and acquisitions
financial markets	investor relations

Table 1: Main areas of finance

Particular emphasis is placed on the difference between the Russian and the Anglo-Saxon financial systems (supervisory bodies, titles of the main laws, most important market players). Each of the blocks is introduced by a lecture in Russian identifying the main terms and culture-bound lexemes. This is followed by a set of activities comprising intensive reading and stylistic analysis, cross-cultural training and group discussions.

The course is intended to embrace both linguistic competence and cross-cultural awareness applied to a specific domain of knowledge. Special attention is paid to the structural differences between English and Russian, the appropriate terminological systems, and the significance of style. The course employs a great range of translation assignments and activities, including the case-study approach, to develop the students' critical thinking. This critical thinking is "an intentional, structured, and directed process that facilitates exploration for deeper, contextualized meaning linked to learning outcomes" (Rice & Pollack 2000: 124). Students are also encouraged to analyse and review translations from specialized journals and websites. Emphasis is placed on translating cultural differences, to which end the students are introduced to various techniques that facilitate the transplantation of texts from one culture to another. The students are expected to participate actively in discussions on the assigned texts and to complete various translation exercises. A part of each class is dedicated to discussing the translations completed by the students.

By the end of the course, the students can meaningfully interpret and apply appropriate translation methods to business and finance texts belonging to different cultures; they can also understand the mechanisms of cross-cultural communication and their successful implementation. They are introduced to the contemporary scene of international business and can articulate different cultural perspectives on global financial markets. Subject to the appropriate modifications, the course may be implemented for other specialized domains of knowledge and language pairs.

In order to boost the students' capacity to feel at ease in situations where participants are divided not only by language but also by cultural barriers, the course aims to build the students' competence around two pillars: "linguistic competence" and "cross-cultural awareness". It is relevant to work on these two pillars because there is a wide gap between the standard training of future translators, on the one hand, and the expectations of potential employers, on the other. Employers' requirements are not limited to strong language skills on the employees' part; they also include knowledge of terminology and discourse practices inherent to a certain professional field, and these are always culture-bound. However, graduates who major in translation, notwithstanding their superior command of a foreign language, often lack these skills. In contrast, finance students generally lag behind in terms of language proficiency but are more conversant with the terminology and the relevant discourse practices.

The contemporary market of language teaching services in Russia offers a plethora of courses under the generic title of "Business English", but none of them educates future translators. This is explained by the fact that teachers are generally trained at pedagogical universities, where they acquire a great deal of theoretical knowledge about methodology and a decent level of English, but do not gain extensive knowledge of the Anglo-Saxon business culture. Besides, UK textbooks such as *Market leader* (Cotton, Falvey & Kent 2010), which are popular for "Business English" courses, do not take into account the specifics of the Russian economic, legal or cultural context or any of the appropriate terminology. In contrast, all job openings for business translators feature specifications such as "specialized knowledge in the fields of economics, banking and finance", "knowledge of/experience in business" or "in-depth knowledge of finance and accounting terminology" as requirements.

This creates a pressing need in Russia to set up a special training programme for future translators and interpreters wishing to specialize in the business area. Before designing such a course, however, it is important to identify the main issues that require special attention, from both a language and a cultural perspective.

2. Linguistic competence

Russia entered the global financial markets only in the 1990s. Therefore, the Russian terminological system in the area of finance and banking is still emerging, and it is strongly influenced by English. One reason for this is that it is heavily reliant on borrowings from English because terms from Anglo-Saxon business law do not have equivalents in the Russian legal system. There is still no unanimity, for example, on how to render in Russian such terms as "due diligence", "covenant" or "roadshow". These terms are sometimes simply transcribed into Russian, making any resulting text look extremely opaque to readers who are not familiar with financial markets. This is especially true for the term "covenant", which is most often transcribed, but whose plural is formed according to the rules of the Russian language (ковенант – ковенанты). Another example is the Russian term "бонд" borrowed from English (bond) and used in lieu of the Russian term "облигация" (bond). However, the first association triggered by the word "bond" for most Russian readers is the name of the famous movie character. This stereotypical association is frequently exploited by the press, where one may find titles based on well-known quotations from the James Bond saga: "Bond. Eurobond" (Chaykina 2009) and "Bond-009" (Rudenko 2009). Another example of an interesting term is the "bible" (a set of documents for a certain transaction), which tends to cause stupefaction on the part of Russians when they hear the term used in this way for the first time.

Texts in the area of banking and finance are also produced at the confluence of various stylistic registers: formal, journalistic, even literary. English business writing tends to employ considerably more metaphors and other tropes than the Russian equivalent, for instance. English metaphorical expressions such as "scorched-earth defences" or "lobster trap" can be translated only by way of description. In this way, they become clear to the reader but look rather cumbersome and lose their initial connotation in translation.

Similarly, public relations (PR) presentations in English tend to avoid 'officialese' in order to attract the readers' attention by making the text more expressive and concise at the same time. In contrast, Russian texts are more grandiloquent. Therefore, the translation of financial texts is a specific type of cultural transfer: here the translator faces not just the problem of achieving terminological equivalence, but also of choosing the appropriate stylistic conventions, which vary across cultures.

3. Cross-cultural awareness

It is a common belief that every language expresses the worldview of the culture it serves. According to Hofstede (2016), Russia is "a nation where power holders are very distant in society", which implies the utmost importance of professional hierarchy. This has a direct impact on business etiquette. Courtesy, in the sense of a somewhat ceremonial show of respect for every individual person, constitutes a cultural value (Wierzbicka 2003: 56). The way one addresses an interlocutor in Russian offers the most obvious case in point: whereas in Anglo-Saxon cultures one uses the first name irrespective of social status, in Russia one does this by name and patronymic[1] if the social gap is large. Apart from names and names with patronymics, unlike English, Russian has two forms of address: "ты" and "Вы", the first one being informal and the second one signalling distance and hierarchy. However, this hierarchical logic often operates only in a one-way mode as the top managers may address their subordinates by intimate "ты", while the managers are expected to be addressed by formal "Вы". It should also be noted, however, that Russian corporate culture is

[1] Russian patronymic is a name derived from the father's first name by adding an affix such as -evich or -ovich. The first name and patronymic constitute the usual official form of address. Most Russian surnames end in -ov or -ev; the equivalent female patronymics end in -ovna or -evna. An example of such transformations in English is the common surname Johnson (son of John).

being influenced by English, which is resulting in a growing trend to use the first name only while still maintaining the formal you ("Вы") mode.

The perception of time also differs radically from that in Anglo-Saxon culture. Russians are quite typical representatives of so-called *polychronic* (Hall 1959) cultures. This means that people are involved in various projects at the same time and the time spent on a certain project depends on its importance at a particular moment. For this reason, UK or US business people frequently complain about last-minute cancellations or rescheduling of meetings that had been fixed and confirmed by both sides weeks before. In addition, Russian official discourse is extremely depersonalized, which may be a throwback to the Communist era, when collective interests were supposed to take precedence over personal ones and direct responsibility was either avoided or passed on. This has resulted in an abundance of passive voice, nominalized forms and impersonal forms of expression. In addition, presentations, even by commercial corporations, tend to be verbose. This is well illustrated by an anecdote cited in a book for young translators:

> Once I acted as an interpreter for a Russian government official who presented a report on the use of the loan to the IMF mission. After listening to the speaker for some time, the head of the mission suddenly said without waiting for the translation: "This is all blah-blah-blah. Ask him how much." And added in a bad Russian: "Cifry, cifry. Skolko?"[2] (Miram 2000: 102)

This being said, it is important to teach a future translator how to deal with clients by explaining to them the need to adapt the phrasing, shift the focus, or even omit some parts in the course of a translation from Russian.

As for English texts, here Russian translators face the opposite challenge, because English texts show a clear preference for active over passive voice and tend to include a profusion of synonyms designed to underscore the company's uncontested leadership in the field. Such a discursive strategy may sound unpleasant to a Russian interlocutor, especially if he or she grew up in the Soviet era. Let us give just one example. The owner of a large Russian private bank was invited to an English-language presentation by a global investment bank. After having been shown about ten slides accompanied by the speaker's comments claiming that "We are No 1 (or, in the worst case, No 2) in the world/Europe/CIS etc", the Russian banker rather loudly slipped the following remark: "You are not going to

[2] "Numbers, numbers. How much?"

show the league tables where you ranked last, are you!?" (Naydenova 2010: 87). Assertive Anglo-Saxon rhetoric may therefore sometimes be inappropriate, especially when it is aimed at an older generation of Russian business owners, who built their fortunes in quite a hostile environment and succeeded in sustaining them despite numerous political and economic crises. These seasoned entrepreneurs prefer to communicate in a simple and straightforward manner, especially when speaking about money.

The examples listed above demonstrate the importance of both intra- and extralinguistic factors for achieving the appropriate level of equivalence in translation. These two factors therefore served as the foundation for designing a training programme for LSP translators and interpreters.

4. Financial translation course (Russian–English): Case study

At the Peoples' Friendship University of Russia, we created a special course in the Translation Bachelor's Programme for third-year students who opted for the banking and finance module. Each topic addressed starts with a brief overview given in the students' native language (Russian) followed by the translation of the key terms into English and a discussion of the topic in English in order to check the students' understanding. The next stage focuses on linguistic competence. It consists of reading authentic texts on the subject in hand, performing linguistic and stylistic analyses on these, identifying culture-bound terms and memorizing certain expressions (Rivera-Mills & Gantt 1999). This helps the students to improve their grasp of the grammar and vocabulary typical of business writing. However, it is crucial that the students also read Russian texts in the field. For this purpose, the students are given the task of finding articles from Russian newspapers translated into English (or vice versa) published on websites specializing in press reviews or research on the economy.

We also place special emphasis on the expansion of the students' personal thesauri. To this end, they draw up their own glossary of terms and expressions most frequently used in business English writing in the course of the semester. For example, they may list the adjectives available to describe a market situation, bearing in mind that this list is much shorter in Russian: вялая рыночная конъюнктура – *dull, lacklustre, languishing, light, negligible, quiet, slow, sluggish, thin, weak*; волатильная ситуация на рынке – *bumpy, choppy, erratic, hesitant, mixed, uncertain, volatile*; оживленная ситуация на рынке – *brisk, heavy, hectic*; крайне оживленная конъюнктура – *frantic, frenetic, frenzied*. The learners are advised to focus particularly on polysemantic terms and collocations. For instance, a commonly used Russian adjective “высокий” can be rendered in English as *ample, robust, solid, sound, high*, depending on the collocate: высокая капитализация – *solid capitalisation*, высокая ликвидность – *ample liquidity, excellent liquidity position*, высокая рентабельность – *robust/strong/sound profitability*.

After intensive reading and the compilation of a glossary, the students are then given a text to translate in order to test the skills they have acquired. An extract from one of the best copies is given below:

	Sentence in the SL	**Student's translation**	**Translation corrected by the teacher**
1	Наши основные цели состоят в увеличении сроков привлекаемого финансирования, а также поддержании эффективности проводимых операций.	Increasing the terms of the raised financing, as well as maintaining efficiency of operations are our main objectives.	Further lengthening of the maturity profile in our funding, as well as continuous efficiency of operations are our main objectives.
2	Наш Банк занимает 10 место среди частных российских банков.	Our institution occupies the 10th place among private banks in Russia.	Our institution ranks among the Top 10 privately owned banks in Russia.
3	В течение продолжительного периода времени мы демонстрируем более высокий уровень капитализации, чем наши конкуренты: за последние 3 года она не опускалась ниже 14,5%. Коэффициент достаточности капитала в настоящее время составляет 16,01%.	For a long time, we have demonstrated a higher level of capitalization than our competitors; it has not been less than 14,5% for the last 3 years. Our Capital Adequacy Ratio currently is 16,01%.	Historically, our capitalization has proven to be superior to our peers; above 14.5% over the last 3 years. Our Capital Adequacy Ratio currently stands at 16.01%.
4	Ресурсная база Банка состоит из: – депозитов физических и юридических лиц; – долговых инструментов внутреннего рынка (таких, как недавно выпущенные облигации на сумму 3 млрд. долларов США сроком на 3 года).	The Bank's funding base consists of: – deposits of individuals and legal entities; – debt instruments of the internal market (like recently issued bonds for the amount of RUB 3 bln for 3 years).	The Bank's funding base is spread between: – retail and corporate deposits; – domestic debt instruments (like a recent RUB 3bn 3-year bond).
5	Кредитование клиентов останется нашим ключевым стратегическим приоритетом, при этом особое внимание мы будем уделять качеству и диверсификации кредитного портфеля.	Customer lending will remain the key strategic priority, and we will pay special attention to loan quality and diversification.	We will maintain customer lending as the key strategic priority, paying special attention to loan quality and diversification.

Table 2: Student's translation

The student's translation is entirely correct from a grammatical point of view, but it requires considerable stylistic corrections, which often draw on cultural considerations. Sentences 1 and 2 demonstrate that the student does not have a grasp on the phrasing inherent in financial research texts such as "to lengthen the maturity profile", or "to rank", and uses the words found in the dictionary. A word-by-word translation of sentence 3 makes the structure of the English sentence appear cumbersome. Again, here the student reveals herself to be unfamiliar with grammatical constructions and lexemes that are typical of business discourse. In many cases, the translation from Russian into English requires compression to make the English text sound more idiomatic: "above" can well be used instead of "it has not been less than". Another important issue is the knowledge of synonyms of the most frequent words such as "to be" in sentence 3, which is replaced by "to stand at". The same remark applies to for sentence 4, where "recently issued bonds for the amount of RUB 3 bln for 3 years" can be compressed to "a recent RUB 3bn 3-year bond". It is also advisable to draw the students' attention to small details such as the abbreviation used for "billion" ("bn" instead of "bln" without a space after the digit), or the use of a full stop and not a comma in decimal numbers. Sentence 5 shows that the student does not take into account the clear preference for animate subjects over inanimate ones in English business writing. This is a common stumbling block for young Russian translators, as passive voice and impersonal constructions are found in abundance in official Russian texts. The inanimate subjects "our aim" and "customer lending" in the source text can easily be substituted by the animate "we".

The results of the test reveal that the student encountered a number of hurdles, which considerably reduced the quality of the translation, even if from a formal point of view the text in the target language sounds correct and ensures a proper understanding of what is being said. After the test, students were invited to compare their translations in groups and choose the most successful among them on the basis of the linguistic and cross-cultural knowledge gained. This kind of task teaches the students how to make informed decisions and draw up clear criteria for evaluation. Below is a sample sentence in Russian followed by three student translations:

> *Sentence in the SL*: Средства клиентов остаются основой ресурсной базой Банка – на 30.06.2015г. на них приходилось 57% совокупных пассивов. Рост объема клиентских средств всегда являлся основной целью Банка.

> *Student 1*: Customers' funds remained the foundation of the resource base of the Bank – as of 20 June 2015, they represented 57% of total liabilities. The growth of the volume of the clients' funds has always been the Bank's main goal.
>
> *Student 2*: The funds of the clients remain the main resource base of the Bank – as of 30.06.2015, they accounted for 57% of total liabilities. The growth of the clients' funding has always been the main objective of the Bank.
>
> *Student 3*: Being at 57% of total liabilities as of 30 June 2015, customer accounts remain the backbone of the Bank's funding base. The growth of the accounts base has always been the Bank's major focus.

Cross-cultural awareness needs to be raised in translator training, for it enables students to feel confident in different cultural contexts (see Angelelli 2004; Hale 2007), and it should aid the efficient and adequate translation of texts produced within different cultural contexts. Of course, misunderstandings cannot always be averted, yet typical communication gaps may be bridged if one boosts cross-cultural awareness on the part of the interlocutors. This awareness can be raised with the help of various intercultural training techniques, one of which is being a *culture assimilator*, which is a cross-cultural training strategy developed by the University of Illinois in 1962. The method it uses is the "critical incident" approach to depicting cultural conflicts between individuals from different cultural backgrounds (Cushner & Brislin 1996: 24). According to Spencer-Oatey and Harsch (2016: 236), a critical incident is

> an event or episode that is significant in some way, such as in its impact on people's emotional reactions or on the subsequent unfolding of events. It can also refer to an event that is perceived as puzzling or surprising by a participant.

The Critical Incident Technique was first developed in the 1950s by the psychologist John Flanagan (1954). Today, the technique is used across a range of fields, including medicine, counselling, international management, organizational behaviour and education. In the intercultural field, it has been extensively used in training. The critical incident approach invites students to perceive cross-cultural conflicts in a focused manner and directs group discussions towards realistic solutions.

In the context of the culture assimilator, critical incidents are short case studies or vignettes that present a cross-cultural interaction and the potential misunderstandings that ensue between culturally different individuals (Dela Cruz et al. 2006: 120). A culture assimilator is a multiple-choice test.

It starts with a brief description of a short real-life situation (a 'critical incident'), in which individuals from different cultural backgrounds interact with the intention of pursuing some common goal, yet they fail in the end. Then the students are offered a number of alternatives and are asked to select the one that best explains the problem. The multiple-choice format of the test allows students to realize that there are many possible perspectives to what at first glance may seem a straightforward case (English & Lynn 1995: vii).

A culture assimilator allows the students to develop conscious strategies for handling cultural differences, taking into account the consequences any of their choices might have. The instrument is developed on the basis of a large sample of critical incidents that reveal the misunderstandings, confusion or even the discord that can occur between people from different cultures. The case studies we select in class provide students with lifelike contexts in which cross-cultural misunderstandings occur, yet present useful business concepts and terms to them at the same time. This is an example of the culture assimilator we used in our course:

> A representative of a British wealth management company arranged a meeting with a Russian business owner in order to offer him investment services. He brought a colourful presentation in English listing the company's credentials and describing its investment schemes with lots of graphs and diagrams. While speaking about the investment opportunities, all of which were based on the Anglo-Saxon law, the presenter used a lot of technical terms, trying his best to convince his potential client to invest. However, at the end of the negotiations, the businessman asked his interlocutor if he could just open several bank accounts with international banks for him. The investment mandate remained unsigned. What went wrong?
>
> A. The businessman did not trust the presenter.
> B. The businessman was confused by the technicalities, both verbal and visual.
> C. The businessman did not understand the investment strategy.

The most appropriate response would be B. Being unfamiliar with complex investment schemes and instruments, the potential client was not able to break through the smokescreen of fancy terms and diagrams. Moreover, the paper presentation was in English, which irritated him as it was regarded as a lack of respect. Response A is not correct as the presenter was given the power of attorney for opening accounts on the client's behalf. Response C is incorrect because the businessman understood the strategy he was offered from his own perspective. Before looking up the correct answer, students have a group discussion. This enables them to delve further into cross-cultural issues related to the situation in hand, such as hierarchy, power distance and uncertainty avoidance (Hofstede 2003). In this way, they are also able to deal with unfamiliar terms in the course of their negotiations. Students usually enjoy this kind of test, because it allows them to develop their creativity as they find solutions to unexpected communicative situations.

5. Conclusion

Teaching translation in any professional field involves a range of aspects, which we can classify into either linguistic or cross-cultural competence. It is crucial to make students realize that even a very good command of English – as acquired during their university years – does not ensure a smooth transition to a professional environment.

Therefore, in addition to translation assignments, the course we designed for the business and finance module and presented in this contribution comprises a set of tailor-made exercises. To enable students to acquire a general understanding of the concepts inherent in the domain in hand, we divided the course into a number of thematic blocks, each of them being introduced in Russian, the students' native language, followed by a translation of the main terms into English. Students were then advised to engage in extensive background reading of the specialist literature and to analyse texts translated by professionals. The course also entailed group discussions in class about translation alternatives for certain sentences or passages, ensuring an understanding of the cultural context in which the texts function. The students were also offered a range of exercises and tests which highlighted communication breakdowns in cross-cultural exchanges, which served to teach them how to avoid the most typical breakdowns so that appropriate translations can be produced. We fully believe the described course provides a solid foundation that students will be able to capitalize on in their future professional lives.

References

Angelelli, Claudia V. 2004. *Medical interpreting and cross-cultural communication.* Cambridge: Cambridge University Press.

Bargiela-Chiappini, Francesca. 2004. Intercultural business discourse. In Christopher Candlin & Maurizio Gotti (eds) *Intercultural aspects of specialized communication*. Bern: Peter Lang, 29–51.

Chaykina, Yulia. 2009. Bond. Eurobond. <http://www.forbes.ru/lichnye-dengi/tsennye-bumagi/13489-bond-evrobond> (accessed 18 September 2017).

Cotton, David, Falvey, David & Kent, Simon. 2010. *Market leader: Intermediate business English*. Harlow: Pearson Longman.

Cushner, Kenneth & Brislin, Richard W. 1996. *Intercultural interactions: A practical guide*. New York: Sage.

Dela Cruz, Kenoalani, Salzman, Michael B, Brislin, Richard & Losch, Naomi. 2006. Hawaiian attributional perspectives on intercultural interactions in higher education: Development of an intercultural sensitizer. *International Journal of Intercultural Relations* 30: 119–140.

Dudley-Evans, Tony & St John, Maggie Joe. 1998. *Developments in English for specific purposes: A multi-disciplinary approach*. Cambridge: Cambridge University Press.

English, Laura M & Lynn, Sarah. 1995. *Business across cultures. Effective communication strategies*. New York: Longman.

Flanagan, John C. 1954. The critical incident technique. *Psychological Bulletin* 51(4): 327–358.

Grosman, Meta. 1994. Cross-cultural awareness: Focusing on otherness. In Cay Dollerup & Annette Lindegaard (eds) *Teaching translation and interpreting. Training, talent and experience*. Amsterdam/Philadelphia: John Benjamins, 51–57.

Hale, Sandra Beatriz. 2007. *Community interpreting*. London: Palgrave Macmillan.

Hall, Edward. 1959. *The silent language*. New York: Doubleday.

Hofstede, Geert. 2003. *Culture's consequences: Comparing values, behaviors, institutions and organizations across nations*. New York: Sage.

Hofstede, Geert. 2016. Russia. <http://geert-hofstede.com/russia.html> (accessed 18 September 2017).

Hua, Zhu. 2016. Identifying research paradigms. In Zhu Hua (ed) *Research methods in intercultural communication. A practical guide*. Malden/Oxford: Wiley Blackwell, 3–22.

Kiraly, Don. 2015. *Towards authentic experiential learning in translator education*. Göttingen: Vandenhoeck & Ruprecht.

Lauring, Jakob. 2011. Intercultural organizational communication: The social organizing of interaction in international encounters. *Journal of Business and Communication* 48: 231–255.

Lefevere, André & Bassnett, Susan. 1990. Introduction: Proust's grandmother and the thousand and one nights: The 'cultural turn' in Translation Studies. In Susan Bassnett & André Lefevere (eds) *Translation, history and culture*. London/New York: Pinter, 1–13.

Liddicoat, Anthony J. 2016. Intercultural mediation, intercultural communication and translation. *Perspectives* 24(3): 354–364.

Miram, Gennady. 2000. *Professija: Perevodchik [Occupation: translator]*. Kiev: Nika Centre.

Naydenova, Natalia. 2010. *Bankovskaja i finansovaja dokumentacija: Posobie po perevodu s russkogo jazyka na anglijskij [Translation for banking and finance: Russian–English]*. Moscow: Vysshaja Shkola.

Palmer-Silveira, Juan Carlos. 2013. The need for successful communication in intercultural and international business settings: Analytic and comparative studies, new trends and methodologies. *Ibérica* 26: 9–16.

Rice, Kathleen & Pollack, Seth. 2000. Developing a critical pedagogy of service learning: preparing self-reflective, culturally aware, and responsive community participants. In Carolyn R O'Grady (ed) *Integrating service learning and multicultural education in colleges and universities.* Mahwah: Lawrence Erlbaum Associates, 115–134.

Rivera-Mills, Susana & Gantt, Barbara. 1999. From linguistic analysis to cultural awareness: A translation framework for the Spanish language classroom. *JOLIB* 10(2): 1–13.

Rudenko, Viktoriya. 2009. Bond-009. <http://cbonds.ru/news/item/422046> (accessed 18 September 2017).

Spencer-Oatey, Helen & Harsch, Claudia. 2016. The critical incident technique. In Zhu Hua (ed) *Research methods in intercultural communication. A practical guide.* Malden/Oxford: Wiley Blackwell, 223–238.

Sun, Yifeng. 2007. (Multi)-cultural context: Interpretation and translation adrift. *Babel* 53(3): 241–259.

Tomozeiu, Daniel, Koskinen, Kaisa & D'Arcangelo, Adele. 2016. Teaching intercultural competence in translator training. *The Interpreter and Translator Trainer* 10(3): 251–267.

Wierzbicka, Anna. 2003. *Cross-cultural pragmatics: The semantics of human interaction.* Berlin/New York: Walter de Gruyter.

JUDITH WOODSWORTH
Concordia University

Transposing Voices: Teaching Interculturalism in a Literary Translation Course

Abstract

Students enrolled in a French–English literary translation course are asked to interview someone from a third culture and then write a story in English. This form of 'translation' makes them aware of the challenges and mechanisms of intercultural transfer, including the translation of orality. Students are faced with a number of technical difficulties: for example, in conveying to a Canadian audience the meaning of certain cultural phenomena, they can use foreign terms, with or without a definition or gloss. Some provide background information; some use conversation to make their stories come to life. The exercise helps to improve translation techniques and English writing skills. The stories of each class are published on the course website for all students to read. The result is a rich compilation of voices and events from around the globe, recorded in compelling tales of departures and journeys, ordeals and celebrations – a reflection of the cultural diversity of the student population and the pluralism of Montreal society in general.

Keywords: Montreal, translator training, literary translation, interculturalism, creative writing

1. Introduction

Since the emergence of the field of Translation Studies (TS) and, particularly, since the much heralded 'cultural turn' in the field (Bassnett & Lefevere 1990) and the ensuing twists and turns that have introduced the perspectives of postcolonial studies, feminism and sociology, among other considerations, it has become increasingly clear, to theoreticians at least, that the act of translation goes far beyond a simple matching up of linguistic units. As the Latin root of translation, *translatio*, suggests, translating involves 'carrying across'. We now realize, to a greater extent than ever before, that the translator carries a heavy burden across borders. Texts have many layers of meaning that transcend the purely linguistic, grounded as they are in geographical, social, political and cultural realities.

Translators in training, familiar to varying degrees with theories of translation, are often stuck in the mode of literal translation. They hang on to every element of the target text (TT), searching – with some level of frustration – for an equivalent for every word or phrase. They tend to proceed in a rather linear fashion, starting at the beginning of the first sentence at the top of the first page, and working their way resolutely to the last line at the bottom.

A literary translation course can serve to remedy this methodological shortcoming by introducing students to a process that involves translating cultural realities rather than merely finding equivalents for words and linguistic structures. This chapter sets out the objectives and content of such a course, part of the translation programme offered by the French Studies Department at Concordia University in Montreal, Canada.[1] In a university such as ours, characterized by a significant mixture of students from diverse backgrounds, in a setting that is increasingly multi-ethnic and multilingual, it is essential to foster interculturalism – the interaction of people from different cultural backgrounds and different language groups in a process of cross-cultural dialogue. This is obviously true for all citizens, but particularly so among future translators who will be called upon to negotiate difference in the course of their professional activities. Over time, there has been a move away from the 'multiculturalism' model to a new understanding and respect for the hybridity of our society, entailing fresh modes of interaction and circulation of cultural values, as Simon has suggested in an essay on hybridity (1999).[2] The focus of this chapter is on one particular component of the literary translation course, the 'storytelling' assignment, and the way in which this particular exercise brings about a familiarity with interculturalism in addition to traditional training in transferring text from one language to another.

In the literary translation course, students translate excerpts from works of literature, as would be expected, but are also required to write an original story. The stories of each class are compiled and published on the

[1] The term 'course' is used in Canada to refer to one of the subjects in a 'programme' of study or degree. In our case, a course is three credits or 13 weeks long.

[2] Interestingly, Simon uses the metaphor of foods on display at Saint-Jean-Baptiste celebrations to illustrate her point – of particular relevance in the context of the students' stories in which the theme of national foods figures prominently (1999: 19).

course website for all to read. The result is a rich compilation of voices and events from around the globe, recorded in compelling tales of departures and journeys, ordeals and celebrations. Each collection is a reflection of the cultural diversity of the student population of our university and the pluralism of Montreal society in general. This storytelling exercise is examined in the pages that follow: the methodological and technical difficulties the students grapple with are discussed, and their wide-ranging solutions and textual strategies presented as examples. The students are also required to comment on the work of their classmates: some of these reactions are cited, as they draw attention to individual fine points of writing as well as to the overall value of the exercise.

In order to give context for this pedagogical experience, it is useful to provide some background on the translation profession in Canada and to show how the pedagogy of translation has developed in response to the evolving practice of translation.

2. Translating in Canada

The language industry generally – translation, interpreting, terminology and revision – has thrived in Canada, particularly in the light of legislation of the late 1960s and mid-1970s that made English and French the official languages nationally and French the sole official language of the province of Québec. In response to a growth in demand for translators across all fields, translation courses (or 'programmes') sprang up in Canadian universities. These are primarily undergraduate, or BA programmes in translation, but several Master's and a handful of PhD programmes have also been established. Intended to train translators for the job market, these programmes contain theoretical courses in addition to a range of practical translation courses – from financial and scientific translation to other offerings that provide skills in translation technology.

Literary translation has fared less well than more pragmatic forms of translation in Canada, despite some important institutional measures, and it has not kept pace with that in other countries.[3] The Canada Council for

[3] Citing the 1986 *Index Translationum*, Jean Delisle points out that Holland publishes eleven times more literary translations than Canada, Sweden six times more, and Finland and Portugal twice as many (2011: 54). A more recent consultation of the *Index Translationum* indicates that Canada is doing better than in the past. However, a comparison based on the 10-year period from 1997 to 2006 (but excluding Portugal whose statistics look problematic) shows that the Netherlands still out-translates Canada 3.5 to 1, Sweden more than 2 to 1, and

the Arts supports publishing companies who choose to publish translations and also provides financial support for the translators. In 1974, the Canada Council launched a prestigious monetary award (now called the 'Governor-General's prize') to one translator a year working in French and another working in English. However, the small population in Canada, combined with economic factors, not to mention the fact that much English translation is done in the neighbouring United States and much French translation in France, continues to result in a relatively low volume of literary translation. Literary translation is therefore not considered lucrative in itself, and remains essentially a subsidized area of activity (Medley 2010). With the exception of a few translators such as Sheila Fischman – Canada's *grande dame* of translation, who at last count had completed more than 150 book-length translations and who, in a *Festschrift* in her honour, is described as having translated "an entire library of Quebec literature" (Simon 2013: xii) – translators are generally unable to make a living doing literary translation alone. Some are also translators of commercial texts; others work as academics, writers or journalists.

If translating literature cannot be considered a viable career on its own, one might ask why it should be taught at all. The role of literary translation in a translation programme is therefore an ambiguous one. However, a good case can be made for its importance within a university programme. It is invaluable, as we shall see in examining the specifics of a literary translation course, in that it not only develops translating and writing skills, but also introduces students to the process of intercultural transfer that is inherent in all forms of translation.

3. Literary translation course

3.1 Objectives

At Concordia, literary translation is a required course in the BA Specialization in Translation, taken in the second year of a three-year degree programme; it is also offered as part of the MA in TS.[4] The literary translation

Finland slightly less than 2 to 1. <http://www.unesco.org/xtrans/bsstatlist.aspx?m=1&lg=1> (accessed 18 September 2017).

[4] The course is quite simply entitled 'Traduction littéraire du français à l'anglais' or 'Literary Translation from French to English'. A parallel course is given from English to French in the stream for Francophones. At the graduate level, in the Master's in Translation Studies (Maîtrise en traductologie), there are two courses on offer: 'Literary translation' and 'Advanced Literary Translation'. Undergraduate courses have an enrolment of 25–30, while graduate seminars will

course I give is intended for students whose primary working language is English. The course offers an overview of the history, theory and practice of literary translation. Through regular practical assignments, students become familiar with a wide range of linguistic, textual and cultural challenges involved in translating various genres of literature. They learn how to produce stylistically and aesthetically acceptable English versions of French originals. Some formal lecturing is supplemented by assigned reading, student presentations and in-class discussions, providing a theoretical framework that enables students to think critically about the art and practice of literary translation. An effort is made to integrate theory and practice in the classroom in such a way as to be beneficial to students in their subsequent professional endeavours. Whether or not they aspire to become literary translators, students gain analytical and writing skills applicable to a variety of translational practices.

3.2 Structure

The course begins with some key principles underlying the nature and forms of literary translation, along with an introduction to traditional and contemporary modes of reflecting on and theorizing translation. Students are asked to read theoretical texts from a variety of sources, each of which is presented by a group of students, who must analyse its key points and lead a class discussion.

Students translate excerpts drawn from different literary genres: prose (including novels, short stories, essays and creative non-fiction), theatre, children's literature, and poetry. I favour contemporary texts, many of them from the Canadian repertoire: more 'canonical' writers such as playwright Michel Tremblay, short-story writer Monique Proux and novelist Dany Laferrière. I also make a point of including content from *la Francophonie*, well-known Algerian author Assia Djebar, for example. On the other hand, in the interests of exposing students to work that has not yet been translated and which is also new and highly regarded, I use excerpts from recently published, acclaimed authors: Abla Farhoud, Dominique Fortier, Françoise De Luca, Martine Delvaux. A portion of the class is also

typically have around 10–12 students. I have taught all three versions of the literary translation course, which each require different levels of workload and grading standards. For the purposes of this chapter, however, I am describing a more or less generic course in literary translation, in which the storytelling assignment is used, albeit with expectations that vary according to the student clientèle.

conducted as a workshop, during which students work together in small groups on in-class assignments. A storytelling exercise complements these practical exercises and provides a way of integrating the various theoretical and practical elements of the course.[5]

3.3 Theory and practice: The foreignization debate

During the course, students are shown how the problems of literary translation have been conceptualized and debated over time and at present. They apply these theoretical notions in commentaries that they are required to write about their own practical assignments and about the stories others have written. Recent discussions around the concept of foreignization are particularly relevant to both practical translations and student stories.

Since the appearance of Venuti's influential book (1995) *The translator's invisibility: A history of translation*, much scholarship in translation has focused on domestication and foreignization – opposite ends of a continuum in translation praxis, depending on whether a translator makes a text fit with the target culture or retains certain elements of the source language and culture to create a sense of foreignness. This is not a new debate. The pendulum has swung from one extreme to the other for centuries and has been discussed in various forms (e.g. the *belles infidèles* movement in 17th-century France and subsequent reactions to it). Venuti has drawn attention to the issue by positioning foreignization as an ethical stance. He has decried fluency strategies in translation, which consist in creating a target text (TT) that reads as if it had been written in the target language (TL), hence masking or erasing that which is foreign in the original text. He advocates, instead, a foreignizing approach, which would make the translator less invisible, and also enrich the receiving culture with elements imported from the source culture. Rather than violently suppressing cultural difference through domestication, he suggests, translators should strive to preserve both meaning and foreignness in the TL text. In this regard, Venuti follows in the footsteps of Berman, well known in French circles, who, drawing

[5] Inspiration for this exercise was drawn from a presentation given by Larkosh at the 1995 Language International Conference held in Elsinore (Larkosh 1996). Larkosh's student project, undertaken in multi-ethnic California, was readily transferable to the Canadian context, and I have put it to good use, in its present form, primarily over the past five years. The exercise was referred to briefly and Larkosh acknowledged in an earlier article about teaching literary translation (Woodsworth 2002).

on the German Romantic tradition, similarly builds an ethics of translation around the idea of embracing the foreign (Berman 1984; 1992).

This makes good sense from a theoretical perspective, but it is hard to teach, particularly to neophytes who sometimes 'foreignize' inadvertently. Examples abound of interference from the other language in a society where two languages are continually in contact, resulting in *anglicismes* in French and Gallicisms in English. While making students conscious of the importance of capturing the significance of all linguistic elements of an original text, crucial in legal or highly technical translation, for example, it is just as important to teach them to grasp meaning in a broader sense and to learn to rewrite or recreate a new, less literal, text that will be effective in the TL and culture.

One of the translation exercises I like to use is an excerpt taken from *À quoi ça rime?*, a novel by Montreal writer André Major (2013), which is set, in part, in Portugal. Translation challenges arise from the local colour as well as the narrator's conversation with his Portuguese driver, someone he has known in Montreal, who speaks 'Franglais'. As American translator Michael Henry Heim points out, "[l]est we forget, foreignization occurs in originals as well as in translations" (2013: 85). Foreignization aside, there is one particular passage in the assignment that stumps even the best students. Weary from his journey from Montreal and feeling the effects of the heat in Lisbon, the protagonist trudges up the stairs carrying a heavy suitcase; he arrives at his apartment hot and tired "*à bout de souffle, les aisselles trempées*" (Major 2013: 14). The tendency, nine times out of ten, is for students to write one of the following: "out of breath, with soaking armpits", "… with wet armpits", "… his armpits soaked", feeling that they must translate every word. This is not foreignization, but rather "dictionary-like servitude to the original" (Heim 2013: 89). What I try to get them to do is imagine themselves in a similar situation and simply recount it in English, in their own words, which would yield the following, or similar, results: "short of breath/gasping for air/and drenched in sweat" or else "huffing and puffing and sweating profusely".

It is important to signal just when foreignization techniques are appropriate and to balance Venuti's somewhat extreme approach to the violence of domesticated translation with a more tempered one. As David Homel, one of English Canada's foremost translators, who is also a novelist, points out, with "[a] translated work, its foreignness is built right in. You don't have to attract attention to the fact that it's a foreign book. It just is by its very existence" (Medley 2010). Heim, also writing about foreignness, attempts to find a middle ground, looking to the text to "indicate to translators whether domestication or foreignization is in order when cultural references in the source language lack counterparts in the target language" (2013: 84). In "Fictions of the foreign", an article on the course reading list, Bellos similarly questions the appropriateness and feasibility of representing the foreignness of a foreign language (2013).

To add further nuance to the debate, I present a 'real-world' situation drawn from my own experience translating a Quebec novel and searching for a publisher. One person with a solid record of publishing translations reviewed the manuscript and suggested that I break up the long, French-style sentences and also create shorter, English-sounding paragraphs. "Make this a work in English. Isn't translation a remake (in the filmic sense of the word)?", he advised. "Remove some precise Montreal settings so as to make the book more open … make it a more any-city type of environment".[6] I did, in fact, cut the sentences and paragraphs into smaller units; however, I refused to take Montreal out of the book. This was a sobering personal lesson, but one which provides an interesting counterpoint to the theoretical discussions that form part of my teaching. Foreignization is not always the decision of the translator alone.

Linking theory and practice helps to illustrate the very wide range of translation strategies available to students when they tackle a literary text and it shows them how to make informed choices. In this respect, the storytelling exercise is an important component of their learning experience.

4. The storytelling assignment

Somewhat unorthodox in a translation course, this is an exercise in creative writing rather than an actual translation from one language to another. Yet, it is a form of translation in the most general sense of the term, since all translation, like this exercise, is fundamentally about communicating across cultures; in other words, it is more a matter of translating cultural realities than finding equivalents for words and linguistic structures. The

[6] Personal correspondence with the publisher. The novel, *Still lives*, a translation of *Des mondes peu habités*, by Pierre Nepveu (Montréal: Boréal, 1992), was ultimately not published by this publishing house but by Nuage Editions in Montreal (1997). I have written about the experience in Woodsworth (2010).

objective of the assignment is to assist students in recognizing and conveying cultural difference, without the constraints of working from a source text (ST). At a theoretical level, it helps students grasp the translation concepts they have been exposed to; at a practical one, they not only improve their translation techniques, but also have an opportunity to exercise their creativity and hone their English writing skills.

The students are given a set of written instructions in which I outline the objectives and parameters of the assignment. I ask them each to interview someone close to them, such as a family member or close friend, about a memorable experience. The interviewee's cultural background should be different from the dominant ethnic groups of Québec/Canada, that is, preferably neither French nor English. The students are to try to elicit a brief personal anecdote or family story, which may be told in a language or dialect other than English or French. The students are required to 'translate' the story into a narrative in English.

In writing their stories, the students are translating from an oral form to a written one, possibly from another language or dialect, and they are expected to find creative ways to explain or 'translate' different cultural realities: food, items of clothing or religious practices, for example. In conveying to a Canadian audience the meaning of certain cultural phenomena, they can choose from a variety of techniques: using foreign terms in the English text, either in italics or not, with or without some kind of definition, gloss or explanation. They are free to add whatever background information they like and to use conversation to make the story come to life. Some even add images.

The story is around 1,000 words. Students are given instructions regarding style and format – font, spacing, spelling and usage – so that I can produce a consistent-looking document for publication on our e-learning platform. Once they submit their stories, I read each draft, make suggestions and indicate any revisions they are to make. They then edit their work and I compile them in a single document for that particular class.

4.1 Anatomy of a story: Some examples

Beyond the editorial instructions, I do not recommend what writing techniques to use, other than suggesting that the students vary the different ways they make use of foreign words, concepts and cultural references.

After interviewing their subject, the students have to decide whether to create a first-person or a third-person narrative. In the first, the interviewee speaks directly about themself; in the second, the narrator (the student) relates all the action using third-person pronouns 'he' or 'she'. A combination of the two is also frequent, with a more formal, written style used for narration by the student and a more spoken one used to capture the perspective of the interviewee, by means of either dialogue or direct or indirect quotations. Some examples, illustrating these and other techniques, follow.

"Forty dollars" (Michel Lam) is a first-person story about a Vietnamese mother who tells the story directly to the student, addressed as 'you'. There are no foreign words per se, only proper names:

> When I got here, I was nineteen years old. I only had forty dollars on me. Your Aunt Lan, however, had left with raw gold leaves which she had to hide in a camera so as not to lose them or have the authorities seize them. I was one of the lucky ones, because I managed to arrive here before '75, as a student. Luckily, your Aunt Ngha and Uncle Thinh had already settled here earlier that year.

"Rwanda day – Toronto 2013" (Erykah Gasaida Werner) is told in the first person. One notes the occasional use of French expressions, as well as a specific use of 'yes' and 'no' which is explained in a footnote.

> *Bon,* the crowd was mostly made up of Rwandans living in Canada and the US, along with those travelling from Rwanda. There were drinks; it was informal, yeah.* … The following day, we went for lunch at a Somali restaurant before heading back to Montreal. When you ask about good restaurants in Toronto, all the Rwandans in Toronto recommend Somali cuisine. I had never had Somali food and it was really good! They had chapati. I also enjoyed the grilled meat and spicy rice. No, it was really good! And … *Après*, that's it. We drove back to Montreal right after that. No, I had a lot of fun that weekend.
>
> *Rwandans have a tendency to use the words 'yes' and 'no', respectively, at the end and at the beginning of a sentence when speaking. It does not mean that we agree or disagree with a statement. 'Yes' is often used at the end of a sentence to simply mark the end of a statement. 'No' is used at the beginning of a sentence for emphasis, usually when expressing a feeling.

"From Austria to the Eastern Townships: A story of transplantation" (Avalon Moore) begins and ends with statements by the narrator, which at my suggestion she has put in italics to keep them distinct from the story itself. The rest is then told in the first person, from the perspective of the interviewee, reporting how she felt about moving to a small town in Quebec and how she ultimately adjusted to her unfamiliar environment. The story is one of many that evoke the immigrant experience in Canada.

> *Gabriele Thomas was born in Vienna, Austria, in 1957. In 1972, when her mother got remarried to an Austrian man living in Canada, the family prepared to move to his farm, in the Eastern Townships of Quebec.*
>
> I remember that it was a pretty exciting time for us, because my mother painted a very rosy picture of what our new life in Canada would be like. Especially since, in Vienna, we lived with our grandparents in one apartment. We would have our own house, with a room to myself, a room for my brother, and *even a bathroom!* ... We were very isolated, about five minutes by car from the closest village – which was very, very, *very* small – and about 10 minutes from Coaticook. Later, I learned to say *quatsi-kook*. The English said *quaddy-cook*, but the French said *quatsi-kook*, so that was what I learned, too.
>
> *It was a startling adjustment for a fifteen-year-old to make: from Austria to Canada, from the freedom of the big city to the isolation of the country, from the familiarity of the German language to the complete foreignness of French. Now, forty years later, Canada has been Gabriele's home for most of her life, and when speaking with her three trilingual children, she switches effortlessly from German, to English, to French, and back again.*

Students are encouraged to convey the voice and character of their interlocutor. One of the challenges in writing up a story that someone has told them is translating the different aspects of this 'orality'. As in much of the diasporan literature produced in Canada, they often resort to code-switching, which helps to simulate real speech and represent the rituals and customs of the community they are writing about. Details abound in these stories, often about food. The authors enumerate the delicious and exotic dishes that are consumed on special occasions, almost providing recipes in some instances. Similarly, festivals, ceremonies and items of clothing are described, often in the foreign tongue.

These alien words are handled in a variety of ways. Sometimes, but not always, they are italicized to draw attention to them, although they are occasionally inserted without any typographical markers, which can make the text more challenging for the reader. The terms can be used with a direct translation adjacent to them, following a dash, or in parentheses, for example. Footnotes can be used to explain concepts or institutions, although this solution is generally too formal or 'academic', and therefore disruptive to readers. Cushioning and contextualization are glossing strategies that can be used instead of translations to make such hybrid texts more accessible. Cushioning involves inserting an English-language explanation to shed light on a foreign word, while contextualization makes the alien term virtually explicit by means of the immediate context (Woodsworth 2008: 109–111; Zabus 2014: 34–37).

The following excerpt from "From Sicilia to Montréal" (Audrey Caramanico) incorporates code-switching, primarily in the form of interjections in direct speech. It depicts, once again, the immigrant experience and concludes with an incisive definition of what it means to be a Montrealer:

> My *nonna* paused for a second as she brought me more cake. "*Comunque*, anyway, *Grazie a Dio*, once we were settled, it became easier. … we brought the entire *familia* from the old country to come live with us, and they came so quickly – you see they need a lot of immigrants to work in factories back then. My *mamma* was miserable and left back home soon after she had arrived." She paused and wiped another tear from her eye and continued: "Canada is our home now. Now, your dad is sixty-six and we're in our nineties. *Gesù Cristo,* it's been so long. *Gesù Cristo*, we're old! OK, let's go back to the living room and take your cake with you."
>
> As I walked back to the couch, I looked at my family and realized that I knew exactly who I was. I was a true Montrealer. And, like so many Montrealers, I had a rich and deeply ingrained past handed down to me by my immigrant family through many different traditions and rituals and recipes.

"The wedding reunion" (Ana Rimac) is a colourful first-person tale that paints a lovely portrait of the immigrant grandmother. The text contains quite a few foreign terms used without translations, leaving the reader to infer that '*mladenac*' is the groom and that '*zastava*' is the Croatian flag, for example.

> Now Kevin, Mariana's fiancé, is Italian. I don't think he knew what he was getting himself into when he agreed to have the wedding in Croatia. But I guess he's a nice guy, all he needs to do is follow along. Kevin, the *mladenac,* was going to pick up Mariana, the *mladenka,* and, according to tradition, they would go together to the church in a limousine led by a procession and a big Croatian flag held by Antonio, the *mladenka's* brother. Of course it was the same *zastava* that was leading the way to the church when Mariana's parents got married. When Kevin got to the *mladenka's* family's house there was a big band of *tamburaši* playing the mandolin, accordion and violin, singing and drinking the famous *rakija*. Mariana's grandfather, *dida* Mirko, had made a bottle of grape *rakija* for each of his grandchildren and it was meant to be opened on their wedding day. This home-made stuff probably had 55% alcohol but the *Šljivovica* sold in Canada only has about 40%. Kevin was in for a surprise, but he survived and was welcomed in the family.

The story ends on a humorous note as the grandmother, in her Croatian accent, chides her modern Canadian granddaughter:

> Basically, Ana, you really missed a big celebration because of work, I think next time you should take my advice: either call in sick or quit that *stuardesa* job. [Ana works for an airline as a 'stewardess'.]

In a story about a Ukrainian Christmas, "*Svyat Vechir*" (Larysa Lacko), both cushioning and contextualization are used:

> '*Ne chipay!*' She could hear her mother slapping away her brother's hands as he tried to sneak some *varenyky*. *Varenyky* are one of the twelve traditional dishes. They are crescent-shaped dumplings of unleavened dough, stuffed with sauerkraut or cheese and mashed potatoes, similar to perogies. … They were also expected to get dressed in their traditionally embroidered blouses called *vyshyvky*. The blouses were decorated with ornamental needlework. Embroidered flowers symbolized prosperity and fertility.

The Romanian story, "Christmas carols in the country of my childhood" (Emilia Lisoschi) once again presents a smorgasbord of Christmas goodies: more than a translation, it is a description of and commentary on differences between these foods and those available in Canada.

> The food was traditional, home-made, of course – there was no other option, anyway – and all of it made with pork, because that is what we traditionally eat for Christmas: sausages (something like the fresh ones with garlic that you can find in some stores here, only those ones were better), *caltabosi* (liverwurst, I guess, which is another kind of sausage, but made from liver and other organs), pieces of roast pork and the must-have *sarmale* (cabbage or vine leaves stuffed with a mixture of ground meat, rice, onion, carrots, eggs and spices).

Another food story, "Doña Siria" (Alina Pietilainen), takes place in Puebla, Mexico. While Spanish words are italicized, they are not translated. The words '*paciencia*' and '*práctica*' are obvious because they are so typologically close to the English 'patience' and 'practice'. In the third sentence, '*galletas*' is used in Spanish, but the meaning, suggested by the context, becomes completely clear in the last sentence when the English word 'cookie' is given.

> Jimena would always tell her daughter that cooking is an art that requires a lot of *paciencia* and *práctica*. When she was old enough to learn how to cook, Marta started cooking very simple things. The first dish she made was oatmeal *galletas* with chocolate and fruits. The *galletas* were so soft, the

> oatmeal, chocolate and fruit would just melt in your mouth. People absolutely loved the cookies and told her that she was definitely her *mamă*'s daughter: she must have the talent of cooking in her genes.

In "Once upon a war" (Andrea Winterhalter), a moving tale of Bucharest in 1944, the author portrays the atmosphere and devastation of war. Code-switching is kept to a minimum, associated mainly with the author's nostalgia for happier times.

> Bare tree trunks and burnt down fields flashed before my eyes as the train rattled past the sad remains of once bustling villages. Still, I could not see the desolation. Looking out through the dirty, foggy windows of the train that was taking me back to Bucharest, I allowed my mind to wander.
>
> As I listened to the rhythmic sound of the train's wheels on the tracks, I was transported into a different world, back to our peaceful life from before the war. I was reliving the lazy mornings of my childhood when, woken up by the delicious smell of freshly baked *poale-n brâu* and steaming hot milk, my brothers and I would run into the kitchen and feel like kings around the table. Nobody could bake cheese pies like Mother did and nobody could eat them as fast as we could.

The students' narratives sometimes take the form of a story about a story. In "A Husband for Djambaro", for instance, Krystèle Gueyaud skilfully weaves the foreignness of Niger into her narrative. In the following introduction, once again italicized to set it apart from the main narrative, she expresses her enthusiasm for the task of translating the folk tale recounted to her by a friend.

> "Eh girlfriend," she said in an exaggerated manner, "I thought long and hard about this assignment of yours, hmph. I even spoke to my sister about it. And you know what? She reminded me of this children's tale they used to tell us at bedtime when we visited our grandmother's village. So, I hope you are ready! This is the story I've decided to tell you."
>
> I smiled, and found myself quite excited at having the opportunity to translate and transcribe the story that follows.

The final example, from "The scent of a lemon" by Melina Carnevale, begins with a conversation about storytelling, after which the writer draws an evocative portrait of her friend, calling attention to the gulf that divides them.

> "Tell me a story."
>
> "A story about what?"
>
> "I don't know. A story about you. Tell me about back home, *le bled.* Tell me why you left."

> Silence.
>
> I look up at my old friend, my pencil poised right above my paper, itching to get started, but he is lost in thoughts too painful to share. I watch him for a moment. He is still that same young man I met seven years ago, *fresh off the boat* and eager to see the world. He hasn't changed one bit; the sun-kissed skin of the North Africans, the mess of loose curls that I know his mother hides beneath her delicate veils, the thin lips that whisper an ancient language that I will never understand, and those eyes. His eyes are dark and deep; they draw everyone in but trust no one because they saw far too much far too soon. They are the eyes of a child robbed of his innocence, of a soldier stuck between causes, a rebel, a martyr, a son and a father; they are the eyes of Algeria.

4.2 Student comments

As an additional task, the students are asked to read all the stories and pick two or three favourites, excluding their own. They are invited to give some examples of how their preferred stories have successfully translated across cultures and are asked to identify the techniques their classmates have used most effectively. The purpose of this part of the assignment is to ensure that students read all the stories and appreciate the full range of writing; they learn not only from reading one another's work critically but also from evaluating selected stories in the light of some of the theoretical concepts they have become familiar with during the course.

Interestingly, each story, with almost no exceptions, tends to be chosen as a favourite by at least one student. I compile the observations and send each student the ones related to his or her own story. This provides everyone with additional positive feedback and, importantly, with input that is different from mine. Some of the students' insightful and enthusiastic comments are provided below.

> "The thirty-first" (Kelly Oliel) beautifully describes the Sri Lankan *Mu-pathi Ondru* ceremony to welcome new-born baby Maya. It is a special and joyful day in a newly expanded family's life. The food ('rice, *ghee*, milk with cardamom, candied sugar') and the sumptuous clothing (the baby's *mullu pavaati* and Sanjana's *panjavi* with its 'mid-thigh-length shirt and harem pants') all convey an impression of plenty.
>
> I really enjoyed '*Stan Wojenny* [Martial law]' (Sylwia Pawlik). The writing style is very warm and draws the reader in. I like the techniques used to retain the foreignness of Polish culture, in a text that is nevertheless accessible to the English reader. For example, she used formal translation in the

following cases: '*osiedle,* neighbourhood' and '*milicja obywatelska*, the governmental militia'. She also used a form of cushioning for "their favourite morning TV program, *Teleranek*" and "the whole district of *Nova Hutá*". I liked the images she used to give her readers further understanding of some of the foreign terms, and I found the footnotes helpful in understanding some of the more complicated concepts.

I liked reading "After the war in Berlin" (Alexandra Grimanis) because the dialogue allows Anne's personality to come through. I imagine her as having a good sense of humour. Also, you can detect her German accent even in written form: "Nobody else had chickens and you are at the age when you look at boys, you know? I mean, you didn't want anybody like this to be seeing you, yeah?"

"*Pasdar*" (Nathalie Le Beller), a story about Iran, dealt with foreign terms in a few different ways. There are direct translations following a short dash, for example: "In the eyes of the government, we were not only Bahá'ís, but also *fararis* – fugitives." She gives the same, direct translation for the term *pasdar,* but later on, when the revolutionary guard speaks, she fluidly works in a 'translation' of his command, "*Bedeh man*", through the character's response, which is to hand over her passport. I thought that this story was very detailed and the intercultural transfers deftly accomplished.

5. Conclusions

From my own perspective, writing these stories contributes in several ways to the learning process. Students develop writing skills; in rewriting the stories and making the changes in the mechanics and style that I recommend, they are simulating a situation in which they must follow an editor's instructions. There are further advantages to giving students a chance to work in this manner: released, as it were, from the constraints of a ST, they have the freedom to follow their creative instincts. The exercise is also rewarding at a personal level, enabling them to get to know, for the first time perhaps, about the experiences of their family or friends as newcomers to Canada.

Most importantly, the students are exposed to the concept and act of interculturalism by entering into a dialogue with someone of another culture. At a professional level, they learn what it means to translate from one culture to another, rather than simply from language to language, acquiring a set of skills that will serve them well not only in working with hybrid texts but also in creating them. They are given an opportunity, finally, to engage in intercultural writing, as defined by Simon in *Translating Montreal*:

"one-way translation, the abandon of the language of origin in favour of a new mixed, imaginative literary language" (2006: 184).

I would like to give the last word to the students, whose comments express their delight in creating these stories as well as in reading them. "I thought all the stories were wonderful to read", commented one student. "I enjoyed and was impressed by all the stories", said another. Beyond personal enjoyment, the students perceived the value of the exercise, as illustrated in the following assessment:

> First, I must say that this assignment was a wonderful exercise. It allowed me to translate the experience of someone of a different background into story form. I had to find ways to express the oral version in a written version. Finally, I had to work with some culture-specific terminology, and decide how to translate it into written English. These efforts enabled me to perfect my translation and writing skills.

Not merely translating, but also transposing another's voice: what the students learn through this exercise, and the literary translation course as a whole, is that translating is always a form of rewriting. It is, in fact, a 're-make', but not in the sense alluded to earlier. It is not a matter of either preserving the foreign or completely erasing traces of it; instead, it is an intercultural process in which the translator weaves elements of hybridity – selectively, thoughtfully and ethically – into their rendering of an original text.

References

Bellos, David. 2013. Fictions of the foreign: The paradox of 'foreign-soundingness'. In Esther Allen & Susan Bernofsky (eds) *In translation. Translators on their work and what it means.* New York: Columbia University Press, 31–43.

Berman, Antoine. 1984. *L'épreuve de l'étranger: Culture et traduction dans l'Allemagne romantique: Herder, Goethe, Schlegel, Novalis, Humboldt, Schleiermacher, Hölderlin.* Paris: Gallimard.

Berman, Antoine. 1992. *The experience of the foreign: Culture and translation in Romantic Germany* (trans. Stefan Heyvaert). Albany: SUNY Press.

Delisle, Jean. 2011. Canadian Tradition. In Mona Baker (ed) *Routledge Encyclopedia of Translation Studies.* London/New York: Routledge, 362–369.

Heim, Michael Henry. 2013. To foreignize or not to foreignize: From a translator's notebook. In Sherry Simon (ed) *In translation. Honouring Sheila Fischman.* Montreal: McGill-Queen's University Press, 83–91.

Larkosh, Christopher. 1996. Teaching – translation – theory: Communicative horizons for critical practices. In Cay Dollerup & Vibeke Appel (eds) *Teaching translation and interpreting 3*. Amsterdam/Philadelphia: John Benjamins, 47–53.

Lefevere, André & Bassnett, Susan. 1990. Introduction: Proust's grandmother and the thousand and one nights. The 'cultural turn' in Translation Studies. In Susan Bassnett & André Lefevere (eds) *Translation, history, and culture*. London: Cassell, 1–13.

Major, André. 2013. *À quoi ça rime?* Montreal: Boréal.

Medley, Mark. 2010. The forgotten mimics: Translating literature "is like writing but with someone else's hand". <http://arts.nationalpost.com/2010/09/24/translators/> (accessed 18 September 2017).

Simon, Sherry. 1999. *Hybridité culturelle*. Montreal: Boréal.

Simon, Sherry. 2006. *Translating Montreal: Episodes in the life of a divided city*. Montreal: McGill-Queen's University Press.

Simon, Sherry (ed). 2013. *In translation. Honouring Sheila Fischman*. Montreal: McGill-Queen's University Press.

Venuti, Lawrence. 1995. *The translator's invisibility: A history of translation*. London/New York: Routledge.

Woodsworth, Judith. 2002. Teaching literary translation: Integrating theory and practice in the classroom. In Eva Hung (ed) *Teaching translation and interpreting 4: Building bridges*. Amsterdam/Philadelphia: John Benjamins, 129–138.

Woodsworth, Judith. 2008. Translating identity in Northern Ontario. In Denise Merkle et al. (eds) *Traduire depuis les marges. Translating from the Margins*. Québec: Éditions Nota bene, 95–120.

Woodsworth, Judith. 2010. Histoire d'une traduction. In Marie-Andrée Beaudet & Karin Larose (eds) *Le marcheur des Amériques. Mélanges offerts à Pierre Nepveu*. Montreal: Paragraphes, 203–213.

Zabus, Chantal J. 2014. "Writing with an accent": From early decolonization to contemporary gender issues in the African novel in French, English, and Arabic. In Simona Bertacco (ed) *Language and translation in postcolonial literatures: Multilingual contexts, translational texts*. London/New York: Routledge, 32–37.

ANNA VERMEULEN AND ANA IBÁÑEZ MORENO

Ghent University and Universidad Nacional de Educación a Distancia Madrid

Audio Description as a Tool to Enhance Intercultural Competence

Abstract

In order to make audiovisual materials accessible to visually or cognitively challenged people, oral comments on the relevant events that appear on screen are included in the gaps in the monologues or between dialogues to compensate for the lack of visual stimuli. This so-called 'audio description' (AD) is a culture-based translating activity. Various professionals and researchers (Pujol & Orero 2007; Udo & Fels 2009) claim that AD is highly subjective, since different cultures see things differently and express them in various ways. As a result, this mode of audiovisual translation makes for a useful tool to enhance intercultural skills. Former research already showed that AD helps to promote language skills. In this contribution, we present the results of various reception studies that were carried out in the framework of the Audiodescripción como Recurso Didáctico en la Enseñanza de Lenguas Extranjeras (ARDELE) project at the Department of Translation, Interpreting and Communication of the Faculty of Arts and Philosophy of Ghent University over the course of three academic years (2011–2012, 2012–2013 and 2013–2014). These studies involved 153 Dutch-speaking Belgian students in their third BA year of Applied Language Studies (B2 level in Spanish). Results show that AD is a good pedagogical tool to raise intercultural awareness because it elicits students' reflections on how important it is to use language accurately in order to communicate effectively.

Keywords: audio description, intercultural awareness, language pedagogy, task-based learning

1. Introduction: ICC and audio description

This article stems from the Audiodescripción como Recurso Didáctico en la Enseñanza de Lenguas Extranjeras (ARDELE) project which explores the benefits of audio description as a didactic tool in foreign language learning (FLL) and teaching (FLT). On the basis of the outcome of former case studies within this project, we discovered that audio description (AD) can be used not only to promote all linguistic competences in an integrated way (Ibáñez Moreno & Vermeulen 2014) – particularly to enhance lexical and phraseological competences (Ibáñez Moreno & Vermeulen 2013) and to raise awareness of grammatical issues such as the use of pronominal verbs in Spanish (forthcoming) – but also to improve (meta)linguistic and intercultural competences in FLL (Ibáñez Moreno & Vermeulen 2017). In this chapter we present the results obtained from the student responses to the question as to how they experienced their participation in the project. Did they become aware that different cultures see things differently and express them in diverse ways? Before presenting the aims of the ARDELE project and the way it was carried out (see section 2), as well as the results obtained (see section 3), we provide an overview of the state of the art of intercultural competence and AD, together with the benefits of their use in FLL.

1.1 Intercultural competence

Intercultural communication is relevant in several disciplines, including Anthropology, Applied Linguistics, Sociolinguistics, and Translation Studies. In the *Common European Framework of Reference for Languages* (CEFR) (Council of Europe 2001: 1) – which also includes translation as a language skill – FLL and FLT are framed within an intercultural approach from the outset:

> In *an intercultural approach*, it is a central objective of language education to promote the favorable development of the learner's whole personality and sense of identity in response to the enriching experience of otherness in language and culture.

In this approach, intercultural competence (ICC) means integrating the learner's personality (that is, their individual side) and sense of identity (i.e. their social side) into the process of learning a language as an enriching experience. The *Common European Framework for Languages* and the European language portfolio include intercultural experiences as part of the language learning process (ibid.: 5): "In particular, the European Language Portfolio (ELP) provides a format in which language learning and intercultural experiences of the most diverse kinds can be recorded and formally recognized." The aim of the learning process is to become a person who is multilingual and intercultural in the sense of being able to mediate between different languages and cultures.

The guidelines of the CEFR (2001) draw on Byram's (1997) proposal for incorporating intercultural competence into communicative competence. Indeed, it stands to reason that intercultural competence is an essential dimension of communicative competence. It implies cultural negotiation. In this sense, and following Holliday et al. (2004: 19), intercultural communication deals with the way we all carry with us our own discourse and perceptions of culture and how we negotiate this in communication. Intercultural communication means understanding people, culture, and society in general:

> Being sensitive to, and understanding, others' cultural productions and the way in which they play with the various identities available to them (discourses on their identities currently available in the context of this interaction) is a crucial part of good intercultural communication.

Following Holliday et al. (ibid.), one of the main pillars of contemporary FLT is Intercultural Communicative Competence (ICC), which seeks to make students aware of the importance of what they express and how they express it. Also, ICC makes them realise that what they say is biased by how they perceive reality, which, in turn, is influenced by their own culture. When we speak or write, we tend to take a particular perspective, that is, our own perspective on the world, which is directly reflected in what we communicate. As Gee says:

> When we speak or write we always take a particular perspective on what the world looks like. This involves us in taking perspectives on what is 'world' and not; what is 'acceptable' and not; what is 'right' and not, what is 'real' and not, what is the 'way things are' and not; what is 'the way things out to be' and not .... (1990: 2)

Beecroft (2013) calls for a shift in the perception of translation in FLT, defining translation as a functional, communicative and inter-transcultural process. Both areas (translation and FLT) are interconnected and point in the same direction: the development of didactic methods that are more discourse-oriented, affective and socio-culturally based. The context of FLT becomes, in Beecroft's terms, a hybrid space for discourse and action, where the inclusion of complex translation tasks, framed within the task-based approach as described by Long (1985), Ellis (2003) and Littlewood (2004), can promote the development of ICC in language learners. In task-based language learning (TBLL), a task is defined as an activity that takes place in the real world, based on authentic materials, with a clearly defined communicative goal, and in which form and content are complementary and, indeed, necessary to achieve successful learning results. Within the field of translation didactics, Hassel (2009) developed some tasks that are communicative, action-oriented and related to translation processes with a view to training translators to acquire (competences that cover) linguistic skills. According to the author, one of these skills is culture-related understanding, that is, "raising awareness of the fact that every utterance is linked to its speaker's culture" (2009: 189). This entails, therefore, promoting ICC, which is also an important goal of FLT, as mentioned.

In this study, we combine translation and language learning by showing how AD, a mode of audiovisual translation, can become a powerful and useful tool in the foreign-language classroom, especially to promote intercultural communication. Intercultural communication is concerned with language learning, because when we learn an FL we are always confronted with culture and, therefore, with the constructs of identity in that culture. In line with Pavlenko and Lantolf (2000), whose work draws on Vygotski (1986), the father of social-constructivist learning theories, we see learning an FL as a way of reconstructing ourselves; in the process of language learning, identities are reconstructed and life stories retold because of the relationship between thought, meaning and words.

1.2 ICC and AD

AD, a technique that was developed in the United States (Benecke 2004: 78) in the 1970s, is a translating activity of inter-semiotic nature that consists in turning the visual content of an event not rendered by an aural channel into speech. In order to make cinema and television productions (films, documentaries, news, sport events), live performances (plays, opera, musicals), or museums and exhibitions accessible to the visually impaired, the audio describer provides oral comments (live or recorded) on relevant events that are happening on screen, the stage, or in a museum to compensate for the lack of visual stimuli. Although the targeted audience originally comprised blind and partially sighted people, AD soon also proved to be beneficial for the elderly, children, immigrants, FL students, etc., as it fosters comprehension and literacy, as well as integration and social inclusion (Snyder 2005: 937).

Since it is a relatively young practice, there is still a lack of scientifically proven guidelines or standards (Orero & Wharton 2007; Vercauteren 2007). Until now, every country or region has drafted its own protocols:

Independent Television Commission (ITC)[1] 2000 and Ofcom[2] in the United Kingdom, the national Standard UNE 053020 issued by the national standard agency Asociación Española de Normalización y Certificación (AENOR) in Spain (2005), *La charte de l'audiodescription*[3] in France (2008) and the Broadcast Authority of Ireland (BAI)[4] 2012 in Ireland. Professionals such as Bernd Benecke (Bayerischer Rundfunk), Veronica Hyks (Independent Media Support), James O'Hara (Independent Television Facilities (itf) Centre), and Javier Navarrete of the Organización Nacional de Ciegos de España (ONCE) have also proposed some guidelines (Dosch & Benecke 2004; Hyks 2005; ADLAB[5] 2014), as have associations such as the American Council of the Blind (ACB), Les amis des aveugles in Belgium, the ONCE in Spain. Recently, the International Standard Organization (ISO) and the International Telecommunication Union (ITU)[6] approved a strategic plan for 2016–2019 to enhance access to telecommunications/ICTs for persons with disabilities and specific needs, including AD. All these documents provide a definition of AD, and indicate what to describe (characters, places, time, action, text-on-screen, camera perspective) and what not (recognizable sounds, technical film or theatre terms), how to describe it (from neutral but not monotonous to creative, additional or integrated), and when to describe it (in the gaps between dialogues at a rate of 160 words per minute). They give additional information on how to select the information (based on relevance) as well as on the language and grammar that should be used (precise, succinct, accurate and idiomatic according to the TL). Above all, a good AD is discreet, does not interfere with the dialogue, sound effects or significant music, and is adapted to the setting and the target audience.

Most guidelines stress that an AD should be 'objective'. According to Snyder (2010: 17), "[t]he best audio describers objectively recount the visual aspects of an image." Subjective or qualitative judgements or comments constitute an unnecessary and unwanted interpretation according to these guidelines. In the same vein, the *ITC guidance on standards for audio description* (2000: 15) states: "describers should not voice a personal opinion

1 <http://www.ofcom.org.uk>.
2 <http://stakeholders.ofcom.org.uk>.
3 <http://www.social-sante.gouv.fr>.
4 <http://www.bai.ie>.
5 <http://www.adlabproject.eu>.
6 <http://www.itu.int>.

or interpret events". The style of an AD should be factual, not interpretative. Udo and Fels (2009: 179) similarly state that an audio describer should "not evaluate or interpret, but rather be like the faithful lens of a camera". However, practice has shown that the objectivity rule is often hard to follow and interpretation cannot always be avoided. For example, when a female character in a film is shown in close-up, tightening her eyelids, drawing together her brows and pressing her lips together, the audio describer is likely to not just accurately describe what they see, as recommended in the guidelines, but derive the underlying emotional meaning of the facial expression and translate the changes in the face of the character into "the lady is angry" (Vercauteren & Orero 2013: 193). As these authors state, the limited characterization afforded by a normal-length feature film (the duration of a film is usually limited to between 90 and 120 minutes) requires a higher degree of inferencing from the audience. Some of the character-related information conveyed by a film is implicit, and describing it will always include a personal and uncertain component. Especially emotions, often expressed in a non-verbal way through gestures, body movements and facial expressions are difficult to verbalize objectively.

This is where the concept of interculturality arises. Creating an AD makes us aware that what we communicate is influenced by our own perceptions of the world. Intercultural communication begins by understanding ourselves as much as we (try to) understand the other: "The weight of responsibility is on 'us' to understand ourselves, rather than on essentialist categories of 'them'" (Holliday et al. 2004: 21). Language plays an essential role here: "We must be careful when talking about, and to, people who we consider to be other, because we may be unaware of the power our words may carry" (ibid.: 30). In the process of the creation of an AD, audio describers need to focus on how images constructed within their own society may influence how they see other people. That is, they need to question themselves and their own perceptions by being aware of the media and institutional influences, and look for alternative representations in order to express them later on; following Holliday et al. (ibid.: 184): "Communication, apart from being about 'what' is said is also about the negotiation of interpersonal relationships, of the signalling of the status of each interactant."

Looking at differences in the cultural value systems that exist in the world is the first step to integrating diversity into communication in a non-essentialist way (that is, departing from the aim to establish a bridge between cultures rather than separate them). That is the reason why Hyks (2006: 1) argues that an AD should not be translated from an existing audio description script (in case of a foreign film), but created directly from the images, because we all see things subjectively different: "even though we all agree on certain basic principles, we do see things differently and we certainly express them in very varied ways" (ibid.). Pujol and Orero (2007) also state that AD is influenced by the individual interpretation of reality, and therefore culturally-bound. In the *Pear tree project* (Mazur & Chmiel 2012), sighted viewers who spoke 12 different languages were asked to watch a short film and recount what they saw. The research shows that they tended to interpret visual events but avoided extremely subjective interpretations that included a moral judgement of the situation. Therefore, instead of applying the binary opposition of objective versus subjective, audio describers should be recommended to work with an objectivity–subjectivity scale, which can help determine those interpretive descriptions that are not redolent of subjectivity and can be used without any risk of coming across as patronizing or even misleading the visually impaired.

Furthermore, the selection of the information to be included in the AD is highly subjective in itself, as it is not only determined by the skills of the audio describers, but also by their personal taste and the target-audience requirements. Here, the question arises whether an AD should offer more information than the sighted audience receives in order to enhance comprehension, or whether it should remind the audience of relevant aspects regarding culture, art, literature, or society (Hernández & Mendiluce 2009). According to the ITC guidance (2000: 15), "occasionally a little additional explanation can help." In the Belgian Dutch series about the World War I, *In Flanders fields* (*In Vlaamse velden,* Jan Mattys, 2014), broadcast on Flemish television (VRT) and available on DVD, the audio describer explains (in Belgian Dutch) that the poppy that appears on screen, is "the symbol of the firsts world war". In the same vein, in the legal drama television series, "*De ridder*", also broadcast with AD on Flemish television (and available on DVD), the audio describer explains that *The Telegraph* is an 'English newspaper'. The sighted audience watching these series without AD does not get that kind of information.

As for AD in translated versions (dubbed or audio subtitled), the translators must decide what is important, what must be explained and what can be sacrificed for the new target audience. Sanz Moreno (2012) illustrates how the Spanish audio describer of *Slumdog millionaire* (Boyle 2008) offers additional information that is not provided in the English AD, assuming that the Spanish audience lacks the cultural background that the English audience has. The audio describer explains that yellow is the colour of happiness, that the Taj Mahal and the Chhatrapati Shivaji station are monuments protected by the United Nations Educational, Scientific and Cultural Organization (UNESCO), that Amitabh Bachchan is a famous actor; he even changes the names of two of the three musketeers, Porthos and Athos, and adds the author's name in question: "el maestro enseña al resto de alumnos el libro *Los tres mosqueteros* de Alejandro Dumas" [in the film the teacher shows the book *The three musketeers*, by Alexandre Dumas, to his students]. In the same vein, the Italian audio describer of the movie *Chocolat* (Hallström 2000) felt the need to add a narrative explanation for the behaviour of one of the main characters, Serge, a rude bar tenant who is abandoned by his wife Josephine and "dopo il duro periodo di rieducazione, Serge è finalmente pronto per tornare da Josephine"[7] (Arma 2012: 51). This information is not given by the English audio describer.

In what follows, we give a brief overview of the ongoing project at the heart of this contribution, focusing especially on the data obtained with regard to intercultural competence.

2. The ARDELE project

2.1 Aims

The aim of the Audiodescripción como Recurso Didáctico en la Enseñanza de Lenguas Extranjeras (ARDELE) project is to explore the benefits of using AD in the FL classroom. It was launched in the Faculty of Applied Language Studies of Ghent University College (Belgium) in 2011 – which was recently integrated as the Department of Translation, Interpreting and Communication into Ghent University – and it has been carried out with Dutch-speaking Belgian students as well as Spanish Erasmus students between the ages of 20 and 22. In the case of the Spanish students, they participated in the pilot study in the year 2010–2011, but most

[7] 'after a very hard time of re-education, Serge is ready to go back to his wife'.

of the students involved in the project are Belgian students learning Spanish as an FL. In the course of three years, 153 Belgian students have participated in the project.

By the time they take part in the project (in their third BA year), the Belgian students' Spanish proficiency can be described as being at B2 level (Independent User) according to the CEFR (2001: 24–28). To help reach our final objective of raising the students' proficiency to a C1 level, we implemented AD-based tasks in the framework of the task-based approach, asking the students to adopt a role which would normally be performed by a professional audio describer.

2.2 Procedures

The pilot study (2010–2011) was carried out as part of the module 'Audiovisual Translation' (3 ECTS) offered in the Master of Translation, in the case of the Belgian students, and in the module 'Screen Translation' (5 ECTS), offered in the postgraduate Dutch and Translation, in the case of the Spanish Erasmus students. All students were asked to create a Spanish AD from scratch (i.e. on the basis of the images) of the film, *Blind*, the first film that was provided with Dutch AD by the director, Tamar van den Dop (2007). The aim of this task was to establish whether Belgian and Spanish students see the same things, select the same information and describe it in the same way. The findings, including the different ways in which the students described the house (*casa/casa de campo/mansión)* or the characters (*negro/moreno/rubio*) proved to be interesting enough to implement the same tasks in the module 'Translation' (3 ECTS) offered in the third BA year, and to set up the ARDELE project.

In the course of the first two years 2011–2012 and 2012–2013, and after we had limited our sample to Belgian students, we asked these students to create a Spanish intersemiotic translation of different clips from *Sin ti*, the first Spanish film that came out with AD (Masllorens 2006). Afterwards, their versions were first compared to each other, and then to the official AD on the Spanish DVD, which was created and read by a native speaker. The lexical and phraseological items were analysed and discussed in class, where native language interferences into Spanish were highlighted, as well as intercultural issues related to the students' way of audio describing. In this way, we could draw the students' attention to the fact that what they communicate is always influenced by their individual and cultural identities. The fact that the recipients of an AD are visually impaired means that the way we express events is even more important than in other communicative contexts, where the recipients can also negotiate the final meaning of our message. In this case, the meaning is negotiated only by the speaker – the audio describer – who must be conscious of the impact of their words on the (visually impaired) recipients, as the latter do not have any other means to interpret the visual events that appear on screen.

Finally, we carried out a controlled experiment during the academic year 2013–2014. An experimental group (EG) created the AD for a clip from *Match point* (Woody Allen 2005) from scratch, while a control group (CG) translated the Dutch AD transcript of the same clip (prepared by the coaches). The results, described in section 5 below, show that the students who created the AD based on images expressed what they saw in a far more specific and accurate way than the students who prepared the AD based on a written text. Furthermore, more students in the EG than those in the CG declared in the post-questionnaire (see below) that they had become aware of intercultural issues.

Each of these projects was set up in three phases: a preparation, production and reflection. The preparation phase, prepared in one classroom session of two hours and extra homework (of approximately another two hours) comprised an introduction to the basics of AD, filling in a pre-questionnaire (in Google Docs), and reading a synopsis of the film. The students also received clear instructions on how to audio describe, based on real AD procedures, as outlined in (1) below:

(1) Describe what you see, not what you think you see.
Be concise (160–180 words per minute).
Use only present tenses.
Describe only sounds that the visually impaired cannot recognize.
Do not use phrases such as "we see".

The pre-questionnaire was designed to retrieve information about the students' proficiency level in Spanish and their motivation to learn and improve their language skills. All Dutch-speaking Belgian participants studied English, French or German as their second language (L2). For most of them, Spanish was their third language (L3). As they stated in the questionnaire, most of them had never heard of AD before. The pre-questionnaire also contained some sentences in Dutch with specific words, phraseological units, and grammatical structures that the students had to translate into Spanish and that would later on appear in the AD of the clips.

The materials selected for the AD task were clips from the films *Blind,* the first film released with AD in the Netherlands/Belgium, *Sin Ti,* the first film released with AD in Spain, and *Match Point,* which includes two long sequences with little dialogue (both of approximately four minutes) that are very similar, which made it possible to repeat the task in order to assess the progress the students had made. Besides, in *Blind* and *Sin ti,* the protagonists are blind, which is likely to make students more sensitive to the issue and hence more predisposed to 'helping' their audience.

The production phase was carried out in two classroom sessions of two hours each. The data gathered consisted of controlled classroom observations and the students' AD scripts. Based on this data, linguistic, communicative and intercultural errors were identified and discussed in class, and the students' AD scripts were assessed as audiovisual translations: the students' ADs were compared to the original, and, based on the evaluation of both their linguistic and audio-descriptive features, the best ADs were selected by the students themselves. The differences in wording and description were discussed in class. Then, the students had to repeat the assignment, rendering a second version of the same clip.

In the reflection phase, the students were required to complete a post-questionnaire (in Google Docs) of 30 statements or questions, divided into several sections, as outlined below:

(2) a. Grid questions related to students' perception of their linguistic learning (rate 1–5)

b. Grid questions related to students' perception of their own AD learning (rate 1–5)

c. Ten language test questions with sentences obtained from their first and second ADs containing their common errors.

d. Grid questions asking for students' general opinion on the project and the tasks (rate 1–5).

As for (2c), the test questions assessed students' improvement at several levels: lexical, phraseological, grammatical, intercultural and audio-descriptive. The students were asked to identify and describe the errors in ten sentences, based on the errors they had made in their own ADs, and to provide a corrected version of these sentences.

3. Results

Although until the present moment the focus of the ARDELE project has mainly been on FLL and FLT, more so than on promoting cross-cultural communication and cultural awareness, it cannot be denied that implementing AD activities in the FL classroom goes beyond language learning and highlights intercultural issues. During the production phase, when the students compared their ADs with the AD made by the Spanish students and the official AD on the DVD (created and read by a native speaker), they were given the chance to observe how different perceptions can be and how important accuracy is when we communicate. For instance, in the film *Blind*, the maid, frightened by the screaming of the blind protagonist, Ruben, runs away and loses the bucket she is carrying. The Spanish students described the scene by saying: "se le cae el cubo", whereas the Flemish students said: "deja caer el cubo" [she drops the bucket], a literal translation of "ze laat de emmer vallen". This is correct in Dutch, but when translated literally into Spanish, it sounds far more intentional than the expression used by the Spanish students. Another example: in the film *Sin ti*, the protagonist, Lucía, frustrated by her blindness, destroys all her paintings, while her daughter Alba looks at her, terrified by so much violence. The AD on the DVD says: "El padre corre hacia su hija temblorosa ante la puerta de la terraza. La zarandea y le da varias bofetadas. Se abrazan con fuerza. Contempla la escena sin separarse de su hija" [The father runs to his trembling daughter, who is standing at the terrace door. He shakes her and slaps her a few times. They embrace tightly. He contemplates the scene without leaving his daughter.]. However, this scene, and especially the way the father reacts to his daughter, "la zarandea y le da varias bofetadas" [He shakes her and slaps her several times], was described by the Belgian students in Spanish in different ways. Some of them are shown below:

- La sacude violentamente y la golpea en la cara. [He shakes her brutally and hits her on the face.] Se abrazan intensamente, y Alba está temblando.
- Toni corre hacia Alba, que también había entrado en la habitación. La zarandea y la reprende [He shakes her and reprimands her]. También le pega ligeramente [He also hits her softly]. Al final le abraza muy fuerte, pero ella quiere escapar. Alba no logra liberarse de sus brazos [..., but she wants to escape. Alba does not manage to free herself from his arms].
- Toni corre hacia su hija reteniéndola y consolándola [Toni runs to her daughter so as to hold and comfort her.] Luego se abrazan. [Then they hug.]

- El marido ve que su hija está en *choque [en estado de shock/in shock]. La pega golpes en la cara y la abraza. La chica se calma [He beats her on the face and hugs her. The girl calms down.]

All these differences between the ADs produced by the Spanish students and the official AD on the DVD were discussed in the class session following the AD exercise. The data gathered as well as classroom observations while these discussions took place show that the Belgian students not only worked hard on correctly conveying the occurrences on screen in Spanish, but they were also given the opportunity to become aware of how the same scene can be described in many different ways; how speakers show, while communicating, their own perception of events.

The answers to some of the statements or questions in the post-questionnaires show that AD tasks enhanced students' self-perception. These questions/statements are provided below (translated into English):

(3) a. Thanks to AD, I have practised my ICC (that is, different ways of communicating, depending on the culture of origin).

b. AD has helped me reflect on how our way of seeing the world influences how we communicate.

c. AD has been useful for me to observe the importance of making all kinds of material accessible to visually impaired persons by using language that takes the recipient's situation into account.

d. Which activity do you think is more useful to developing ICC? AD or translation?

Based on the students' answers, we can deduce that they thought they had become more aware of and had enhanced their cross-cultural communication. The first statement (4a), presented only in the tests of 2011–2012 (49 students) and 2012–2013 (52 students) to a total of 101 students, is explicit, where students were asked to assess whether they were practising their ICC. As can be seen, a brief definition of what ICC is was provided. Chart 1 shows students' responses to the statement professing AD to be an effective tool for promoting ICC.

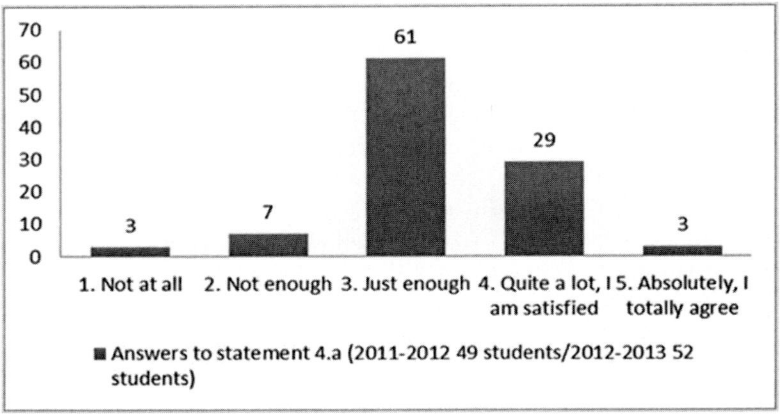

Table 1: Thanks to AD, I have practised my ICC

In the years 2011–2012 and 2012–2013, out of 101 students, ten gave a negative response (three believing that AD did not help at all and seven claiming that AD did not help enough). Sixty-one students stated that AD helped just enough (rating 3). Twenty-seven students gave a rating of 4, and three students gave a rating of 5 to this statement. Given these data, the mean (3.15) shows that most students were positive, whereas the median is 3.

This first statement was not presented to the students who participated in the experiment in 2013–2014 (52 students). As we explained before, we changed the experiment and used a between-group experimental design, with each group performing different activities: one group performed AD-based tasks and the other translation tasks. Therefore, the statements were also adapted. The question these students had to answer was the one shown in 4d.

The second and third statements (4b) and (4c), presented to all students in the three years, are implicit; although they are related to ICC, this is not explicitly stated. Students were asked about the development of their social awareness and their sense of citizenship, more specifically the importance of helping the visually impaired persons, both of which constitute essential elements of ICC. The charts below show the students' answers to these statements/questions over the three years.

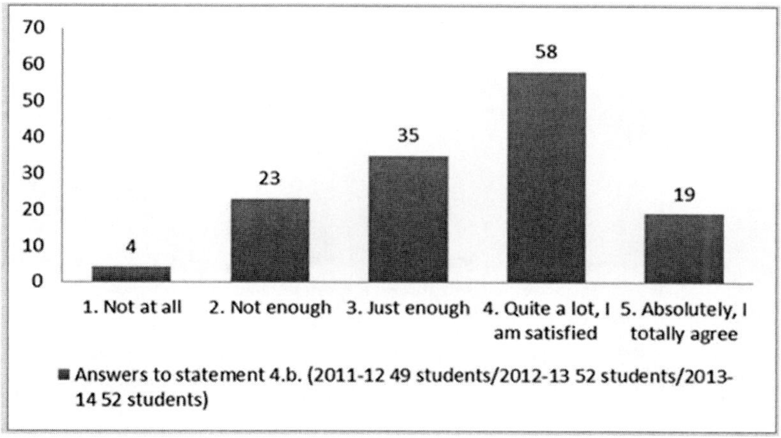

Table 2: AD has helped me reflect on how our way of seeing the world influences how we communicate

Statement (4b), about AD as a tool to reflect on how our way of seeing the world influences how we communicate, implicitly reflects some aspects of intercultural communication, and yielded more positive results than statement (4a). Four students over the course of three years (a total of 153 students) rated it with a 1; 23 rated it with a 2; 35 students rated it with a 3, stating that it was enough; 58 students rated it with a 4, stating that they were satisfied, and 19 students claimed that they were absolutely satisfied with the use of AD to reflect on how what we communicate is influenced by our own view of the world. The mean (3.15) of all responses is again positive, whereas the median in this case is slightly higher than previously, at value 4.

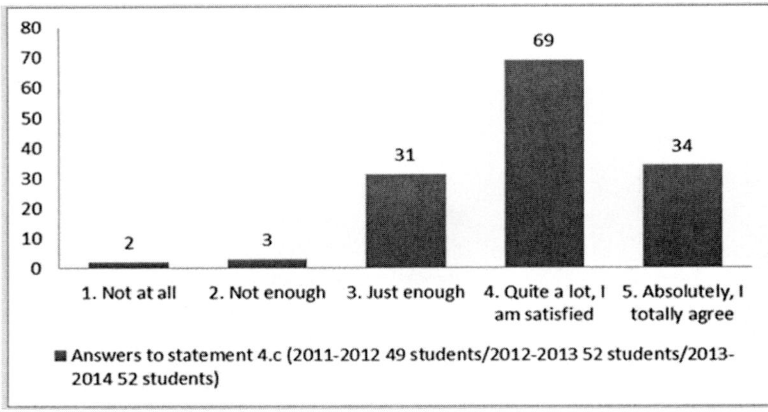

Table 3: AD has been useful for me to note the importance of making all kinds of material accessible to visually impaired persons by using language that takes the recipient's situation into account.

Statement (4c) was concerned with making students aware of the usefulness of AD for its target audience, and of communication as essential for accessibility purposes in general. The students' answers showed AD had helped them become more concerned with accessibility, given that 69 of them gave a rating of 4 and 34 rated the statement with a 5. Only two students out of 153 declared that AD did not contribute to making them aware of the communication needs of the visually impaired. Also, three students rated the statement with a 2 (that is, AD helped them, but not enough). Therefore, the mean is higher than in statements (4a) and (4b), namely, 3.58, whereas in this case the median is value 4.

It is remarkable that, although students' selection of ratings 4 and 5 was more frequent when they were asked about their ICC implicitly (statements 4b and 4c) rather than explicitly (statement 4a), the means in all cases were quite similar. In the case of statement (4a), where they were directly asked to rate their improvement in terms of ICC, none of the students chose the maximum rating (5: Absolutely), and 3 students gave the minimum rating (1: Not at all). However, in statement (4b), there were ten students who circled the 5 (20% of all the students) and none of them rated it with a 1. The same goes for question in (4c), where 34 students answered with a 5 (34%) and only two (1% of all the students) answered with a 1.

Finally, question (4d) was present only in the post-questionnaire of year 2013–2014, the year in which, as described above in point 2, we conducted a controlled experiment, where one group of students had to carry out a task based on AD (the EG), while the other group (the CG) had to perform an interlingual translation task by translating the original AD script into Spanish. The results are that 34 out of the 52 students of the EG declared that they had improved their ICC thanks to their AD-based task, whereas in the CG only 18 students out of 52 claimed the same with regard to translation. This is shown in the chart below:

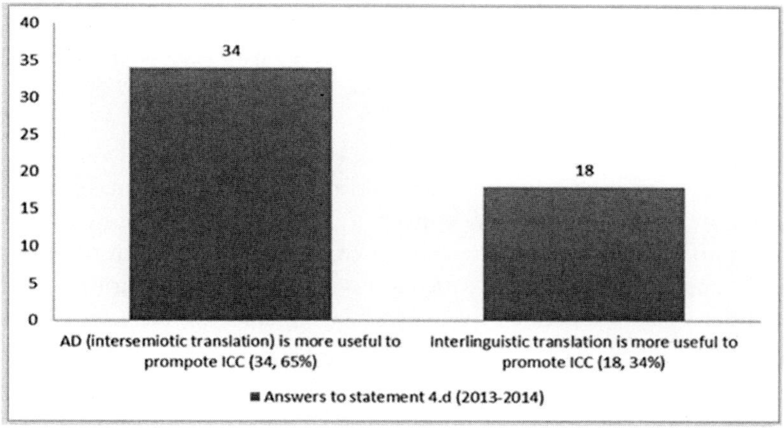

Table 4: Which activity do you think is more useful to developing ICC? AD or translation?

Based on the mostly positive responses of the participants to these statements and questions, we conclude that AD can be a valuable tool to address intercultural issues in the classroom.

4. Conclusion

The results of the ARDELE project have shown that applying a complex intersemiotic translation task, in this case creating an AD of a clip taken from a film, is successful in the promotion of ICC. Task-based learning is adequate for this type of action-oriented teaching, because the tasks emulate authentic settings. In this case the students have to assume the tasks of an audio describer in all their different phases: preparation, production and reflexion. The reflection phase promotes increased awareness and helps learners to negotiate meaning between several individual and cultural points of view. In addition, tasks can be carried out both individually and in groups, eliciting class discussions on how each of us sees and expresses events in different ways. As Beecroft (2013: 164) points out, one of the important elements of these tasks is that learners are put in a position to identify and develop cultural expressions of meaning, and to make choices:

> Thus, learners are in a position to recognize, relate and develop cultural expressions of meaning. Furthermore, the learners' role as translators who have to make explicit choices whilst carrying out the tasks should help them realise that putative culture-specific phenomena only occur through the act of comparison. Therefore, these phenomena are neither absolute nor representative, thus contributing to one of the goals of ICC to raise awareness of the factiousness of essentialist concepts of culture and identity.

Implementing AD in the FL classroom makes students realize that the messages they communicate are addressed to an audience from another culture, so they have to 'deconstruct' their own messages, analyse which parts of these messages are subjective, and rephrase them by taking their audience into account. In order to do this, we first need to become aware of our own cultural identity, as Holliday et al. (2004) state.

On the basis of the results of our study, AD proves itself to be a useful tool to help in this process. Intercultural communication is a two-way process of negotiation, where cultural and personal identities are called into question and their impact on the actual communication process is assessed. Following Holliday et al. (2004), what we see is a projection of our resources from a familiar culture onto the unfamiliar culture.

In general, the students perceived AD activities as a useful tool that requires proficiency in all areas of language use: listening, speaking, writing, reading and translating. In the post-questionnaires, the students stated that the activities made them aware of the importance of accuracy of language as an essential part of communicative competence. Results also suggest that the task promotes an awareness of cultural differences between what we see as well as how we describe what we see. The way we interpret and express what we see directly echoes our perception of reality, and this is in turn informed by culture. Although most AD guidelines agree that additional information that is not available to the sighted audience should be avoided since it might be interpreted as condescending and patronizing, it cannot be denied that different audiences might need different descriptions, including additional explanations to fully understand the events on screen.

In order to provide further evidence of the benefits of implementing AD as a tool to enhance linguistic competences – both in the FL classroom and in translation training – and to increase language learners' awareness of any knowledge gained about the target culture, we will continue working on the ARDELE project and broaden the corpus. We also plan to adapt the questionnaires by adding questions that measure online ICC and sensitivity rather than relying only on reported measures of ICC.

References

Arma, Saveria. 2012. Why can't you wear black shoes like the other mothers? Preliminary investigation on the Italian language of audio description. In Elisa Perego (ed) *Emerging topic in translation: Audio description.* Trieste: EUT Edizioni Università di Trieste, 37–55.

Beecroft, Raphaëlle. 2013. From intercultural speaker to intercultural writer: Towards a new understanding of translation in foreign language teaching. In Dina Tsagari & Georgios Floros (eds) *Translation in language teaching and assessment.* Cyprus: Cambridge Scholars Publishing, 154–172.

Benecke, Bernd. 2004. Audio-description. *Meta* 49(1): 78–80.

Byram, Michael. 1997. *Teaching and assessing intercultural communicative competence.* Clevedon: Multilingual Matters.

Council of Europe. 2001. *Common European framework of reference for languages: Learning, teaching, assessment.* Cambridge: Cambridge University Press and the Council of Europe.

Dosch, Elmar & Benecke, Bernd. 2004. *Wenn aus Bildern Worte werden – Durch Audio-Description zum Hörfilm.* Munich: Bayerischer Rundfunk.

Ellis, Rod. 2003. *Task-based language learning and teaching.* Oxford: Oxford University Press.

Gee, James Paul. 1990. *Social linguistics and literacies: Ideology and discourses.* London: Falmer Press.

Hassel, Ursula. 2009. Fremdsprachenlernen, Übersetzen und Dolmestschen: Das Konzept einer translationorientierten Fremdsprachendidaktik. In Ernest WB Hess-Lüttich, Peter Colliander & Ewald Reuter (eds) *Wie kann man von 'Deutschen' leben? Zur Praxisrelevanz der interkulturellen Germanistik.* Frankfurt am Main: Peter Lang, 179–202.

Hernández Bartolomé, Ana & Mendiluce Cabrera, Gustavo. 2009. How can images be translated? Audio description, a challenging audiovisual and social gap-filler. *Hermeneus. Revista de Traducción e Interpretación* 11: 1–17.

Holliday, Adrian, Hyde, Martin & Kullman, John. 2004. *Intercultural communication. An advanced resource book*. London/New York: Routledge.

Hyks, Veronica. 2005. Audio description and translation. Two related but different skills. *Translating Today* 4: 6–8.

Hyks, Veronica. 2006. *Translation versus origination, creativity within limits*. <http://www.languagesmedia.com/lang_media_2006/protected/Veronika_Hyks.pdf> (accessed 18 September 2017).

Ibáñez Moreno, Ana & Vermeulen, Anna. 2013. Audio description as a tool to improve lexical and phraseological competence in foreign language learning. In Dina Tsagari & Georgios Floros (eds) *Translation in language teaching and assessment*. Newcastle upon Tyne: Cambridge Scholar Press, 41–65.

Ibáñez Moreno, Ana & Vermeulen, Anna. 2014. La audiodescripción como recurso didáctico en el aula de ELE para promover el desarrollo integrado de competencias. In Rafael Orozco (ed) *New directions in Hispanic linguistics*. Newcastle upon Tyne: Cambridge Scholars Press, 263–292.

Ibáñez Moreno, Ana & Vermeulen, Anna. 2017. The ARDELE project: Audio description as a didactic to improve (meta)linguistic competences in foreign language teaching and learning. In Jorge Díaz Cintas & Kritjan Nikolic (eds) *Fast-forwarding with audiovisual translation*. Clevedon: Multilingual Matters, 114–123.

ITC guidance on standards for Audio Description. 2000. <http://www.ofcom.org.uk/static/archive/itc/itc_publications/codes_guidance/audio_description/index.asp.html> (accessed 18 September 2017).

Littlewood, William. 2004. The task-based approach: some questions and suggestions. *ELT Journal* 58(4): 319–326.

Long, Michael H. 1985. A role for instruction in second language acquisition: Task-based language teaching. In Kenneth Hylstenstam & Manfred Pienemann (eds) *Modelling and assessing in second language acquisition*. Clevedon: Multilingual Matters, 77–99.

Masslorens, Raimon. 2006. *Sin ti*. Barcelona: Lavinia Production, Bausan Films, Catalonia Television.

Mazur, Iwona & Chmiel, Agnieszka. 2012. Audio description made to measure: Reflections on interpretation in AD based on the Pear Tree Project data. In Aline Remael, Pilar Orero & Mary Carroll (eds) *Audiovisual translation and media accessibility at the crossroads. Media for all 3*. Amsterdam/Atlanta: Rodopi, 173–188.

Orero, Pilar & Wharton, Steve. 2007. The audio description of a Spanish phenomenon: Torrente. *JosTrans* 7: 164–178.

Pavlenko, Aneta & Lantolf, James. 2000. Second-language learning as participation and the (re)construction of selves. In James Lantolf (ed) *Sociocultural theory and second language learning*. New York: Oxford University Press, 155–177.

Pujol, Joaquim & Orero, Pilar. 2007. Audio description precursors: Ekphrasis and narrators. *Translation Watch Quarterly* 1: 7–18.

Sanz Moreno, Raquel. 2012. "Slumdog millionaire" *(Boyle, 2008): Análisis contrastivo de dos guiones de audiodescripción inglés y español.* Trabajo de fin de Máster, Facultad de Filología, Traducción y Comunicación, Universidad de Valencia (unpublished).

Snyder, Joel. 2005. Audio description: The visual made verbal. In *International Congress Series* 1282, 935–939.

Snyder, Joel. 2010. *Audio Description guidelines and best practices. A work in progress.* https://www.acb.org/adp/docs/AD-ACB-ADP%20Guidelines%203.1.doc. (accessed 18 September 2017). ADP%20Guidelines%203.1.doc

Udo, John Patrick & Fels, Deborah. 2009. Suit the action to the word, the word to the action: An unconventional approach to describing Shakespeare's Hamlet. *Journal of Visual Impairment and Blindness* 103(3): 178–183.

Vercauteren, Gert. 2007. Towards a European guideline for audio description. In Jorge Díaz Cintas, Pilar Orero & Aline Remael (eds) *Media for all. Subtitling for the deaf, audio description, and sign language.* Amsterdam/Atlanta: Rodopi, 139–149.

Vercauteren, Gert & Orero, Pilar. 2013. Describing facial expressions: Much more than meets the eye. *Quaderns. Revista de Traducción* 20: 187–199.

Vygotsky, Lev. 1986. *Thought and language.* Cambridge, MA: MIT Press.

The Assessment of Transcultural Competence in Translation

CATHERINE WAY

University of Granada

Teaching and Assessing Intercultural Competence: From Common Ground to Divergence

Abstract

While intercultural competence has been considered fundamental to translator training, especially in initial training modules, research and training have often been limited to basic cultural references. In the later stages of translator training, little has been done to scaffold this training and systematise the introduction of a framework of decision-making for cultural problems. These problems require more than the trainees' basic knowledge of obvious cultural differences as they face more deeply embedded and obscure culturally divergent elements. These may not only be overseen by trainees, but may also be misinterpreted through dependence on their own cultural framework, with serious consequences for the target reader. In this chapter I discuss intercultural competence and the importance of empathy in translator training before describing a tried-and-tested framework that gradually introduces the more complex culturally divergent elements. Finally, I give examples of how intercultural competence can be included in an assessment system within the suggested framework through the use of rubrics.

Keywords: intercultural competence, cultural empathy, translator training, assessment

1. Introduction

In this chapter I first discuss intercultural competence (ICC), linking it to translator training, Translator Competence Models (TrC), and the importance of empathy for translator trainees. I then discuss a threefold approach to translator training in ICC, which includes awareness of the more deeply embedded cultural elements in texts. Finally, I present examples of how ICC may be assessed in translator training through rubrics that contemplate ICC at all stages of the translation process.

Despite many years of debate, academia still struggles with the search for definitions of *culture* and *intercultural competence*. Many approaches have been suggested and applied in different fields, while in Translation Studies (TS) the 'cultural turn' of the 1990s (Bassnett & Lefevere 1990) drew attention to the ways in which translators approached culture and, particularly, cultural references in the texts they translate. Katan (2009: 74–92) provides an excellent overview of how TS has approached culture and translation as intercultural communication, which is ultimately the mission of translation.

A model of ICC that is especially pertinent – in that it underlines the importance of negotiating the distance between cultures – is the one proposed by Byram (1997: 73; 2003 and Byram et al. 2001). This model draws on linguistic, sociolinguistic and discourse competences to attain ICC. This competence, in turn, draws on interpreting/relating skills; discovery/interaction skills; knowledge, and critical cultural awareness and attitudes. Byram then describes the intercultural mediators with most competence as

> [t]hose who have an understanding of the relationship between their own language and language varieties and their own culture and cultures of different social groups in their society, on the one hand, and the language (varieties) and culture(s) of others, between (inter) which they find themselves acting as mediators. (2003: 61)

This must surely be applicable to translators, as they are intercultural mediators who aim to facilitate communication through texts originating from, and targeted at, different languages and cultures. In translator training, we find that the three competences suggested by Byram (1997) are often included, with most emphasis being placed on linguistic and sociolinguistic competence in the early stages of training and, to a lesser extent, on discourse competences in the later stages (Way 2012). These I return to in the threefold training approach I describe in section 4.1.

Among some TS authors and translator trainers, however, there has been a certain tendency to consider the translation of cultural items or references as being restricted to certain texts. House (2006: 347), for example, suggested the use of cultural filters[1] in tourist texts in particular. This rather limited view of what constitutes a cultural element is often reflected in

[1] House (2006: 249) defines 'cultural filters' as "a means of capturing cognitive and socio-cultural. differences in expectation norms and discourse conventions between source and target linguistic–cultural communities".

initial translator training courses, which devote time to the translation of institutional names, weights and measures and recipes, or to the translation of cultural references, such as Spanish *tapas*. This is obviously valuable and necessary in the early stages of translator training, particularly before trainees have a chance to experience mobility programmes or to widen their experience of the languages and cultures that they study. Others, however, such as Nida (1964: 130), have suggested that the text type is less important than the linguistic and cultural distance between the languages and cultures concerned. This gives rise to the perpetual dilemma of the translator who must create an image of the target reader and imagine how much knowledge is shared, what their cultural background is, and how they will perceive the target text (TT). As I discuss in section 4, this is no easy task.

More recently, attention in TS has shifted somewhat towards authentic experiential learning, as can be seen in Cynrim (2016), who discusses how to develop ICC through authentic projects in the translation classroom. Besides lamenting the lack of progress in defining ICC in translator training, Cynrim presents a six-stage developmental model based on Witte (1995; 2000), Bennett (1998; 2001), Grosch and Leenen (2000) and Thomas (2003).

Stages	Development of translator's ICC
Stage 1	Develop an awareness of culture-specific differences.
Stage 2	Accept these cultural differences (in the sense of cognitive tolerance).
Stage 3	Develop awareness of our own culture-boundedness.
Stage 4	Develop the ability to modify one's own way to perceive the other culture (including interpretation and evaluation).
Stage 5	Develop the ability to modify one's own behaviour with regard to the other culture (consciously and purposefully).
Stage 6	Develop the ability to interpret and produce behaviour for the (interaction) needs of others in order to establish communication between members of (at least) two different cultures.

Table 1: Developmental model of the specific ICC of translators and interpreters (Cynrim 2016: 135)

Providing such a categorization of the steps towards ICC is enormously useful for trainers when structuring their courses. If we consider these six stages in translation, our learning outcomes would expect trainees to:

1. Identify cultural problems and differences
2. Understand them in their cultural context
3. Contrast them with their own cultural frames
4. Accept and view the differences objectively
5. Adopt a less culture-bound stance
6. Resolve cultural problems in translations.

The first three stages are frequently found in early translator training courses with fairly obvious cultural references or problems (often under the umbrella of 'General Translation' courses). The final three stages, however, require a much more substantial leap, especially in more specialized translation courses. When trainees progress to scientific, technical, economic or legal texts, for example, they often become so immersed in acquiring thematic or field competence and instrumental competence (technology/terminology) that culture seems to vanish from their priorities when approaching a text. Stage six, particularly, also implies two other, often forgotten factors which Cynrim (2016: 132, 136) draws our attention to:

1. The need for translators to manage intercultural communication between members of a variety of professions (depending on the field and text type in question).
2. The fact that translators are not communicating themselves, but are communicating for the agents[2] involved in the translation process.

The first question requires translators to be aware of the differences between not only the languages and cultures involved, but also the varieties of different fields and professions, in that way complicating intercultural communication even more. The second touches upon the complex matter of how the translator can gauge the intercultural knowledge of the agents involved in order to compensate for or circumvent any discrepancies that may arise. As Cynrim (ibid.: 136) states:

> Translators and interpreters need to be knowledgeable about the perceptions of the partners involved in the process in order to adequately and professionally ensure successful communication between them.

[2] The agents involved in the translation process are the initiator/commissioner, ST author(s), TT producer(s)/translator(s), and the final users or receivers. See Holz-Mänttäri (1984: 109–111).

But how, then, exactly is intercultural competence reflected in the Competence models (TrC) models that are most widely used?

Despite many of the problems posed above, several authors have designed TrC models that include cultural and/or ICC.[3] Although Cynrim (2016) deplores the limited scope of the definitions of ICC in TrC models, for the sake of brevity I will use the model proposed by Kelly (2002; 2005; 2007: 248–249) where *cultural and/or intercultural competence* (CIC) is more widely described than in other TrC models as: including awareness of the main institutions of the trainees' A, B and C languages; awareness of the shared values, myths, perceptions and beliefs which condition the behaviours of the A, B and C language cultures; understanding the relations which exist between cultures and their texts and the development of intercultural communicative competence that can identify and deal with the differences found. Again, much more attention is paid to the first part of this description in training, with less emphasis on the relations existing between cultures and their texts, identifying and dealing with how culture has shaped these differences, and the effects that not detecting or resolving them successfully may have on a translation.

Research by the Avances en Traducción e Interpretación (AVANTI) Research Group (2009)[4] and, more recently, by Cano (2012a; 2012b), has observed the acquisition of CIC and the trainees' perception of how this is achieved. It shows that a wide variety of external factors beyond training (student mobility, cultural baggage) are involved. Nonetheless, from a flexible threshold, given the diversity of trainees that we find in the classroom, we can use all of the elements above to create a framework for training in CIC that may be adapted to embrace, particularly, the last three stages described above, and to accommodate the heterogeneous translator training classroom. Before I describe the framework for training in CIC, however, there is one more vital element necessary for successful training in CIC: empathy.

---

[3] For an overview see Gregorio Cano (2012a).

[4] The Acquisition of Cultural and Intercultural Competence in Translator Training ACCI/HUM 2006-04454/FILO, R&D Project funded by the Spanish Ministry of Education, Culture and Sport.

2. The importance of empathy

One final ingredient for our recipe to achieve CIC successfully is *empathy*. Zhu (2011: 116) considers intercultural awareness to be the foundation of communication. Its importance in the later stages of translator training is, however, often overlooked. Zhu proposes intercultural empathy to be the situation in which a person is capable of putting him- or herself in the cultural situation of the TL or target culture and of achieving effective communication from the SL. For Zhu (ibid.: 117), intercultural empathy is "the prerequisite and assurance for effective cultural communication". This implies the first four stages proposed by Cynrim where, translated into learning outcomes, trainees would learn to (1) identify cultural differences, (2) understand them in their cultural context, (3) contrast them with their own cultural frames, and (4) understand and accept the differences objectively in order to produce effective cultural communication. Empathy should never be confused with sympathy, however: "Being culturally empathic means being non-judgmental and recognizing that although differences may exist based on culture, communication can still continue" (Cynrim 2016: 119). Eliminating the barriers of culture-boundedness is the first major step towards objectivity, since this allows trainees to accept cultural differences and to be more effective intercultural communicators. Vreeke and Van der Mark (2003: 177) consider that "empathy is aided by a twofold control system, comprised of judgements and forms of self-control", both of which may be overcome through achieving stages 1–4 of Cynrim's model. The authors consider that situating empathy "in a communicative context also allows one to relate empathy and its development to interpersonal relationships and subsequently to socio-cultural processes" (ibid.: 180).

There is often a moment in translator training when trainees become obsessed with the Skopos, suddenly swinging from focusing completely on the SL and the source text (ST) to shifting their perspectives completely to accommodating the TL and target text (TT) or the target culture. This will generate TTs that sacrifice content and meaning from the STs in order to 'please' the TT reader by adapting completely to target culture expectations. One such example would be when trainees omit information from a Spanish birth certificate in their translations as it does not appear in a British birth certificate. Enticing trainees back to the middle ground of objectivity is one of the most complicated tasks in training CIC. Vreeke and Van der Mark (2003: 188) also consider "the judgemental system and the ability to control or regulate feelings" to be the control systems which are involved in empathy and which we need to nurture. A further factor mentioned by the authors (ibid.: 199–200) is compliance, or the ability to regulate our behaviour according to external standards. In translation, these external standards or forces, with all the expectations, norms and constraints that the three may entail, are threefold:

1. the ST (language, culture and social process);
2. the translation brief (requirements of the Skopos and of the agents involved);
3. the TT (language, culture and social process).

Complying with, or at least taking into account, all three forces, plus other external forces such as "accepted translation behaviour", is akin to juggling three balls at the same time and a source of a great deal of trainees' indecision when choosing translation solutions.

With regard to translator training, Hague (2015: 20) has recently discussed empathy and, more specifically, "empathic accuracy", which he describes as "the ability to imagine others' perspectives". Hague proposes different activities to include training in empathic accuracy in the translation classroom, two proposals of which are of interest for our approach:

1. the studies the author cites by Kiraly (2000), Austermühl (2008) and Stewart et al. (2008), which all indicate that collaborative translation in teams can help trainees to imagine the minds of others, and
2. the work by Jones (2011: 194), who reminds us that translators "write within and for a certain culture" or subgroup of a culture which he calls 'imagined communities'.

Both of these elements are integrated into our threefold approach (see section 4), which supports Hague's statement that "translation instructors have the responsibility to help students develop this empathic capacity" (2015: 9).

3. Threefold approach

It never ceases to amaze me that, despite the enormous facilities available nowadays to read and hear about, and see, other cultures thanks to the internet, cable and satellite television and increased mobility, trainees are often very anchored, not only in their own cultures, but also in their own personal experience, often believing it to be 'just how things are' rather than only one possible version of cultural reality. In an attempt to palliate this, I adopted a threefold approach that combines a Critical Discourse Analysis (CDA) approach (Way 2003; 2005a; 2005b; 2012); a decision-making course structure approach (Way 2014); and a student-centred (Kiraly 1995; 2000) project management-based approach which monitors the trainees' individual TrC development (Way 2008; 2009). This approach has been successfully used in specialized translation courses, particularly for Law and Economics translations.

To describe this threefold approach I will use the translation of law texts as an example of how it can be successfully integrated into courses. As legal translation trainees often have little or no grounding whatsoever in the field of Law, trainers of legal translators face enormous problems in their efforts to introduce their trainees into the legal discourse community, requiring them to translate texts that are completely unfamiliar, given their limited prior experience and social practices (Prieto Ramos 2014). It is often said that legal translation requires the 'bridging of cultures' skills of the translator more than other fields of specialized translation, particularly given that legal terms may have surface similarities (e.g. marriage and *matrimonio*), but considerable conceptual differences (legal age for marriage/same sex or not). After more than 25 years of training legal translators, I have identified three major causes of the difficulties that trainees encounter:

1. prior pedagogical translation experience in language learning leads to an obsession with words;
2. in the later stages of their training this becomes an obsession with terminology, and
3. their lack of vital experience, given their youth (Way 2003; 2005b; 2012; 2016).

Our trainees are generally in their early 20s and, as a result, unlikely to have participated in everyday legal or administrative social activities such as court cases, buying a house or signing a contract. As a result, trainees tend to rely excessively on external resources, such as terminology databases, as their first option in an effort to understand their STs. Familiar resources tend to boost their confidence when they make decisions in unfamiliar terrain. Legal, and particularly administrative, texts are replete with suppositions and references to social practices that the students have never experienced. Therefore, their searches are rarely successful as they find it tremendously difficult to judge and choose between the possible solutions they encounter.

Dam-Jensen's (2012) recent process research discussing decision-making and dictionary use by MA students in Denmark highlights the fact that students often make unjustified decisions of which they are not particularly convinced. Our threefold approach is designed to mitigate these difficulties during training and to equip the students with a methodology they can use and adapt when faced with new fields and texts in their professional practice.

3.1 The CDA approach

Different fields of translation have applied discourse analysis in the past, analysing texts through their discourse, understood as a means of structuring social practices or fields of knowledge. CDA, on the other hand, occurs much less frequently in TS research. During my PhD research I used the perspective of CDA (Way 2003; 2005a; 2005b) to study the problems posed in a social practice that requires the intervention of a certified/sworn translator. For the methodological basis I adopted the three-dimensional model proposed by Fairclough (1992; 1995), which suggests a model of analysis that includes the description of a text, the interpretation of the discursive practice (production, distribution and consumption of the text), and the explanation of how the discursive practice is related to the social process, besides how the three elements relate to one another. This is particularly useful for translators who need to go beyond a simple internal analysis of a text to take into account all the agents involved in the communicative process. The model was adapted by introducing translation as a further complicating element in the process and is represented as follows:

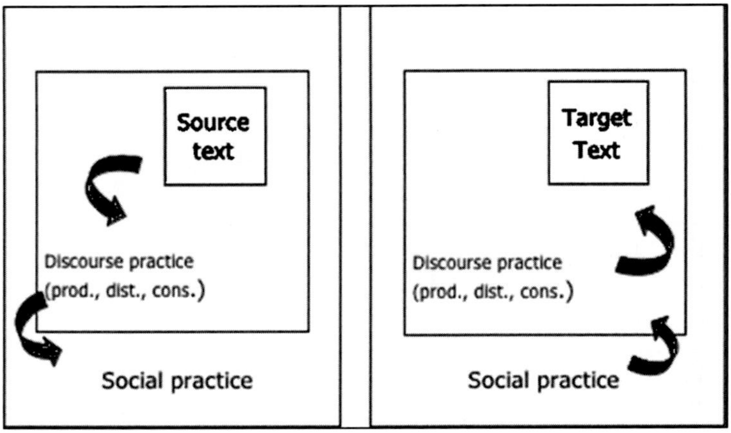

Figure 1: A discourse-analysis approach to translation (Way 2012)

The model guides trainees through a step-by-step procedure which first situates the text within the social process and the social events that surround it.

An example:

Translation of a Spanish birth certificate for the United Kingdom

The ST in Spain

1. Production: Students research who produces this document in Spain and any rules or regulations governing its production. This clarifies the content included in the document, the format and how concepts are represented. They also research the workings, in this case, of the Spanish Civil Registries.
2. Distribution: How is the document distributed? How is it issued? To whom?
3. Consumption: When and for what purposes is it required? Who are the (multiple) possible receivers of the text in Spain?
4. In which social practices (with special emphasis on the social process included in the translation brief: adoption/marriage/filiation/etc)? How does the social practice involving the text to be translated work?

The TT in the United Kingdom

5. How does the social practice involving the translated text work?
6. Consumption: When and for what purposes is it required? Who are the (multiple) possible receivers of the text in the United Kingdom?

7. Distribution: How is the document distributed? How is it issued? To whom?
8. Production: Students research who produces this document in the United Kingdom and any rules or regulations governing its production. This clarifies the content to be included in the document, the format and how concepts are represented. They also research the workings, in this case, of the British Civil Registries.

By situating the text within the discursive practice (production, distribution, consumption) and the social practice, the trainees become acquainted with the internalized discourse and social structures and conventions governing the text, allowing them to gain access to what Fairclough (1995) calls 'members' resources'. When this information is combined with the social practice in which the text participates, seemingly obscure elements in the original text become immediately clearer as the trainees acquire the knowledge, terminology and discourse necessary for their task. The process is then also applied in the TL and the target culture to discover whether parallel discursive and social practices exist. This leads to parallel or similar texts. It is only at this point that the translation process proper may begin.

This approach provides a tool to help trainees develop a structured analytical process when translating legal texts. Many translation classes hinge upon the text to be translated and, more specifically, the terminology that is problematic for or unfamiliar to trainees. This three-stage discourse analysis approach delicately disengages trainees from the three main reasons for their difficulties mentioned above. As the trainees become versed in the discursive and social practices surrounding the ST and the parallel process in the target culture, many of the potential problems they first detect in the ST vanish. Consequently, the stumbling block posed by their lack of vital experience is overcome. What's more, as the approach attenuates trainees' weak grasp of the terminology and the discourse required, applying it largely eradicates the need they may feel to search for unfamiliar terms. As a result, the ingrained habit of immediately resorting to a dictionary disappears too.

3.2 Decision-making approach

The second approach involves the complex question of decision-making as a cornerstone of the translation process. Several scholars of TS (e.g. Jumpelt 1961: 169, 186; Levý 1967: 1171–1172; Toury 1980; 1995: 55–56; Séguinot 1991: 79–88; Wilss 1994; 1998: 57; Darwish 1995; 1999: 19) have discussed this delicate matter from diverse perspectives. Recently, I have focused on creating a framework for decision-making in the translation classroom, based upon TrC, that trainee translators may then use to assess and improve their own competences in their translation courses and, ultimately, throughout their professional practice.

Translator trainers often find it difficult to help trainees to establish an overarching framework for decision-making, rather than concentrating on specific decision-making processes for individual translation problems. An overarching framework of decision-making rests upon combining different sub-competences to solve different problems, and consequently provides strategies central to the translation process. Decision-making is vital to the translator's performance (process) and to the final translation (product). Indeed, our assessment methods ultimately measure the success or failure of our trainees' decisions. The shift from a product-oriented to a process-oriented approach implies that we place more emphasis on assessing the process than the final product itself at different points in training, but both approaches still rely heavily on the trainees' decision-making. Decision-making and problem-solving are obviously intertwined (Wilss 1998), drawing upon both declarative/theoretical and operative/practical knowledge, as suggested by González Davies and Scott-Tennent (2005). If we want to solve a problem, we must inevitably make a decision at some point by choosing between possible solutions.

Research on TS has mainly concentrated on decision-making for individual translation problems (institutional names, metaphors) as opposed to establishing an overarching framework. Because decision-making is vital in many fields, such a framework had to exist elsewhere. One such field is Decision Theory, where I discovered a possible solution: organizing the presentation of translation problems to trainees by categorizing decision-making situations based, in our case, on a TrC model (Way 2012; 2014). The Cynefin framework for leaders[5] developed by Snowden and Boone (2007) has been instrumental in this organization of translation problems. This framework proposes five contexts for decision-making defined by the nature of the relationship between cause and effect: simple, complicated, complex, chaotic and disorder. According to the authors, leaders should diagnose situations and act in contextually appropriate ways in the first

[5] '*Cynefin* is a Welsh word that signifies the multiple factors in our environment and our experience that influences us in ways we can never understand' (Snowden & Boone 2007: 2).

four contexts, while in the fifth, disorder, it is difficult to decide which of the first four contexts would prevail (ibid.).

If we were to apply these categories to translation, we could consider that *simple* contexts involve stable problems where clear cause-and-effect relationships are evident. In other words, situations in which translation norms or accepted behaviour could be employed (translating an institutional name, for example). In the simple context, the decision-makers identify the problem, categorize it, and then resolve it by using established translation practices. Simple contexts, however, may sometimes be more complex than expected: if the problem is not identified correctly or if the decision-makers fall into the trap of what Snowden and Boone (2007) call 'entrained thinking'. In other words, they may use a conditioned response based on prior experience or training and success, or they may use their 'automatic pilot' when facing apparently familiar problems (see the example of an alarm system in Robinson 1997). An example of simple contexts resolved by following accepted translation norms:

It's raining cats and dogs – Il pleut des grenouilles – Está lloviendo a cántaros

In *complicated* contexts, as the name implies, multiple correct solutions may exist to the problem, requiring the decision-maker to analyse the different possible solutions before deciding on which one to implement. This is often time-consuming, as more than one correct answer may be feasible. These complicated problems should be introduced gradually in translation courses as they require more advanced diagnostic skills and expertise. An example of complicated contexts with multiple solutions:

You may vote on reaching full legal age.

Puedes votar al alcanzar la mayoría de edad.

Full legal age may vary from one country/culture to another. To deal with this, the translator could include the age in brackets, add a footnote or make the age explicit in the text, depending on the brief and the receiver.

Complex contexts include problems with a wide variety of interacting elements, which (in turn) are dynamic and nonlinear. This implies that minor changes could produce extremely serious consequences, often hampering a prediction of the possible results. They are unpredictable and often call for creativity and innovation. An example of complex contexts where at least one correct solution may be possible, but must be found. Such an example is when a client requests a translation without outlining the brief clearly. In this case, if the client is not contacted, the translator will have to make multiple decisions which may or not be appropriate. These problems, I believe, are less common in translation than in interpreting, but may be encountered occasionally.

Chaotic contexts are full of unknowns because of their constantly changing circumstances. These contexts are characterized by enormous pressure, multiple decisions and demanding time constraints, as, for example, in interpreting. An example of chaotic contexts with changing circumstances: A speaker tells a joke with references to certain nationalities which will not make sense in the TL. The interpreter is unaware of the nationalities of those attending the conference and is therefore unable to adapt the contents of the joke to the audience.

Contexts with *disorder* are extreme – likened by Snowden and Boone (2007) to the events of 9/11 – and unpredictable. These are unlikely to occur during translation or interpreting. Furthermore, once a course has been structured according to the suggested framework (Way 2014), it is still flexible and can embrace different trainee profiles by, for example, simply changing the translation brief for a text. In this way the difficulty or scope of a given decision-making context can be incremented or different sub-competence requirements can be introduced. One set of course materials may also be adapted to the requirements of different decision-making contexts for different student groups, such as Law graduates or Translation undergraduates at different stages of training, by focusing more on one sub-competence or another. Progression can also be readjusted as a course progresses by reinforcing certain decisions through repetition or by introducing added difficulty to others, depending on how a given group is coping with the problems posed. We can also introduce texts that may pose a particular problem at one sub-competence level (e.g. subject-area competence), but still be able to use the text at an early stage by providing more support materials and explanations for students to counteract this added difficulty in that one sub-competence area alone. For instance, if we want to translate a court document on marriage that includes the more complex concept of marriage settlements, we simply provide more resources (e.g. background reading, parallel texts on marriage settlements) to help them perform their task.

The use of this framework to select translation problems in a training course allows us to increase the complexity of the problems posed progressively. When carefully scaffolded, the problems can also illustrate the dangers of making decisions based only on our past patterns of success and failure instead of on a clearly defined framework of decision-making. For example, it is not uncommon for trainees on introductory legal translation courses to rely heavily on glossaries, which are often presented as lists of static equivalences without contextualisation. If the trainees do not reflect carefully upon the ST and Skopos, we will find them misusing a term which had been used successfully and appropriately in another context. Building a framework for guided decision-making, especially in the initial stages of legal translator training, must be central to our teaching. Frequently, the degree of abstraction of legal terms and concepts has been used to identify a text as being more or less specialized, and therefore as the basis for structuring legal translation courses.

The framework suggested here, alternatively, provides a sequencing pattern of increasing difficulty dependent on the activation of all the subcompetences and not just on subject area/thematic competence. This allows translator trainers, then, to help trainees create their own decision-making framework that will gradually enable them to internalize problem-solving strategies through structured decision-making and controlled training. These processes gradually become automatic to a certain degree, facilitating trainees' work as a translator, besides increasing their efficiency and confidence. Through these initially controlled processes trainees will internalize certain mechanisms to provide solutions as reflex actions or habits and reduce their decision-making load – and therefore their uncertainty when making decisions.

3.3 Project management methodology

The third approach I propose is instrumental in drawing trainees away from focusing on the product to focusing on the translation process. Rather than asking trainees to correct a translation (or more than one version) of a text as the central activity in a class, I use a system based on project management. Trainees are provided with a Project Management Sheet (see Way 2009) and in an introductory class and tutorials the different roles involved are discussed and delimited, with stress being placed on the usefulness of taking advantage of any strengths group members may have for peer learning.

Collaborative translation groups share out the roles of project manager, researcher/documentalist, terminologist, translator(s), reviser and editor; they then rotate these roles for each task with additional guidance on any overlapping and the need for coordination between the roles. A Project

Management Sheet is also distributed online and must be completed for each task, detailing the time taken and any difficulties that arose with each task. This forces the students to reflect on the different elements that can come into play during the translation process. It also enables trainees to perceive their strengths and weaknesses and see where there may be a need for improvement in their competences, particularly for embedded cultural elements, as discussed in section 5.

The Project Management Sheet is presented in class by each member, in their respective roles, before the translation and its revised version are seen. Therefore, greater attention is drawn to the process before even considering the product. The groups present their description of the translation process and the whole class discusses the difficulties encountered, suggesting solutions that may be useful for the same (or different) difficulties in the future. In this way the whole class may benefit from the experience of only one or two groups who have undertaken a particular translation project and may share their own experiences and suggestions.

As the semester progresses and each group's difficulties are discussed before assessing their translations, the students progressively reduce the time needed for each task, despite the fact that the translations become gradually longer and more complex. This approach not only allows trainees to systematize their work methods, but also, through rotating their roles, enables them to pinpoint their own strengths and weaknesses in their different areas of competence (Way 2008). The students are encouraged to review their earlier Project Management Sheets and to track their evolution, especially concerning the time taken to complete tasks and in their ability to identify and find solutions to problems. These visible results boost self-confidence (psychophysiological competence), while at the same time instrumental and interpersonal competences (see Kelly 2007: 248–249) improve and the students feel more confident about joining the professional market. Furthermore, the presentation of others' difficulties and proposed solutions leads to lively debate and also helps trainees to imagine the minds of others, in that way also improving empathy.

4. Embedded cultural elements

How does this then work in practice for the more deeply embedded and obscure culturally divergent elements present in the STs? The CDA approach obliges students to compare and contrast not only words (one of their primary obsessions) but also, as shown in section 3.1, a wider range of cultural differences that permeate the ST and their planned TT. The decision-making approach ensures that cultural problems designed to improve their CIC appear in a carefully structured course of increasing difficulty. As mentioned above, culture pervades all the competences that trainers aim to improve, far beyond the traditional notion of cultural references. Therefore, the project management approach serves to highlight differences and similarities – for example, in instrumental or strategic competence as group members learn to collaborate from their different work method backgrounds. The blend of all three approaches means that trainees become much more aware of how important culture is, even in highly specialized texts.

To achieve the first four stages suggested by Cynrim (2016) training courses will start with relatively familiar fields, such as Family Law. As trainees follow the CDA approach, they discover that marriage, for example, which they may not have identified initially as a problem, is in fact not as simple as they thought. Historical and cultural influence will determine the conceptual content and therefore call for translation strategies (such as explicitation – different age requirements/same or different sex) that enable the target reader to fully understand the ST's meaning. Other embedded elements that are introduced gradually may include: measuring time; space/deixis; perceptions hidden in adjectives, or intensity.

As far as time is concerned, the trainees are usually aware of the different uses of am or pm, for example, but they may not be as aware of different perceptions of punctuality. 'Please arrive on time' may be understood as arriving ten, 15 or 30 minutes after an appointed time or precisely at the given time. Likewise, space or deixis is frequently overlooked so that 'it's near' or 'it's not far' may have vastly different meanings in different cultures and may need to be modified accordingly. Perceptions underlying adjectives – for example, in a witness report – again, may vary considerably: Was the thief tall or short? Did he or she have blonde or brown hair? The term *rubio* (blonde) is used in Spanish to refer to many shades of even light brown hair and would certainly not match the northern European concept of blonde.

In communicative and textual competence, the CDA approach again allows students to see that whereas future adoptive parents may use three or more adjectives or adverbs to describe why they wish to adopt in Spanish (*un niño alegre, risueño y contento*), this would simply be considered overkill in a similar text in English, where one or two adjectives or adverbs would suffice. Texts also vary in their organization depending on the culture in which they are used: attention lines, for example, are often placed at the bottom of formal Spanish documents but at the top of similar English documents, requiring textual re-organization.

There are many more examples of culturally embedded problems which require CIC than we, or trainees, may initially think, yet the threefold approach has nevertheless proved enormously successful in not only achieving Cynrim's first four stages, but in progressing to success in stages five and six.

5. Assessment/rubrics

Many translator trainers assess CIC by verifying whether trainees have identified a cultural problem, correctly understood the problem in its cultural context, and provided a successful solution in the TT. This does not allow us to gauge, however, whether trainees have contrasted this problem with their own cultural frames; accepted and now view the differences objectively; adopted a less culture-bound stance, and resolved the cultural problem successfully in the TT. The project management approach requires students to describe their difficulties and justify their solutions. Furthermore, the rubrics assess the students' progress in each project management role. The oral defence of their decision-making allows the trainer to see clearly which part of the process requires more attention rather than simply assessing the final outcome of their choices in the translation. This allows trainers to see how far trainees have progressed in Cynrim's six stages and to respond accordingly to trainees' needs.

Recently I have designed rubrics for assessing trainees' class work, again divided into the roles used in project management, with an additional rubric for the TT product. As CIC pervades all competences, it is also present in all the rubrics. One extract from the project manager's rubric includes:

Collaborative work	Almost always listens to, shares with, and supports the efforts of others. Tries to keep people working well together.	Usually listens to, shares with and supports the efforts of others. Does not cause 'waves' in the group.	Often listens to, shares with and supports the efforts of others, but sometimes is not a good team leader.	Rarely listens to, shares with and supports the efforts of others. Often is not a good team leader.

This collaborative learning component of the rubric would draw attention to resolving differences among the group members owing to the diverse cultural baggage and work methods of the members. Or in the case of the attitude component of the rubric trainers and trainees can address the enormous cultural differences when it comes to criticism or constructive criticism or losing face:

Attitude	Never is publicly critical of the project or the work of others. Always has a positive attitude about the task(s).	Never is publicly critical of the project or the work of others. Always has a positive attitude about the task(s).	Occasionally is publicly critical of the project or the work of other members of the group. Usually has a positive attitude about the task(s).	Often is publicly critical of the project or the work of other members of the group. Often has a negative attitude about the task(s).

All of these are highlighted and discussed in the team presentations, raising awareness and modifying trainees' behaviour. Similarly, in the researcher's rubric, we find the following component:

Presentation of information for translator	All sources are accurately documented in the required format. Information is recorded and organized well.	Most sources are accurately documented, but a few are not in the required format. Information is recorded and is reasonably organized.	Some sources are accurately documented, but many are not in the required format. Information is recorded, but is fairly disorganized.	Few sources are accurately documented, but many/none are not in the required format. Information is not recorded and/or is disorganized.

Asking the researcher to imagine what information the translator needs increases empathic accuracy by forcing the researcher to reflect on their own needs and the different needs other team members (often from different cultures) may have.

In the TT rubric the category 'Writing – mechanics' is included:

Writing – mechanics	Capitalization and punctuation are correct throughout the translation.	Capitalization and punctuation are mostly correct throughout the translation even after the reviser/editor has read and corrected the translation.	There are some capitalization and/or punctuation errors in the translation even after the reviser/editor has read and corrected the translation.	There are several capitalization or punctuation errors in the translation even after the reviser/editor has read and corrected the translation.

This is not merely a question of using punctuation or capitals correctly. Legal texts in Spanish and English often overuse capitalization, but in different ways. The visual cultural differences in the texts are often there for historical reasons. Understanding this and contrasting it leads to achieving the final stages of Cynrim's proposal for developing CIC. Therefore, errors often attributed to language misuse are identified as emanating from a lack of CIC, which causes hiccups in the intended successful communication of the ST to the target culture.

6. Conclusion

Moving from the safe common ground of easily identifiable cultural references to the much more treacherous ground of embedded cultural elements leads us to diverge from more common practices in training and assessment. The proposed threefold approach combining CDA, decision-making and project management is actually extremely straightforward to use, despite its apparent complexity. Trainees quickly adapt to the methodology, with excellent results (as proven by the remarkable drop in examination failures from approximately 30% to 2% since its introduction). Once an initial investment is made in careful text selection and scaffolding of the multi-competence decision-making framework, it is remarkably flexible and, more importantly for trainees, effective.

References

Austermühl, Frank. 2008. A collaborative approach to the teaching of terminology management. In Frank Austermühl & Joachim Kornelius (eds) *Learning theories and practice in Translation Studies.* Trier: Wissenschaftlicher Verlag Trier, 261–280.

Avanti. 2009. The acquisition of cultural and intercultural competence in translator training ACCI/HUM 2006-04454/FILO, R&D Project funded by the Spanish Ministry of Education, Culture and Sport. <http://www.ugr.es/~avanti/produccion_proyectos.html> (accessed 18 September 2017).

Bassnett, Susan & Lefevere, André (eds). 1990. *Translation, history and culture.* London/New York: Pinter.

Bennett, Milton J. 1998. Intercultural communication: A current perspective. In Milton J Bennett (ed) *Basic concepts of intercultural communication. Selected readings.* Yarmouth: Intercultural Press, 1–34.

Bennett, Milton J. 2001. Developing intercultural communication for global leadership. In Rolf-Dieter Reineke & Christine Fussinger (eds) *Interkulturelles Management. Konzeption-Beratung-Training.* Wiesbaden: Gabler, 205–226.

Byram, Michael. 1997. *Teaching and assessing intercultural communicative competence.* Clevedon: Multilingual Matters.

Byram, Michael. 2003. On being 'bicultural' and 'intercultural'. In Michael Byram, Geof Alred & Mike Fleming (eds) *Intercultural experience and education.* Clevedon: Multilingual Matters, 225–239.

Byram, Michael, Nichols, Adam & Stevens, David (eds). 2001. *Developing intercultural competence in practice.* Clevedon: Multilingual Matters.

Cano, Ana Gregorio. 2012a. La competencia cultural e intercultural en traducción: estado de la cuestión. *Íkala, revista de lenguaje y cultura* 17(2): 129–144.

Cano, Ana Gregorio. 2012b. Becoming a translator: The development of intercultural competence in Spain. *Cultus* 5: 154–170.

Cynrim, Andrea. 2016. Developing intercultural competence through authentic projects in the classroom. In Don Kiraly & Silvia Hansen-Schirra (eds) *Towards authentic experiential learning in translator education*. Germesheim: V&R Mainz University Press, 129–145.

Dam-Jensen, Helle. 2012. Decision-making in translation. A pilot study of students' translation processes. *Fachsprache* 3–4: 146–164.

Darwish, Ali. 1995. A model for designing decision-based translation tests. <http://www.translocutions.com/translation/constraints_0.1.pdf> (accessed 18 September 2017).

Darwish, Ali. 1999. Towards a theory of constraints in translation. Available at <http://www.translocutions.com/translation/constraints_0.1.pdf> (accessed 18 September 2017).

Fairclough, Norman. 1992. *Discourse and social change*. Cambridge: Polity Press.

Fairclough, Norman. 1995. *Critical Discourse Analysis: The critical study of language*. London: Longman.

González Davies, Maria & Scott-Tennent, Christopher. 2005. A problem-solving and student-centred approach to the translation of cultural references. *Meta* 50(1): 160–179.

Grosch, Harald & Leenen, Wolf Rainer. 2000. Bausteine zur Grundlegung interkulturellen Lernens. In Bundeszentrale für politische Bildung (ed) *Interkulturelles Lernen. Arbeitshilfen für die politische Bildung*. Bonn: Bundeszentrale für politische Bildung, 29–46.

Hague, Daryl R. 2015. Empathic accuracy and translator training: Helping students imagine other minds. *ITT* 9(1): 20–29.

Holmes, James S. 1988 [1972]. The name and nature of Translation Studies. In *Translated! Papers on literary translation and Translation Studies*. Amsterdam/Atlanta: Rodopi, 67–80.

Holz-Mänttäri, Justa. 1984. *Translatorisches Handeln. Theorie und Methode*. Helsinki: Suomalainen Tiedeakatemia.

House, Juliane. 2006. Text and context in translation. *Journal of Pragmatics* 38: 338–358.

Jones, Francis R. 2011. *Poetry translation as expert action: Processes, priorities and network*. Amsterdam/Philadelphia: John Benjamins.

Jumpelt, R Walter. 1961. On the objectivization of translation. In Andrew Chesterman (ed) *Readings in translation*. Helsinki: Oy Finn Lectura Ab, 33–36.

Katan, David. 2009. Translation as intercultural communication. In Jeremy Munday (ed) *The Routledge companion to Translation Studies*. London/New York: Routledge, 74–92.

Kelly, Dorothy. 2002. Un modelo de competencia traductora: bases para el diseño curricular. *Puentes* 1: 9–20.

Kelly, Dorothy. 2005. *A handbook for translator trainers: A guide to reflective practice.* Manchester: St Jerome.

Kelly, Dorothy. 2007. Translator competence contextualized. Translator training in the framework of higher education reform: In search of alignment in curricular design. In Dorothy Kelly & Kyongjoo Ryou (eds) *Across boundaries: International perspectives on Translation Studies.* Newcastle upon Tyne: Cambridge Scholars Publishing, 128–142.

Kiraly, Don. 1995. *Pathways to translation. Pedagogy and process.* Kent: Kent State University Press.

Kiraly, Don. 2000. *A social constructivist approach to translator education. Empowerment from theory to practice.* Manchester: St Jerome.

Levý, Jiřý. 1967. Translation as a decision process. In *To honor Roman Jakobson: Essays on the occasion of his seventieth birthday* (Vol II). The Hague: Mouton, 1171–1182.

Levý, Jiřý. 1988. Translation as a decision process. In Andrew Chesterman (ed) *Readings in translation theory.* Helsinki: Oy Finn Lectura Ab, 37–52.

Nida, Eugene A. 1964. *Toward a science of translating with special reference to principles and procedures involved in Bible translating.* Leiden: Brill.

Prieto Ramos, Fernando. 2014. Parameters for problem-solving in legal translation: Implications for legal lexicography and institutional terminology management. In Le Cheng, King Kui Sin & Anne Wagner (eds) *The Ashgate handbook of legal translation.* Farnham: Ashgate, 121–134.

Robinson, Douglas. 1997. *Becoming a translator. An accelerated course.* London/New York: Routledge.

Séguinot, Candace. 1991. A study of student translation strategies. In Sonja Tirkkonen-Condit (ed) *Empirical research in translation and intercultural studies.* Tübingen: Narr, 79–88.

Snowden, David J & Boone, Mary E. 2007. A leader's framework for decision making. *Harvard Business Review.* <https://hbr.org/2007/11/a-leaders-framework-for-decision-making> (accessed 18 September 2017).

Stewart, John, Orbán, Wencke & Kornelius, Joachim. 2008. Cooperative translation in the paradigm of problem-based learning. In Frank Austermühl & Joachim Kornelius (eds) *Learning theories and practice in Translation Studies.* Trier: Wissenschaftlicher Verlag Trier, 9–32.

Thomas, Alexander. 2003. Interkulturelle Kompetenz – Grundlagen, Probleme und Konzepte. *Erwägen Wissen Ethik – Streitforum für Erwägungskultur* 14(1): 137–228.

Toury, Gideon. 1980. *In search of a theory of literary translation.* Tel Aviv: Porter Institute.

Toury, Gideon. 1995. *Descriptive translation studies and beyond.* Amsterdam/Philadelphia: John Benjamins.

Vreeke, Gert J, Van der Mark, Ingrid L. 2003. Empathy, an integrative model. *New Ideas in Psychology* 21: 177–207.

Way, Catherine. 2003. *La traducción como acción social: el caso de los documentos académicos (español–inglés)*. Granada: Universidad de Granada [Doctoral dissertation]. <http://digibug.ugr.es/bitstream/10481/4591/1/Tesis.pdf> (acces-sed 18 September 2017).

Way, Catherine. 2005a. Researching professional practice: An insight into translation norms in Spain. In Ian Kemble (ed) *Proceedings of the fourth conference 'Translation norms in translation. What is normal in the translation profession?'*. Portsmouth: University of Portsmouth, 146–158.

Way, Catherine. 2005b. *La traducción como acción social: el caso de los documentos académicos (español–inglés)*. Granada: Editorial Universidad de Granada.

Way, Catherine. 2008. Systematic assessment of translator competence: In search of Achilles' heel. In John Kearns (ed) *Translator and interpreter training: Issues, methods and debates*. London: Continuum, 88–103.

Way, Catherine. 2009. Bringing professional practices into translation classrooms. In Ian Kemble (ed) *The changing face of translation*. Portsmouth: University of Portsmouth, 131–142.

Way, Catherine. 2012. A discourse analysis approach to legal translator training: More than words. *International Journal of Law, Language & Discourse* 2(4): 39–61.

Way, Catherine. 2014. Structuring a legal translation course: A framework for decision-making in legal translator training. In Le Cheng, King Kui Sin & Anne Wagner (eds) *The Ashgate handbook of legal translation*. Farnham: Ashgate, 135–152.

Way, Catherine. 2016. The challenges and opportunities of legal translation and translator training in the 21st century. *International Journal of Communication* 10: 1009–1029.

Wilss, Wolfram. 1994. A framework for decision-making in translation. *Target* 6(2): 131–150.

Wilss, Wolfram. 1998. Decision making in translation. In Mona Baker (ed) *Routledge encyclopaedia of Translation Studies*. London/New York: Routledge, 57–60.

Witte, Heidrun. 1995. Contrastive culture learning in translator training. In Cay Dollerup & Vibkee Appel (eds) *Teaching translation and interpreting 3: New horizons papers from the third language international conference, Elsinore*. Amsterdam/Philadelphia: John Benjamins, 73–79.

Witte, Heidrun. 2000. *Die Kulturkompetenz des Translators. Begriffliche Grundlegung und Didaktisierung*. Tübingen: Stauffenburg.

Zhu, Honglin. 2011. From intercultural awareness to intercultural empathy. *English Language Teaching* 4(1): 116–119.

Geoffrey S Koby

Kent State University

Intercultural Errors and Translation Assessment: Two Small German–English Case Studies

Abstract

Errors in two sets of German to English translations with source texts (STs) at similar reading levels were examined to discover the types and frequencies of error due to culture-specific items: 27 translations from examinations by undergraduate translation students (translation novices) and 28 translations by candidates for the 2006 American Translators Association (ATA) certification examination who have experience in professional translation. Student translations marked by the author (an ATA grader) and ATA texts marked by ATA graders were scored on the basis of the ATA error categories and marking scale. Each set was examined for errors with a cultural component, defined as factual errors requiring knowledge of the source and target cultures in order to arrive at an accurate translation. Student texts showed errors of over-specification, failure to recognize cultural differences or a lack of cultural experience, whereas the ATA examination texts contained errors of over-specification, shifts in cultural register, non-lexicalization of cultural terms and a lack of historical knowledge. Both sets of translations showed relatively few errors relating to culture-specific items, almost all of which involved the 'terminology' or 'misunderstanding' categories, whereas a majority of the translations showed correct translations of cultural items. The two groups are compared and contrasted, resulting in suggestions for more detailed ATA cultural-error categories.

Keywords: translation assessment, intercultural awareness, error analysis, culture-specific errors

1. Introduction

The categories used today in professional translation assessment – such as those found in the ATA *Framework for standardized error marking* (see Appendix I), the Canadian Translators, Terminologists and Interpreters Council

(CTTIC) *Standard certification translation examination marker's guide,* the Chartered Institute of Linguists (CIOL) *Handbook for candidates* or the South African Translators' Institute (SATI) *Framework for marking of translation accreditation examinations* – do not specifically classify translation errors resulting from deficiencies in intercultural awareness or a lack of knowledge of specific cultural items in the source or target culture. Depending on their level of linguistic or cultural knowledge, however, translation students or examination candidates may commit errors in single words, phrases, idioms or sentences owing to a lack of knowledge of specific cultural items. These translators may also, more seriously, translate entire passages with serious disruptions because of fundamental cultural misunderstandings. Indeed, inexperienced or student translators may not know the terminology of a particular domain in a particular country, including shared technologies that are culturally different or similar, such as the cultural usages related to the concept *Straßenbahn* ('streetcar, tram' – a relatively rare means of transportation in the United States). They may therefore be unable to select appropriate terminology even when it is available in a resource such as a dictionary, termbase, or an online or a printed reference work.

This chapter reports on translation errors with an intercultural component that were produced in actual examination situations by two different sets of translators using different source texts (ST). The data were obtained naturalistically, that is, from already existing records made in natural classroom or examination settings. The readability of the two texts was measured using the Björnsson readability index for German, which resulted in scores of 50.25 and 51.42, respectively, both of them in the 'medium' range of readability (on a scale of 0 to 100). They are therefore largely equivalent in difficulty (Psychometria n.d.). Translations from German into English were produced (1) by undergraduate students of translation in final take-home examinations and (2) by candidates for the ATA certification examination. Although the examination situation and the presumed skill level of the groups differ, the similarities in reading level and the frequency of errors make it possible to draw some comparisons between the two different groups. Both sets of translators produced relatively few errors caused by cultural differences or a lack of cultural knowledge.

The author, an ATA grader, marked the student papers using standard ATA criteria and methodology, while regular ATA graders marked the ATA examinations. The papers were marked using the ATA Certification Program error categories (ATA 2015), assessed for severity using the ATA

Flowchart for error point decisions (Appendix II), and a score was calculated using the ATA *Framework* (Appendix I). The ATA tools use a variety of error categories (such as mistranslation, addition, omission or misunderstanding), but lack a specific category for cultural error.

Two limited case studies were produced based on the two groups of translators. Each case study examines one set of German–English translations for errors caused by cultural misunderstandings. The first group comprised 27 third-year undergraduate translation majors, students from my classes, who translated an advertising text I had selected. The second group comprised 28 candidates who took the ATA certification examination in 2006 and who translated three texts.[1] The errors caused by culture-specific items[2] were discovered in only one of the ATA texts, which is the object of study here.

The two sets of translated texts were reviewed to discover errors that may have been caused specifically by a misunderstanding or a lack of knowledge of culture-specific items in the ST. 'Culture-specific item' was defined as any object, idea or action that exists in the source culture but not in the target culture, or any such object, idea or action that exists differently in the target culture in usage, frequency or characteristics. The two texts are of different lengths (156 ST words vs 219 ST words), the student text being roughly 30% shorter than the ATA text; but both texts are so short that it was considered unlikely for more than one or two additional cultural items to have occurred in the student text had it been longer. Our hypothesis was that because undergraduate students normally have less experience in the culture of the ST than candidates taking a professional examination such as the ATA certification examination, the errors caused by culture-specific items could be expected to occur more frequently in the student translations. To my knowledge, no study has as yet examined the differences in errors caused by culture-specific items between student translations and certification examination candidates.

Since students will ultimately become professionals, this study describes the variation in the production of errors caused by culture-specific items between a small sample of students majoring in translation and a small sample of examination candidates. It will, in addition, show if there

---

[1] The STs used by the students and examination candidates are reproduced in Appendices III and IV.

[2] Katan (2009: n1) indicates that the literature often classifies errors relating to a particular country or culture as 'culture-specific'.

are any patterns in the production of such errors and examine whether current error-description categories are sufficient for translation pedagogy. Because of the small sample, this can be considered only a pilot study indicating general trends.

Although there is a great deal of literature on culture in translation, relatively little work has been done on analysing individual errors caused by culture-specific items and how they affect either the micro- or the macro-context of a given translated text. Katan (2009: 1) suggests differentiating between generic intercultural competence (ICC) regardless of country and specific cross-cultural competence (CCC) relating to a particular country or culture. Ochs argues that any error in translation (either of meaning or of language) is a cultural error, since "using language is integral to social life and participating in society is integral to the process of making sense of linguistic constructions" (1996: 407). Although Ochs is not incorrect in a larger abstract sense, errors caused by culture-specific items as defined here are more likely to produce insights that would enable teachers of translation to develop effective strategies for teaching students to identify cultural disparities and handle them correctly while translating. Therefore, this study will not use the notion that any error in a translation is fundamentally a cultural error.

Investigations of cultural errors in translation have dealt with a variety of aspects. Séguinot (1989: 79) reports that

> [s]econd language students seem to make errors that can only be explained in terms of a recognition block. They seem to let individual words and phrases take prominence, so that they are unable to see the larger conceptual meaning on re-reading.

Hietaranta (2000), however, argues that experienced translators are less likely to violate cultural maxims in their work than novice translators who do not see where cultural adaptation is necessary. His study showed that cultural errors are particularly likely to occur in translations that are *not* into the translator's native language, a fact which he used as an argument to justify the central role of teaching culture in translator training. This call for more cultural training is also echoed by Bahumaid, who advocates that "specific objectives and outcomes of postgraduate English–Arabic translation programmes should be set in such a manner that reflects the relative importance of cultural issues in the training of would-be translators" and calls for a "compulsory course on culture in translation". (2010: 583)

Hietaranta notes that "cultural problems are not signalled to the translator by any overt cues, the way language-specific syntactic structures are" (ibid.: 100). This leads him to conclude that the prevalence of cultural errors may be caused, at least in part, by the fact that, for translation students, simply listing error types is not explanatory; so much so that, as he argues, "there is no possibility … to try to provide students of translation with algorithms that would automatically enable them to detect the presence of culturally sensitive material in texts" (ibid.: 101).

At the same time, while in this chapter the idea of 'cultural' errors does not extend as far as Ochs's, it must include at least potentially any product by any culture. For instance, Altay notes that "the most daunting aspect of legal translation common to almost every language is the culture-specific quality of the texts" (2002); Schmitt (1999) dedicates 50 pages to discussing various culture-specific aspects of automotive technology as an example of technical translation requiring cultural knowledge, and Al-Kharabsheh et al. (2008) cite many examples of error-ridden shop signs translated from Jordanian Arabic into English that were translated with little knowledge of English and a lack of cultural information about the English-speaking world. Aside from spelling errors changing or completely obscuring the intended meaning, they identified three types of translation error: word order, terminology and informativity errors. Also in the Arabic context, Bahumaid (2010: 570) defines culture

> merely as one of several sources of the problems faced by translators in their arduous task of tackling morphological, syntactic, lexical, textual and discoursal features of different source-language texts.

Bahumaid describes an experiment in English–Arabic translation of 15 culturally bound items by 10 students in MA programmes at two universities in Sharjah, United Arab Emirates (UAE). He reported "rather low performance in their Arabic renditions" (2010: 574). The ability of the ten students in the study to render the 15 cultural items correctly ranged from one item to a maximum of five items, with the average being a low 2.6 items (17%) (ibid.: 575). Bahumaid found that the most common type of error was 'incorrect meaning', renditions in which "informants failed to provide the correct meanings of their Arabic counterparts" (ibid.: 576), which he found to be caused by five factors:

1. Lack of knowledge of SL culture-specific terms.
2. Lack of awareness of differences between SL and target language (TL) cultures.
3. Copying from a dictionary.

4. Inadequate proficiency in English.
5. Lack of awareness of the brief (ibid.: 577–579).

Other types of error were under-translation – the omission of required compensation, amplification, explicitation – which Bahumaid also saw as failure to recognize the importance of the translation brief (ibid.: 579–580); the omission of a necessary element (although Bahumaid points out that several commonly used English–Arabic dictionaries lacked the cultural terms in question) (ibid. 580), and illogical formulations in the target text (TT). This detailed examination led Bahumaid to conclude that there were six fundamental areas of error, three of which are inadequate knowledge (of aspects of SL and TL culture, of differences between SL and TL, and of translation procedures), two are a lack of awareness (of the importance of the brief and of lexical gaps), and one is incorrect dictionary use (ibid.: 583).

In the following case studies, we will consider whether and how these areas of error, as revealed by Bahumaid's results, apply to students and ATA examination candidates. The unit of analysis in this study is *coupled pairs of replacing + replaced segments* in the sense of Toury, who refers repeatedly to this concept in his book (1995: 103 and passim). He states:

> Mapping each assumed translation onto its assumed source (in this order!) would thus result in assigning the status of translation solutions to various constituents of the target text, which would so far have been considered, rather vaguely, as 'translational phenomena'. Owing to this procedure, which yields a series of (ad hoc) coupled pairs of replacing + replaced segments, a target-text solution would not merely *imply* the existence of a corresponding problem in the source text. Rather, for the purposes of the study, *the two should be conceived of as determining each other* in a mutual way. (1995: 102–103; emphasis in original)

Following Toury, each translation was compared with the ST, and coupled pairs were discovered in each translation using the definition of 'culture-specific item' above (any object, idea or action that exists in the source culture but not in the target culture, or any such object, idea or action that exists differently in the target culture either in usage, frequency or characteristics). They were then extracted on an ad hoc basis and analysed with respect to the corresponding problems in the ST.

2. Case study 1: Student data

The first set of data comes from 27 third-year German–English translation students, almost all of them native speakers of US English studying at an American university. They were assigned the text: "Sie haben mehr mit Bosch zu tun, als Sie denken" (reproduced, along with the accompanying translation brief, in Appendix I) as a final project in their first practice course in translation. The students were permitted to use any resources desired, including the internet. The 156-word ST is an 'image' text with some technical terminology, designed to introduce the text's audience to the variety of products manufactured by the Bosch company. At the time these translations were produced, the students had also just completed an introductory translation theory course and therefore could be considered novice translators who were relatively unfamiliar with German cultural items and therefore likely to commit greater numbers of cultural errors in translation. Technical texts can also carry a great deal of cultural information that must be adapted.

The texts were graded by the author using standard ATA tools. The number of marked errors in the passage ranged from 2 to 50. Because the 156-word text is shorter than a standard ATA examination, the scores were adjusted by a factor of 0.0624 to match the standardized 250-word ATA passage length, resulting in a range of 3–80 points. Since the students could not be expected to perform at the level of professional quality, the 17-point ATA pass/fail threshold was set as the boundary between a grade of 'A' and 'B', with higher numbers of error points resulting in lower grades (see Koby & Baer 2005 for the complete methodology for adjusting ATA error points).

Student final project results – normalised to ATA 17-point passing score

Score range	*Number of examinations*
0–17 (grade of A)	11
18 and higher (grade of B or lower)	16

Table 1: Breakdown of student scores

A review of the errors in the TTs produced by the students revealed that only four culture-specific items caused errors. Other errors in the TTs that lacked culture-specific items were ignored. The culture-specific errors are listed and analysed in the following paragraphs:

- *bei der nächsten Inspektion*

This item refers to a required inspection of automobiles. Most of the students (22 of 27, or 81%) correctly selected *next inspection*, plus one who explicitated acceptably and produced *next car inspection*. Another two selected *next service*, and one the *next time it is serviced*, which were penalized with 1 or 2 points in the terminology category because a required inspection is not automotive service. Although automotive service and required inspections occur in both cultures, the cultural misunderstanding is caused by differences in the characteristics of the inspections, which are required everywhere in Germany but not necessarily in every US state. One student, however – a native speaker of German – translated this item as the *next scheduled e-Check*. e-Check is an emissions testing programme specific to the state of Ohio, and would therefore only be appropriate in a translation targeted only at residents of that state. The student inappropriately narrowed the scope of the translation vis-à-vis the source and was penalized 4 points in terminology.

- *daß Sie im Supermarkt <u>von unseren Maschinen verpackte Lebensmittel</u> einkaufen*

The translation problem in this example is both grammatical and cultural. Grammatically, the underlined section of the phrase is a complex embedding of a relative clause as an adjectival phrase, literally "by-our-machines-packaged food". The cultural challenge becomes apparent when students produce translations that represent situations that would not occur in a German supermarket, and they must recognize this fact. They may either draw an analogy to their own supermarkets (which may or may not be correct) or they may have experience in supermarkets in the foreign culture. Therefore 15 students correctly translated this phrase as *food/groceries packaged/packed by our machines*, one used *wrapped up,* and another applied transposition to produce *that our machines packed the food you buy from the supermarket*, meaning that 63% of students successfully handled this challenge. Another three students rendered this phrase as *machine packaged/packed* food, which is correct as far as it goes but omits the action of the machines. The remaining students had various difficulties where cultural knowledge of supermarkets (in either culture) should have been applied, which should have suggested that their version was impossible: four indicated that the reader was purchasing foods *from our machines* (implying that Bosch machines store the food), one had the reader purchasing *packaged food … with our machines,* and one had the reader buying *packed groceries in one of our machines.* Finally, one student presented the reader with *that you wrapped up grocery shopping in the supermarket of our machinery*, indicating that the student was entirely unable to make sense of the passage. All of these errors were penalized with four points in the mistranslation or misunderstanding categories, as the error scope exceeds mistranslation of a mere term.

- *die Marke ist Bauer … mit Bauer-Projektoren Filme vorgeführt* (4th and 5th sentences)

Whereas 26 of the 27 students successfully translated these items as something similar to "the brand name is Bauer" … "films shown using Bauer projectors" (which are technical items that could be expected from a company such as Bosch), one student seemed to be unaware of the technical context and did not realize that *Bauer* was a brand name, as *Bauer* is also a word in German meaning 'farmer'. This student produced *the mark is a farmer … presented with a Farmer-Project movie.* By mistranslating the word *Marke* as *mark* instead of *brand name,* the student was unable to retrieve cues from the macro-context that would have precluded such an absurd solution. This breakdown in communication, essentially the illogic error mentioned above, was penalized 16 points in misunderstanding (of the ST), four each for *Marke* and *Bauer,* and eight points for *Farmer-project movie.* In addition, the same student also translated the brand name *Blaupunkt* in the next sentence as *blue point.*

- *Straßenbahnen* (9th sentence)

This term is translated either as *streetcars* or *trams*, depending on the country of the target audience. Collins (2008) notes that *tram* is 'esp Brit' and *streetcar* is 'US'. Despite the fact that in the American context these vehicles are generally called *streetcars*, given the very restricted distribution of public transportation systems in the United States, many students in suburban contexts (such as the students in this study) may never have seen a streetcar and are unfamiliar with the terminology. This resulted in 13 students (48%) using the correct *streetcar*, 12 (44%) choosing the foreign term *tram* (which was accepted, but commented on) and one student each choosing *cable car* (terminology, 2 points) and *trolley* (register, 1 point). The penultimate choice is a technically different vehicle (pulled by a cable), perhaps known to the student from those found uniquely in San Francisco, and the last is a somewhat antiquated term used in the United States that would not be appropriate in an advertisement for a modern technical company. No student selected the technically correct *light rail vehicle* or *LRV* that would not have matched the requirements of the brief.

In summary, the data in Case study 1 (students) showed four instances where errors occurred due to culture-specific items. Three of these locations centred on a single word, whereas the fourth was due to the students' misunderstanding of both a process and a grammatical structure. The three single-word errors were problematic in terms of culture-specific items only for a small number of students (*Inspektion,* 1 student; *Bauer,* 1 student; *Straßenbahn,* 2 students), while the more complex ideas expressed in *machine-packaged groceries* were a challenge for 26% of the students.

These four instances, however, reflect four different error types in terms of culture-specific items. The *Inspektion* item caused an error of overspecification, that is, the translation was too specific to a very narrow locale. The *Bauer* and *Straßenbahn* items share some features: *Bauer* caused an error of cultural recognition in that, having mistranslated the principal cue *Marke* = *brand name* and lacking sufficient experience with the source culture, the student did not recognize it as a name; the *Straßenbahn* item caused an error in technical terminology because the students lacked sufficient experience with this cultural item in both the source and the target cultures. Finally, since we cannot assume that students lack cultural experience with supermarkets, we may surmise that a lack of cultural knowledge about the similarities and differences in supermarkets in both cultures triggered this error. The embedded modifier construction can be seen as a likely contributing factor.

3. Case study 2: ATA data

The second set of data in this analysis comes from the ATA certification examination, specifically the German–English examination in the 2006 testing year. The ATA examination requires candidates to complete a mandatory passage on a general topic, labelled 'A', and to choose between a scientific or technical passage 'B' and a legal or commercial passage 'C' (see Koby & Champe 2013 for a complete description of the ATA testing programme). In this testing year, the A passage focused on food, the Mozart family and everyday life; the B passage on vision and the brain, and the C passage on European stock exchanges. Candidates produced a handwritten translation using only paper resources (at that time, no internet access was allowed). Each passage was graded by two trained graders, who assigned points and categories in accordance with the ATA programme.[3] The maximum error score for passing the ATA examination is 17 points. In the German–English language pair, 28 candidates completed the examination, with 11 selecting the B passage and 17 selecting the C passage. The native language of the candidates is unknown, because ATA does not collect this information. The breakdown of scores is shown in Table 1.

2006 German–English ATA Examinations

Passage letter / Score range	Number of examinations A	B	C
0–17 (Pass)	16	4	8
18 and above (Fail)	12	7	9

Table 2: Breakdown of scores by passage for 2006 German–English ATA examinations

Therefore 16 candidates passed the A passage, but only four and eight passed the B and C passages, respectively. Ten candidates (35.7%) passed the examination as a whole (i.e. both passages were scored at 17 or fewer error points).

For the purposes of the present analysis, the three STs were examined to identify where cultural knowledge was required in order to translate the text successfully, and particularly where a lack of such knowledge led to the graders marking errors in the candidates' TTs. Culture-specific items and related errors caused by such items were found only in the general A text and not in the scientific or economic texts. In the following para-

[3] Variation in points assigned by graders is a topic for further research and is not discussed here. It may be attributed to the fact that graders are asked to evaluate the impact of an error on the text as a whole, and their assessments vary subjectively to some degree. Still, the markings show general agreement among the graders that an error exists. Little research has been done on inter-rater (grader) reliability in evaluating translations. One recent study was done by Colina (2009).

graphs, each item is identified and discussed, with particular emphasis being placed on the analysis of the errors and the knowledge gaps that may have caused them. This will be followed by an analysis and an attempt at classifying the errors.

Passage A contains three cultural items that are terminological in nature, that is, cultural artifacts that need to be adapted to the target culture. Their solutions and the graders' error markings are:

- *Muschel-Suppe* (1st paragraph, 1st sentence)

In this case, 20 of the 28 candidates (71%) selected *mussel soup* as the solution, which is straightforward and was also accepted by the graders. The remaining candidates variously used *mussel stew*, which was accepted as a variant solution, *shellfish soup, clam soup* and *clam broth,* all of which were penalized two points in the mistranslation category, and *clam chowder*, which was penalized with four mistranslation points. In addition, there was one instance of *muscle soup*, which was penalized two points in the spelling category.

The variants occurring in the 16 passing examinations are *mussel soup* (13) and one instance each of *mussel stew, muscle soup* and *shellfish soup*. The examinations with deficient variants using *clam* in some form also generally have the highest error point scores. One of the examinations using *clam chowder* contains the following grader comment: "Correct: mussel soup. Why do anything else? (This is Salzburg, not New England; plus, the ingredients are listed a few sentences later and they don't match clam chowder)." It may be surmised that the five candidates (18%) choosing the clam options, particularly clam chowder, are members of the US culture, where clams and clam chowder are well known, and that they lack sufficient knowledge of European cuisine to be able to avoid cultural interference. *Clam chowder* carries connotations of US New England culture that are incorrect in the Salzburg context.

- *Delikatessengeschäft* (1st paragraph, last sentence)

Here, 21 candidates (75%) selected the word *delicatessen*, which was accepted by the graders. Other accepted variants were *deli* and *purveyor of fine foods*, while *deli-store* was penalized one point for usage. Therefore a total of 86% of the candidates selected an acceptable option according to the grader markings. *Delicacy shop* was penalized two points as a wrong word choice (terminology), whereas *gourmet food store* was penalized four mistranslation points, as was *specialty food store.* One candidate used *gourmet food store (grocery)* and was also penalized one additional point in the indecision category. It is unclear why *purveyor of fine foods* was accepted whereas *gourmet food store* was not.

In this example, it is apparent that the candidates needed to understand the German cultural context in which the term was embedded in order to assess accurately the type of establishment that native speakers of German would understand from *Delikatessenladen,* in terms of both size and type of goods sold, and match it to an equivalent – which is straightforward – in English.

- *Suppengrün* (2nd paragraph, 3rd sentence)

This term is an example of a concept that is lexicalized in the SL but not in the TL. It appears in bilingual dictionaries with a periphrastic definition such as *herbs and vegetables for making soup* (Langenscheidt Collins 2008), which was selected by eight (29%) of the candidates. Three instances of this acceptable usage were included in a larger error marked by graders in the ambiguity category, presumably because in the phrase *Herbs and vegetables for making soup, butter, and wine* it is potentially possible to interpret the clause as indicating that herbs and vegetables could be used in making butter and wine. However, other instances of this usage were not marked by other graders.

Other accepted variants were *soup herbs and vegetables* 3 (11%), *herbs and vegetables for the soup, herbs and vegetables needed to make the soup, herbs and vegetables for soup making.* The phrase *bunch of herbs and vegetables for making the soup* was penalized one point for terminology for the use of the word *bunch,* which is not in the source. Collectively, all of these solutions include the three relevant characteristics *herbs, vegetables* and *soup.* Fifteen candidates (54%) used this set of solutions. Another five candidates used *herbs and vegetables,* while one used *bunches of herbs and vegetables.* All six (21%) of these solutions were penalized one or two points for omitting the concept of *soup.*

For this item, graders also accepted *soup greens,* which four candidates (14%) used. However, the solution *green vegetables for making soup* was marked by one grader in the ambiguity category (but not by the other grader of the same examination), presumably for omitting *herbs,* whereas *soup-herbs* was similarly marked by one grader as omission (presumably of *vegetables*). Therefore these two solutions lack one or another of the components (*herbs* or *vegetables*), whereas *soup greens* subsumes *herbs and vegetables* into the concept of *greens*. Finally, the term *herbs for soup* was penalized four points in the mistranslation category.

This group of responses shows that when a term is not lexicalized in the TL, a variety of solutions appear. This may be due to the various dictionaries that the candidates used, which are unknown. However, it is clear from the grader markings that the key elements of the concept must be included in the periphrastic solution in order to be accepted.

- *Salonleben* (3rd paragraph, 1st sentence)

In order to translate this item successfully, it was necessary for the candidates to have historical knowledge, specifically of the literary salons that were a popular feature of society life in Mozart's time. A hint of this knowledge is available in dictionaries, for example Langenscheidt Collins (2008), where the five translation options available for the word *Salon* all include indications of the relevant domain:

a) *(= Gesellschaftszimmer)* drawing room; *(NAUT)* saloon

b) *(= Friseursalon, Modesalon, Kosmetiksalon etc)* salon

c) (HIST= *literarischer etc Zirkel)* salon

d) *(= Messe, Ausstellung)* show; *(= Messestand)* stand, exhibition stand

e) *(= Kunstsalon)* exhibition room

Ideally, the abbreviation 'HIST' (*historical*) would cue the candidates to choose item 'c' (or a similar item in another dictionary) and *salon* as the correct option. In fact, 11 candidates (39%) did select this option, either as *salon life* (7), *life in the salon(s)* (3) or *salon culture*, all of which were accepted by the graders. In contrast, those five candidates (18%) who chose option 'a' and wrote *drawing room life* or similar wordings (one wrote *parlor life*) were penalized one or two points, as the point of the literary or cultural salon was not where it occurred (i.e. the drawing room) but rather the kind of discourse that characterized it, which is relevant in the sentence in question.

Finally, two options were penalized more heavily: *social life* and *society life*. Seven candidates (25%) selected *social life*, which was penalized mostly with four points, but also with one or two points, while five (18%) selected *society life*, which was penalized in the same way. Both solutions suffer translation loss by failing to convey the historical phenomenon of the literary salon.

Combining all of the penalized solutions shows that 61% of candidates lacked the cultural knowledge to translate this lexical item successfully. Two factors may have contributed to this: if the reference works they had at their disposal lacked this knowledge, they could not obtain it under the examination circumstances; or if the information was available, the candidates may not have been able to recognize it in order to use it effectively.

In summary, the data in case study 2 (ATA candidates) showed four locations where errors occurred due to culture-specific items. All of these locations centred on a single word. Two were problematic for a relatively small group (*Muschel-Suppe,* with 18% incorrectly choosing *clam chowder*, and *Delikatessengeschäft* with 14% choosing *delicacy shop, gourmet food store* or *specialty food store*). Two other locations were more challenging to candidates: *Suppengrün*, with 46% creating various incorrect solutions due to non-lexicalization, and *Salonleben,* with 61% choosing incorrect options due to a lack of historical knowledge relating to the source culture.

The four locations, however, reflect different error types in terms of the culture-specific item. The *Muschel-Suppe* caused errors of over-specification, that is, the incorrect translation (*clam chowder*) was culturally specific to the target locale. The *Delikatessenladen* item caused errors to be marked due to a shift in cultural register, that is, a *delicatessen* is not a *gourmet food store* in the Austrian. The *Suppengrün* item is a culturally specific concept that is not lexicalized in the target culture and therefore requires analysis in order to provide a paraphrase of its conceptual components. Finally, the *Salonleben* item required specific historical knowledge that many candidates lacked and were unable to retrieve from their reference sources.

4. Comparison and analysis

The two case studies work with data produced naturally in the course of instructional examinations or translation certification examinations, respectively, and therefore with different texts. (It is unlikely that the same text would be selected for the two activities. At the time, it was also not possible to use ATA texts in the classroom, although this may become possible in the future.) The length of the two texts differs due to the type of task assigned.

Although the two case studies differ, the two groups – translation students and ATA candidates – are of similar size (27 vs 28), which facilitates comparisons. The two texts are of different lengths, but both texts are so short that it seems unreasonable to assume that there would have been more than one or two additional cultural items in the student text had it been longer. Another difference is that the student text deals with marketing and technology, whereas the ATA text deals with history and gastronomy. Despite these differences, however, seven of the eight cultural issues causing errors are terminology errors requiring cultural knowledge of specific phenomena and the eighth, *von unseren Maschinen verpackte Lebensmittel*, requires at least general knowledge of supermarkets in both cultures.

Regarding categorization, the four student errors were classified as over-specification, cultural recognition error, cultural experience deficiency and general lack of cultural knowledge, whereas the ATA errors also included over-specification, plus cultural register, culturally specific topic and historical knowledge. Therefore, although the small size of the samples in the two case studies means that broad generalizations are impossible, culture-specific items generally seem to trigger these errors, which break down into a variety of more specific types. A comparison of the errors is shown in Table 3.

Student			ATA		
Error	ATA Type	Distribution	Error	ATA Type	Distribution
bei der nächsten Inspektion	"Terminology": Term requiring comparative knowledge of auto inspections – error of cultural over-specification	85% correct 11% incorrect 4% very incorrect	*Muschel-Suppe*	"Mistranslation": Term requiring comparative knowledge of regional cuisine – error of cultural over-specification	75% correct 25% incorrect
von unseren Maschinen verpackte Lebensmittel	"Mistranslation" / "Misunderstanding": Phrase requiring use of logic and cultural knowledge of supermarkets in both cultures	63% correct 37% incorrect	*Delikatessengeschäft*	"Usage" / "Terminology" / "Mistranslation": Term requiring knowledge of relative cultural significance of shopping options – error of cultural register	86% correct 14% incorrect
Bauer	"Misunderstanding": Term requiring concept of brand names – error of cultural recognition	97% correct 3% incorrect	*Suppengrün*	"Ambiguity" / "Terminology" / "Omission" / "Mistranslation": Non-lexicalised term requiring knowledge of components and adaptation – cultural item unlexicalised in target culture	68% correct 32% incorrect
Straßenbahn	"Terminology" / "Register": Term requiring awareness of usage in various English cultures – error of cultural familiarity	48% correct 44% culturally misleading 8% incorrect	*Salonleben*	"Terminology": Term requiring historical-cultural knowledge	39% correct 61% incorrect

Table 3: Comparison of cultural errors in student examinations and ATA examinations

Two questions can be answered using the data:

- first, given the variety of cultural errors committed, whether the ATA error categories that were assigned to these errors characterize the errors sufficiently in cultural terms, and
- second, whether the student errors differ in kind or distribution from the examination candidate errors.

The answers to these questions may give indications for future research on whether this kind of cultural error can be prevented.

Table 3 shows that the primary ATA error categories used in classifying these translation errors – both those assigned to the students by the author[4] and those assigned by the graders in 2006 – were 'terminology' and 'misunderstanding', both of which are subcategories of the general 'mistranslation' error. According to the ATA Framework:

> [A] **terminology** error occurs when a term specific to a special subject field is not used when the corresponding term is used in the ST. This type of error often involves terms used in various technical contexts. This also applies to legal and financial contexts where words often have very specific meanings. In more general texts, a terminology error can occur when the candidate has not selected the most appropriate word among several that have similar (but not identical) meanings.

In addition, "[a] **misunderstanding** error occurs when the grader can see that the error arises from misreading a word, for example, or misinterpreting the syntax of a sentence" (emphasis in original). These categories are designed for examination testing, not formative assessment, and therefore, although these errors 'fit' into that framework, the categories do not provide sufficient information to allow students to consider what type of error they have committed.

Seven of the eight errors are fundamentally terminology errors, so in a way 'terminology' makes sense as an error category. This also fits with two of Bahumaid's six categories, inadequate knowledge of aspects of SL and TL culture and of differences between SL and TL. However, assigning a 'mere' terminology error fails to recognize that there are three different possibilities for error causation in a cultural sense:

[4] The author is a current ATA German–English grader. He was not a grader for the 2006 ATA examinations investigated here.

1. the translator understands the SL and the TL and culture, but selects an incorrect word or term due to, for example, linguistic deficits (no cultural influence);
2. the translator fails to understand the source cultural reference (SL cultural deficit, as in the *e-Check* example above, leading to over-specification), or
3. the translator fails to provide a culturally adequate translation even though they understood the SL reference (TL cultural deficit, e.g. the *clam chowder* example above; again, over-specification).

In other words, while for examination purposes a separate cultural error (or even two) is not necessary, additional culture-specific error categories would be useful in a pedagogical context in order to indicate to students where they should seek additional cultural knowledge. Based on this small sample, we could propose at least 'over-specification', 'cultural experience/recognition/topic' and 'historical/cultural knowledge' as error categories for consideration.

In contrast, the other main ATA category fits somewhat into this cultural area, but also highlights the challenges of classifying this type of error: 'misunderstanding'. Often anecdotally described by ATA graders as 'mind reading', the category does require the grader to reconstruct a defective thought process on the part of the translator, which is different from the other categories that make no such demand. In other words, graders must recognize not only that the translation of a particular item is incorrect, but also infer from the incorrect solution that a misunderstanding has occurred, in effect back-translating the mistranslated item to attempt to infer what the candidate understood instead of the actual ST item, perhaps by misreading the spelling or misremembering a similar item.

Finally, the other ATA categories used – register, usage, ambiguity and omission – occur only in individual cases and are caused by the circumstances of a particular candidate's solution. This may imply that such categories are not fundamentally used to classify cultural errors, and are instead used because of the specific features of a particular error.

As analysed above, the errors caused by culture-specific items share some features across the two studies, since both sets of errors resulted in the assignment of similar error categories and require specific knowledge idiosyncratic to the culture and the text in question. In addition, the severity of the errors (as measured by the ATA *Flowchart*) does not differ significantly between the students and the examination candidates, except for the one outlier in the *Bauer* example, where the candidate's solution fell far outside the technical scope of the brief. This confirms Bahumaid's argument about the importance of the brief. Barring the outlier who committed several serious errors, the translations that contained one error caused by culture-specific items did not necessarily contain others. Therefore, the presence of such an error is apparently not a good predictor of a general tendency to commit culture-specific errors.

It may be that cultural errors are entirely idiosyncratic to each individual translator's pattern of knowledge.[5] If this is the case, then a fruitful approach might be to examine cultural errors in the larger context of all errors in a given translation or by a given student. The presence of many general (non-cultural) errors could indicate a general lack of facility dealing with the source language, so that any cultural errors committed might not be due specifically to a lack of cultural knowledge, but rather to this general lack of linguistic proficiency. On the other hand, a pattern of relatively few non-cultural errors coupled with several cultural errors might indicate a linguist who acquired the SL outside of the source culture. Here again, further research is needed.

It should be noted that, owing to the nature of the assignment, and similarly to Bahumaid's students, the students in case study 1 had full access to the internet and also to all electronic and internet resources, and therefore should have been (and mostly were) able to solve cultural errors using research. The four cultural issues were successfully resolved by 85%, 63%, 97% and 48% of the students respectively.

Although they lacked internet access, the ATA examination candidates in case study 2 were permitted to bring any printed resources they wished to the examination. This would have limited their ability to solve translation problems to the resources that they considered necessary. Nevertheless, they successfully solved the four culture-specific items in 75%, 86%, 68% and 39% of the cases respectively. This pattern is similar to the pattern of percentages in case study 1. The similar variation in both groups requires further study of the reasons for such fluctuation.

[5] Niedzielski and Chernovaty concluded that in one experiment no significant difference could be found between bilingual technicians who become translators and linguists who are trained to translate in technical fields. They found that two factors contributed to successful translation: (1) age and experience in a technical field, and (2) original and creative thinking (1993: 128). Overall, however, their experiments showed that the technical background resulted in more accurate translations (ibid.: 139). This would imply that training linguists to be technical translators is the cause of many errors relating to 'technical culture' in translation.

5. Conclusions

Both of these small-scale case studies, though separate and distinct, showed similar patterns in the frequency and severity of the errors caused by culture-specific items. This would suggest that, while the teaching of culture is important in a general sense in all language teaching and specifically in translation teaching, it would be difficult to predict just which piece of information will be required in a given translation – therefore confirming Hietaranta's argument against algorithms for detecting cultural material. The data are also indicative of a possible need, at least in translation pedagogy, for more detailed categories for cultural errors. More study is needed, for instance, on a larger corpus of ATA examinations, such as those available in the Spanish–English or English–Spanish combinations, or across multiple examination years, to see whether these preliminary results are validated in larger studies.

It would also be interesting in future research to attempt to classify culture-specific errors in the ST according to their 'knowledge distance' from the translators' experience, in advance of translation, and then to compare this with the frequency of errors. The challenge in such research would be to devise a reliable method for measuring the cultural knowledge needed for translation. Fundamentally, this research would have to focus on methods of identifying cultural errors and strategies for solving them, since it is impossible to predict which cultural phenomenon will cause an error in any given text. It is similarly impossible to create a corpus of all possible cultural phenomena that may cause errors.

Finally, the preliminary results from these two naturalistic case studies could be validated or refined in two experiments: one in which students use the same text as the ATA candidates, with similarly limited materials, and another in which ATA candidates have full internet access. Culture-specific items in the texts could be identified beforehand, and retrospective interviews focusing on these items could collect information on the translators' knowledge and decision-making process. At the time of writing, most ATA examination sittings scheduled for 2017 and beyond will allow candidates full internet access. This promising development will provide future data that can be analysed for differences in the success rate of translating culture-specific items.

References

Al-Kharabsheh, Aladdin, Al-Azzam, Bakri & Obeidat, Marwan M. 2008. Lost in translation: Shop signs in Jordan. *Meta* 53(3): 717–727.

Altay, Ayfer. 2002. Difficulties encountered in the translation of legal texts: The case of Turkey. *Translation Journal* 6(4). <http://translationjournal.net/journal/22legal.htm> (accessed 18 September 2017.

American Translators Association (ATA). Nd. Framework for standardized error marking. Explanation of error categories. <http://www.atanet.org/ certification/aboutexams_error.php> (accessed 18 September 2017).

Bahumaid, Showqi. 2010. Investigating cultural competence in English–Arabic translator training programs. *Meta* 55(3): 569–588.

Canadian Translators, Terminologists and Interpreters Council (CTTIC). 2005. CTTIC standard certification translation examination marker's guide. <http://www.cttic.org/examDocs/guide.markersE.pdf> (accessed 18 September 2017).

Chartered Institute of Linguists. 2014. Diploma in translation. Handbook for candidates. <http://www.ciol.org.uk/sites/default/files/Handbook-Dip Trans.pdf> (accessed 18 September 2017).

Colina, Sonia. 2009. Further evidence for a functionalist approach to translation quality evaluation. *Target* 21(2): 235–264.

Hietaranta, Pertti. 2000. Thwarted expectations: Investigating translational mishaps with reference to cultural disparities. *Target* 12(1): 83–107.

Katan, David. 2009. Translator training and intercultural competence. In Stefania Cavagnoli, Elena Di Giovanni & Raffaela Merlini (eds) *La ricerca nella comunicazione interlinguistica. Modelli teorici e metodologici*, Milan: Franco Angeli, 282–301.

Koby, Geoffrey S & Champe, Gertrud. 2013. Welcome to the real world: Professional-level translator certification. *Translation & Interpreting* 5(1): 156–173.

Koby, Geoffrey S & Baer, Brian J. 2005. From professional certification to the translator training classroom: Adapting the ATA error marking scale. *Translation Watch Quarterly* 1(1): 33–45.

Langenscheidt Collins. 2008. *Langenscheidt Collins e-Großwörterbuch Deutsch–Englisch 5.0*. Berlin/Munich: Langenscheidt KG and HarperCollins Publishers.

Niedzielski, Henry & Chernovaty, Leonid. 1993. Linguistic and technical preparation in the training of technical translators and interpreters. In Sue Ellen Wright & Leland D Wright Jr (eds) *Scientific and technical translation*. Amsterdam/Philadelphia: John Benjamins, 123–150.

Ochs, Elinor. 1996. Linguistic resources for socializing humanity. In John Gumperz & Stephen C Levinson (eds) *Rethinking linguistic relativity*. Cambridge: Cambridge University Press, 407–437.

Psychometria. Institut für psychologische Diagnostik. Nd. Lesbarkeitsindex. <http://www.psychometrica.de/lix.html> (accessed 18 September 2017).

Schmitt, Peter A. 1999. *Translation und Technik*. Tübingen: Stauffenburg Verlag.

Séguinot, Candace. 1989. Understanding why translators make mistakes. *TTR* 2(2): 73–81.

South African Translators' Institute (SATI). n.d. Framework for marking of translation accreditation examinations. <http://translators.org.za/ sati_cms /downloads/dynamic/marking_guidelines_translation_english.pdf> (accessed 18 September 2017).

Toury, Gideon. 1995. *Descriptive Translation Studies and beyond.* Amsterdam/Philadelphia: John Benjamins.

Appendix 1: American Translators Association *Framework for standardized error marking*

ATA CERTIFICATION PROGRAM

FRAMEWORK FOR STANDARDIZED ERROR MARKING
Version 2009

Exam Number: __________

Exam Passage: __________

Check here if for Review ☐

1	2	4	8	16	Code	Reason
Errors that concern the form of the exam						
Treat missing material within the passage as an omission.					UNF	Unfinished (If a passage is substantially unfinished, do not grade the exam.)
					ILL	Illegibility
					IND	Indecision, gave more than one option
Translation / strategic / transfer errors: Negative impact on understanding / use of target text.						
					MT	Mistranslation (use a subcategory if applicable)
					MU	— Misunderstanding of source text (if identifiable)
					A	— Addition
					O	— Omission
					T	— Terminology, word choice
					R	— Register
					F	— Faithfulness
					L	— Literalness
					FA	— Faux ami (false friend)
					COH	— Cohesion
					AMB	— Ambiguity
					ST	Style (inappropriate for specified type of text)
					OTH	Other (describe)
Mechanical errors: Negative impact on overall quality of target text. Points may vary by language. Maximum 4 points.						
					G	Grammar
					SYN	— Syntax (phrase / clause / sentence structure)
					P	Punctuation
					SP / CH	Spelling / Character (usually 1 point, maximum 2; if more than 2 points, another category must apply)
					D	— Diacritical marks / Accents
					C	— Capitalization
					WF / PS	Word form / Part of speech
					U	Usage
					OTH	Other (describe)
	x 2 =	x 4 =	x 8			**Column totals**

A grader may stop marking errors when the score reaches 46 error points.	A grader may award a quality point for each of up to three specific instances of exceptional translation.	Quality points are subtracted from the error point total to yield a final score. A passage with a score of 18 or more points receives a grade of Fail.
Total error points (add column totals):	**Quality points (maximum 3):**	**Final passage score (subtract quality points from error points):**

Appendix 2: ATA *Flowchart for error point decisions*

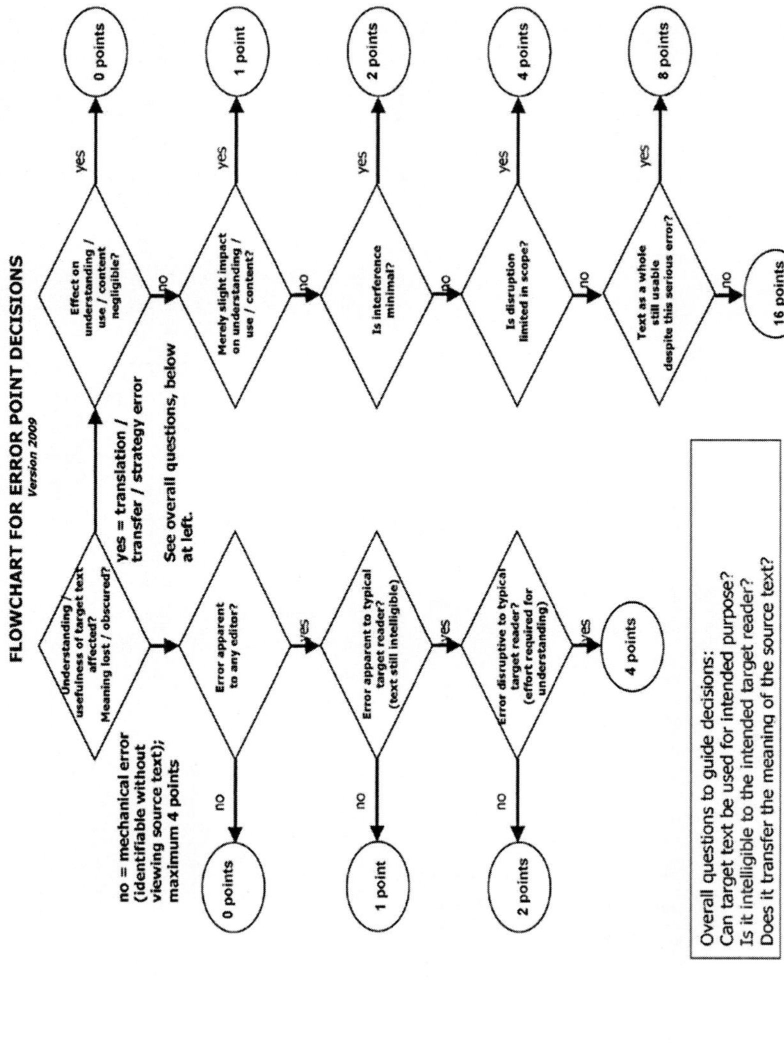

Appendix 3: ST and sample correct TT for the student assignment (156 ST words)

Translation brief: *The following text is intended for a brochure advertising Bosch products in the United States, which will be placed in print magazines and on websites. Translate the following 156-word text from German into English, using the appropriate style and wording. It should be of the highest quality and as ready for publication as you can make it.*

Sie haben mehr mit Bosch zu tun, als Sie denken

Mit ziemlicher Sicherheit enthält Ihr Auto einiges von Bosch und wird bei der nächsten Inspektion mit Bosch-Prüfgeräten kontrolliert.

Die Wahrscheinlichkeit ist groß, daß Sie im Supermarkt von unseren Maschinen verpackte Lebensmittel einkaufen, sie dann in Ihrer Bosch-Küche verarbeiten und in einem Bosch-Kühlschrank aufbewahren.

Vielleicht filmen Sie mit einer Filmkamera von Bosch, die Marke ist Bauer. In vielen Kinos bekommen Sie mit Bauer-Projektoren Filme vorgeführt. Oder Ihr Fernseher ist von Blaupunkt, also von Bosch. Wenn nicht, haben Sie vermutlich die Olympischen Spiele trotzdem mit unseren Augen gesehen. Viele der Wettkämpfe wurden mit Bosch-Fernsehkameras übertragen.

Bosch Elektrowerkzeuge helfen beim Bau von Wohnungen, Badezimmer werden mit Junkers-Anbaumöbeln eingerichtet, Straßenbahnen fahren mit Bauteilen von uns, Kliniken bringen Blutkonserven mit Bosch-Geräten auf Körpertemperatur. 5700 Wissenschaftler und Techniker arbeiten bei Bosch allein in der Forschung und Entwicklung. Zur Zeit besitzen wir 10 000 Patente in aller Welt, weitere 15 000 sind beantragt.

You Have More to Do with Bosch Than You Think

It is very likely that your vehicle contains a few things from Bosch and will be checked with Bosch testing devices during its next inspection.

There is a strong likelihood that you buy food in the supermarket that is packaged by our machines, which you then prepare in your Bosch kitchen and store in a Bosch refrigerator.

Perhaps you make movies with a video camera from Bosch; the brand is Bauer. In many movie theaters, you see movies shown with Bauer projectors, or your television is by Blaupunkt, thus, by Bosch. If not, you probably still watched the Olympic Games through our eyes – many of the competitions were broadcast with Bosch television cameras.

Bosch power tools help with the construction of homes, bathrooms are equipped with Junkers modular furniture, streetcars run with parts made by us, and clinics bring units of stored blood to body temperature with Bosch appliances. At Bosch, 5700 scientists and technicians work exclusively in research and development. We currently hold 10,000 patents worldwide, and another 15,000 are pending.

Appendix 4: ST and sample correct TT from the 2006 German–English ATA examination – general passage (219 ST words)

Translation brief: *The following text is taken from a guidebook on the city of Salzburg addressing foreign visitors. Translate it for an American readership.*

Wenn sich heute eine Salzburger Familie eine Muschel-Suppe wünscht, ist der Weg vom Wunsch zur Erfüllung kurz und unkompliziert. Die Muscheln finden sich in gleich mehreren Fischläden, die übrigen Zutaten sind in jedem Delikatessengeschäft zu bekommen.

Der gleiche Wunsch, geäußert von der Familie Mozart, konnte die Mutter vor einige Probleme stellen. Vor allem die Muschel-Beschaffung ließ sich nicht zu allen Jahreszeiten bewerkstelligen. Zwar waren Suppengrün, Butter und Wein stets erhältlich, Olivenöl hingegen war eine Seltenheit. Das Menü der Familie richtete sich weniger nach dem Wunsch der Tafelrunde, als nach den Angeboten der Händler, die sich wiederum nach Jahreszeiten, Straßenzuständen, Krieg und Frieden zu richten hatten.

Der Alltag der Familie Mozart im 18. Jahrhundert mit seinen Sorgen und Freuden, Liebe und Klatsch, Bierpreis und Salonleben ist uns dank einiger fleißiger Briefschreiber und Tagebuchführer vertraut. Die wichtigsten und interessantesten Beobachtungen gehen auf die Familie Mozart selbst zurück. Im Zusammenhang mit dem Alltagsleben der Familie haben die Briefe des Vaters das größte Gewicht. Er hat den Lebensweg seiner Kinder, so lange und so weit es ihm möglich war, begleitet, und er hat seinen Freunden, seinen Kindern und besonders seiner Frau geschrieben, was ihm des Berichtens wert schien. Und so ist die Lektüre der Briefe Leopold Mozarts nicht nur sehr unterhaltsam, sondern zuallererst ein Weg, einen Menschen in seiner Zeit kennen zu lernen.

Today, when a Salzburg family wishes to have mussel soup, it is a short and uncomplicated process to turn this wish into reality. The mussels can readily be found in several different fish shops, and the remaining ingredients are obtainable in any delicatessen.

The same wish, expressed by the Mozart family, presented the mother with some problems. Mussels, in particular, could not be found at all times of the year. Although herbs and vegetables for soup, butter and wine were always available, olive oil was a rarity. The family menu was based less on the preferences of those seated around the table than on what was offered by the shopkeepers, who in turn were dependent on the seasons, the road conditions, war and peace.

Thanks to several people who were diligent in writing letters and keeping diaries, we are familiar with the day-to-day life of the Mozart family in the 18th century—its joys and sorrows, love and gossip, the price of beer and salon life. The Mozart family itself is the source of the most important and interesting observations. The father's letters carry the greatest weight with regard to the family's everyday life. He accompanied his children on their journey through life as long and as far as it was possible for him, and he wrote to his friends, his children and especially his wife whatever he deemed worth reporting. Reading the letters of Leopold Mozart is therefore not only very entertaining but, first and foremost, a way to get to know a person in his time.

JUNE EYCKMANS

Ghent University

Cultural Competence in Translation Studies and its Assessment

Abstract

In this chapter, I consider the role that cultural competence has been given in different translation competence models and I will discuss different options for assessing cultural competence, both as a separate construct and as part of translation competence as a whole. With regard to the latter option, I will contend that a norm-referenced assessment method is best suited to put cultural competence on a par with all other sub-competences of translation ability. Not only does this method allow the reliability of the assessment to be checked, but it also has two important advantages when it comes to the validity of measuring (cultural) translation competence: it takes into account that sub-components of translation ability are more or less inextricable in actual performances, and it subscribes to the notion that the manifestation of cultural competence is always dependent on the interaction of a particular translator with a particular text.

Keywords: cultural competence, translation competence, phraseology, translation assessment, norm-referenced assessment method

1. Introduction

In Translation Studies (TS), a number of scholars have attempted to conceptualize and define translation competence, focusing on the knowledge and skills it requires. A lineup of prevailing definitions (PACTE 2000; Arango-Keith & Koby 2003; Angelelli 2009; ISO 17100 2015) reveals that most contemporary conceptualizations of translation competence follow a functional rather than a linguistic approach. They emphasize the mediating role of the translator who has to transpose a particular text that was written to perform a function in the source language (SL) and culture into a new form in order to perform a function in the target language (TL) and culture. Therefore, sub-competences with names such as 'transfer competence', 'pragmatic competence', 'strategic competence' or '(inter)cultural competence' (ICC) figure in virtually all current definitions (Eyckmans et al. 2009). This development has decidedly been influenced by the cultural turn in TS, in which every text is seen as the result of the "total beliefs and practices of a society" (Nida 1994: 157). In view of the fact that the conventions of text production and reception vary from culture to culture, the practice of translation has been described as a cross-cultural event (Snell-Hornby 1988: 46) and the role of the translator has been redefined in the sense that they have become an intercultural mediator who needs to be proficient in SLs and TLs as well as have a profound knowledge of source and target cultures.

If the ability to convey meaning from a source text (ST) to a target text (TT) according to socio-cultural appropriateness lies at the heart of translation ability, it stands to reason that assessment procedures should encompass this element. However, reports on the assessment of cultural competence are sparse in the TS literature, and cultural competence as a sub-competence has rarely been studied experimentally.

This chapter consists of two parts. In the first, the increased popularity of cultural competence both as a term and as a skill is discussed and the descriptions and definitions that have been put forward in TS literature are described. Next, the question whether linguistic dimensions form part of cultural competence is dealt with by considering the attention that is paid to idiomatic language use in second language acquisition (SLA) literature as well as in TS. In the second part of this chapter, the assessment of cultural competence will be addressed. To this end, current practices in translation assessment are discussed and proposals for measuring the sub-competence 'cultural competence' are reviewed. Finally, the potential of a norm-referenced method for identifying items that are culturally laden and for measuring cultural competence in a valid and reliable way is outlined.

2. Cultural competence within Translation Studies

2.1 Background

One of the most discussed issues within TS is translation equivalence and the translatability/untranslatability of language, with Nida (1964) and Newmark (1981) as well-known theorists in the field. After a period in which TS was dominated by ethnocentrism, poly-system theory emerged and became mainstream in the field. Even-Zohar's (1979) ground-breaking work on the interplay between diachronic (historical) and synchronic (contemporary) dimensions heralded the shift in TS towards a more complex analysis of socio-cultural systems. As such, and in the wake of concurrent developments in Cultural Studies, key concepts such as gender, youth, power, cultural identity and ideology found their way into translation theory and translation scholars began to emphasize the cross-cultural aspects of translation (Snell-Hornby 1988; Bassnett 1991).

Today, it is generally accepted that the quality of a translation does not depend on the TT alone but also on the reception of the text by the implied reader. This implied reader brings along an idiosyncratic collection of social, socio-cultural, political and ideological characteristics. With a view to improving translation pedagogy, translator trainers such as González Davies and Scott-Tennent (2005) have put forward proposals to increase student translators' cultural competence. They advocate the necessity for students to familiarize themselves with cultural references (such as those exemplified in Nida's taxonomy, Nida & Taber 1969) as well as to improve their knowledge of translation strategies. This, they hold, will increase the students' chances of arriving at good solutions to translation problems.

Their pedagogical proposal for student translators includes a wide range of activities in which students are trained in 'translation problem-spotting' and developing written protocols to make their decision-making processes in translating cultural references explicit. In these written protocols translation problems are identified and different solutions are put forward and justified. With these activities the authors aim to (1) develop an awareness of the limitations of any definition of the concept of cultural reference, (2) reconcile students' assumptions about their own community and those of the target culture, and (3) establish the perception in students that culture as a behaviour and as a way of perceiving the world permeates the whole text, not just loose words and expressions (ibid.: 175).

2.2 Terminology

The importance of cultural competence has yielded a plethora of terms in Cultural Studies: multiculturalism, cross-cultural adaptation, cross-cultural awareness, cultural competence, intercultural sensitivity, ethnorelativity, global competence and transcultural communication are but a few of those listed to refer to the ability to communicate across language–culture differences (Fantini 2009). Of course, the definition of 'culture' itself is problematic. It is reported to be one of the most complicated words in the English language (Williams 1976: 87). For their 1952 publication, Kroeber and Klockhohn had already gathered 165 different definitions (1952).

Within TS the European Norm for Translation Services (ISO 17100 2015) is holding on to the generic term 'cultural competence', whereas the European Master of Translation (EMT) expert group prefers 'intercultural competence' (ICC) (2009). The proponents of the Trans-European Voluntary Certification for Translators (TransCert) project (Budin et al. 2013), in turn, use the term 'transcultural competence' in their competence description as integrated in the framework of the European Certification and Qualification Association (ECQA). Meyer (1991) also uses the term 'transcultural competence' and defines it as the highest level of cultural competence. He asserts that learners acquire cultural competence by degrees:

- At a monocultural level they use behavioural schemes that are merely adequate for their own culture and this results in a stereotyped, cliché-ridden and ethnocentric view of the foreign culture.
- At the intercultural level, learners are able to explain cultural differences between their own and the foreign culture.
- At the transcultural level, learners are able to evaluate intercultural differences and negotiate their meaning.

In this chapter, the more generic term 'cultural competence' will be used instead of its many derivatives (i.e. transcultural, cross-cultural or ICC) in order to refer to all the aspects of the translator's cultural knowledge and the strategies he or she uses to transform the cultural dimension of the source text into an appropriate target text (TT).

2.3 Cultural competence in translation models

Although translation scholars and translation trainers have put forward different conceptualizations of translation competence, most of them give a prominent role to cultural knowledge and cultural skills in the translation models they have developed (Nord 1988; Bell 1991; Hewson & Martin 1991; Kiraly 1995; Neubert 2000). Publications in the past decade point to the generally accepted consensus that translation competence should be defined as the combination of advanced language competence in SL and TL language, subject- and culture-specific knowledge, knowledge of text-typological conventions in the SL and the TL cultures, and translation skills (PACTE 2005; Göpferich & Jääskelainen 2009; Malmkjær 2009; Schäffner & Beverly 2000).

In what follows, the definitions of cultural competence from three current and prominent frameworks within Europe are listed to illustrate that organizations also recognize cultural competence as an integral part of translation ability:

1. ISO 17100 2015 describes the professional competence of translators as encompassing five sub-competences: translating competence, linguistic and textual competence in the SL and TL, research competence, cultural competence and technical competence. 'Cultural competence' is defined as the ability to make use of information about the locale, behavioural standards, and value systems that characterize the source and target cultures.
2. In the document "Competences for professional translators and experts in multilingual and multimedia communication", the EMT expert group (2009) defines six sub-competences of translation competence, which are presented as interdependent: translation service provision competence, language competence, ICC, information mining competence, thematic competence, and technological competence (see also Rosiers, this volume). Within this framework, ICC comprises sociolinguistic and textual dimensions. The sociolinguistic dimension pertains to recognizing function and meaning in language variation (social, geographical, historical and stylistic) and knowing how to employ a register that is appropriate to a given situation. The textual dimension encompasses the ability to grasp presuppositions, implicit allusions and stereotypes and to identify culture-bound values and references, and also the ability to compare cultural elements and methods of composition.
3. Within the European Life-Long Learning Programme, TransCert (Budin et al. 2013), translator scholars and translator trainers aim to develop a complete certification and training programme for translators at a European level. In order to arrive at such certification the framework from the ECQA is used. This is an international certification scheme for professionals that provides the same examination pool, rules and electronic system for all certification examinations in its member countries. By creating an ECQA skill card for the Certified Translator, TransCert envisages its certification to be recognized in all European Union (EU) countries. The skill card distinguishes seven

skills: language, translations, domain-specifics, information mining and terminology, personal translation management, technological and transcultural. These transcultural skills are explicitly related to the values of the EU, for "including transcultural skills in the training scheme brings innovative European added value to the TransCert program" (Peraldi 2014).

Notwithstanding the different terms that are used in these models and descriptions, it can be concluded that the terms refer to the same construct – cultural competence – which is invariably defined as a combination of knowledge, attitudes, behaviour and know-how. However, the second and the third model mention a (socio)linguistic dimension in their definitions of (trans)cultural competence, whereas the first does not. The role of linguistic knowledge and skills in the conceptualization of cultural competence is discussed in the next section.

2.4 Phraseology

Although the link between language and culture is complex and the directionality of the relationship is still often debated (language can be seen to reflect as well as influence a community's pattern of thought), not many contemporary linguists would dispute the close relationship between a language's lexicon and the cultural segmentation of reality of its speakers. Not only does a language's lexicon contain keywords that reveal key concepts of core cultural values in any given language community (Wierzbicka 2001); it also possesses an important cultural dimension in the sense that it consists of a wide range of (semi-)preconstructed word combinations that are language-specific. These include idiomatic expressions, collocations, phrasal verbs, metaphorical expressions, similes, proverbs, compounds and discourse markers. Together they constitute what is called a language's idiomaticity or a language's phraseology. As Stubbs puts it: "our knowledge of a language is not only a knowledge of individual words, but of their predictable combinations, and of the cultural knowledge which these combinations often encapsulate" (2001: 3). Studies of first-language (L1) discourse have revealed overwhelming evidence of collocational tendencies, and adult native speakers' phrase lexicon is estimated to consist of many thousands of chunks (Pawley & Syder 1983; Foster 2001; Wray 2002; Schmitt 2004). Corpus linguistic research into the English language, for example, has revealed that half of all written English is made up of lexical phrases (Erman & Warren 2000; Butler 2005).

Within second-language (L2) acquisition research, language learners' struggle with the phraseological dimension of language is well attested. They have been found to acquire the phrasal component of the TL only very slowly (Durrant & Schmitt 2009; Li & Schmitt 2010; Yamashita & Jiang 2010). Even at quite advanced levels, learners are known to produce word combinations that sound odd to native speakers (e.g. **say the truth*; **throat ache*) and that require effortful interpretation on the part of the latter (Millar 2010). Often, such non-nativelike word combinations can be traced back to the learner's L1 (Nesselhauf 2005; Laufer & Girsai 2008). Studies of native and non-native speakers' use of phrases in writing (Granger 1998) have demonstrated non-natives' overuse of certain lexical phrases (*the fact that* and *as far as X is concerned*), their great reliance on a limited repertoire of what may be called 'fixed anchorage points', and their inability to detect deviant collocations from standard collocations.

In translator training, idiomatic language use is at least as important as it is in L2 acquisition. The translation of fixed phrases constitutes a double challenge: the ability to establish the meaning of the fixed phrase, and the ability to find an equivalent and idiomatic formulation for fixed phrases in the TL. When one skims the research on the linguistic dimension of cultural competence, one finds accounts of translation challenges in published works that include phraseology (Katan 2004; House 2006; Colson 2008; Bahumaid 2010; Park et al. 2015). One fairly recent example is Dinçkan's analysis of the translation of culture-bound collocations in bestsellers (2010). In his study the author points to the challenges of culture-bound collocations in the two directions of translation: when translating from one's native language into a foreign language the choice of the appropriate collocation may be problematic; when translating from a foreign language into one's native language the recognition of culture-bound collocations might prove too challenging. Both situations may result in erroneous translations. The English collocation *terraced housing*, for example, may be understood by Dutch- and French-speaking translators as referring to houses with patios whereas it refers to a row of joined houses.

Dinçkan observes in his corpus that both foreignizing and domesticating strategies are used by his participants when translating culture-bound collocations. Among the foreignizing strategies he counts loan collocations, literal translations, footnotes, translations by paraphrase and translations by a collocation with a similar meaning. The domesticating strategies that the translators in his study employ are translation by cultural substitution and omission. His analysis of the participants' performance revealed that the collection of mistranslations contained examples of both categories.

Dinçkan's analysis reveals how the boundaries between language competence and cultural competence are difficult to maintain when analysing SL–TL examples. Translation problems that concern culture-bound collocations in different areas of life such as beverages or food (*spring roll*), holidays (*Bank Holiday*), and leisure (*Happy Hour*) illustrate the linguistic component of cultural competence. This inevitable mixture of cultural and linguistic competence also concerns the connotations of language-specific collocations. In Dinçkan's English–Turkish corpus, the English collocation *single mother* was often mistranslated as "a widowed mother" in Turkish since in Turkey having children is usually directly associated with being married: if a mother lives alone, she is thought to be either divorced or widowed. The Turkish student-translators either did not appear to know the connotations of being a *single mother* in the source culture or they passed on their own value judgments during the translation process (Dinçkan 2010: 466–467).

The listed examples illustrate that the cultural component of translation ability includes both culture-bound terms (the so-called *culturemes*; Vermeer 1983) and phraseology at large. In fact, phraseology can be considered as an interface between culture and language. As Katan (2004: 11) puts it:

> The role of language within a culture and the influence of the culture on the meanings of words and the structures of discourses are so pervasive that scarcely any text can be adequately understood or effectively presented in a translating process without careful consideration of the factors of culture in it.

In view of the acknowledged cultural dimension of formulaic language (see also Skandera 2007), it is clear that linguistic competence and cultural competence show significant overlap. This needs to be taken into account when the assessment of translation competence is considered.

3. The assessment of cultural competence

Before the options for assessing cultural competence as a dimension of translation competence are discussed, some general assessment issues within the domain of TS need to be considered.

3.1 Issues in translation assessment studies

Notwithstanding the enormous turnover that translation activities represent in today's society and the concomitant number of translation courses around the world, surprisingly little attention has been paid in TS to the assessment of translation. This is probably attributable to the fact that prescriptive translation theory and translation criticism have prevailed within TS since its inception. It is not difficult to come across publications that discuss the translation choices made by translator X or Y as they tackled a literary novel, but publications on the subject of translation assessment within translator training programmes at university are rare. Beeby attributes this dearth of publications to the fact that translation competence is not yet fully defined and that it includes sub-competences which seem to include "the world, the universe and everything" (2000: 185). An alternative explanation (Anckaert et al. 2008) is that the teaching and testing of both translation and interpreting skills has generally been in the hands of practitioners rather than researchers, which has led to a situation in which assessment has been informed by practice rather than by empirical research.

An important issue resulting from the lack of empirical research in translation assessment is the omission of reliability indices from translation tests. In foreign-language assessment the introduction of psychometrics has led to the development of numerous studies on the reliability of language tests, yet these issues have been addressed only sparingly in TS. As a result, questions about the reliability of assessment methods have remained largely unanswered (Eyckmans et al. 2009; Eyckmans et al. 2012; Eyckmans et al. 2016). This deficit of reliability indices has a negative influence on the presumed validity of translation tests, since one of the fundamental principles of measurement theory is that no test can be considered valid if it is not proven reliable (Bachman 1990: 238).

Another matter of importance when considering translation assessment is the issue of certification. Most translators are nowadays trained and certified in educational settings. Both the training of translators and the certification of translation skills first require translation competence to be defined. Within educational methodology it is generally accepted that the assessment of a competence in any field entails five steps: (1) defining the competence, (2) defining its sub-components (sub-competences), (3) formulating competence descriptors for each of the sub-competences, (4) linking the competence descriptors to observable behaviour, and (5) developing instruments to elicit and score this behaviour (Bachman 1990). Since the last decades of the 20th century, several TS scholars have taken up the challenge to describe the sub-components of translation competence (Bell 1991; Campbell 1991; Pym 1991; Shreve 1997; PACTE 2000); yet to our knowledge to date no methodology has been proposed in which competence descriptors of the several sub-competences are turned into instruments that enable translation performance to be scored reliably. Moreover, although scholars have suggested that the overarching construct of translation competence and its set of interrelated sub-competences can be studied both in isolation and in combination with others (Schäffner & Beverly 2000), both theoretical and empirical studies about this are also notably absent from the literature. In fact, to the best of my knowledge, sub-competences such as cultural, heuristic and technical competences are almost never measured separately in the assessment practices of translation training programmes. Neither are the psycho-physiological components that are deemed to be important components of strategic competence (PACTE 2005). Therefore, let us first look at the separate measurement of cultural competence before moving on to contextualized ways of measuring it – ways that translation practitioners at large generally deem to be more valid.

3.2 Measuring cultural competence as a separate construct

One of the few reported initiatives for measuring cultural competence as a separate component in translation is that of Bahumaid (2010). This researcher developed a "Test of Cultural Competence in Translation" to verify the translator's knowledge of the target culture, linguistic and otherwise. In his test, Bahumaid targets knowledge of British life and culture among Arabic native speakers and incorporates translation problems that cover various areas of life (food and drink, sport) or genres (literary, political) and include several linguistic culture-specific expressions (metaphors as well as similes and proverbs). According to his analysis of the test scores, the Arabic students had inadequate knowledge of the political, social and religious aspects of both the source and the target culture. They also suffered from a lack of awareness of certain semantic problems such as culture-specific idioms and similes.

Tests such as Bahumaid's that measure cultural knowledge of the TL and culture separately from the act of text translation can take many forms (e.g. multiple-choice formats, true/false format) and can be developed for different SL–TL combinations. Such tests would typically target critical items that cover knowledge of the target culture or the difference between the source culture and the target culture (e.g. terms and references such as 'trick or treat' or 'Speaker of the House of Commons' are to be translated into Arabic in Bahumaid's Test of Cultural Competence). Tests of declarative knowledge such as these have their merits but they carry the disadvantage that it is impossible to predict whether these critical items will surface in an actual translation exercise or what the relationship is between knowledge of these critical items and the translator's skill in applying it (or to use heuristic competence skills to find a solution to a particular cultural translation problem) when confronted with the multifaceted process of translating a text.

Another approach to measuring cultural competence separately – one that is becoming increasingly popular in Communication Studies – is the appraisal of individuals' cultural attitudes and abilities. On the basis of questionnaires that tap into the meta-cognitive and behavioural aspects of personality, indices of cultural intelligence or cultural effectiveness are calculated (see also Rosiers in this volume). These indices serve as quantitative indicators of the way in which an individual functions in culturally diverse settings, or the degree of mental flexibility and open-mindedness an individual has (with reference to remaining unprejudiced towards different cultural norms and values). Within TS, Olalla-Soler (2015) has included this dimension in his PhD research on cultural competence. Apart from having students translate a text that contains five culturemes, he administers a (cultural) declarative knowledge test and asks the students to fill in a number of surveys (such as the Cultural Intelligence Scale and the Multicultural Personality Questionnaire) with a view to triangulating these data. Although these surveys may provide valuable information about the conative characteristics of translators, they constitute a very indirect way of gauging a translator's cultural competence.

With a view to test and task authenticity, the measurement (of the subskill) of cultural competence might be best served by contextualized assessment, that is, as part of a test that requires students to demonstrate their cultural competence by translating a text (or part of a text). This is explained in the next section.

3.3 Measuring cultural competence by means of text translation

3.3.1 The holistic and analytic method

In most translator trainer programmes, the translation product is seen as evidence of the student translator's competence (Waddington 2001; 2004; PACTE 2005). Although the field currently lacks the necessary psychometric underpinnings to affirm this nexus (one of the pitfalls of the equation between product and competence being that the source text – and the resulting translation product – may not be sufficiently challenging to reveal a translator's competence), one may assume the ecological validity of the argument that the quality of translation products can be used to infer student translators' translation skills.

During translator training, student translators' texts are evaluated in order to give the students feedback on their translation practice or, in an examination, to decide on their final mark. The methods used to score these translations are almost always based on either a holistic or an analytical assessment approach. When applying a holistic approach, the assessor reads the product and awards it a score on the basis of a general impression of its quality. There is no reason to think that cultural knowledge and skills would not form part of the assessor's global impression. It is up to the assessor to decide intuitively the degree to which the translations they appraise show evidence of cultural competence on the part of the student translator. However, research has shown that the highly subjective nature of the holistic approach, together with the reality of having to score many translations, may cause translations to receive diverging scores from different assessors (Waddington 2004; Garant 2009).

In an analytical approach assessors use a scoring protocol in which translation errors are categorized and weighted. Such a scoring protocol enables a detailed analysis of the translation performance and it can be used as a justification of the given scores. Again, it is fairly easy to imagine the incorporation of cultural competence in such an assessment protocol. The construct of cultural competence would simply be added to the list of assessment criteria that make up the assessment grid or the scoring protocol. Mistakes against the translation of culturemes or errors that are the result of a lack of phraseological competence can be categorized separately and the assessor can decide on their weight. The disadvantages of the analytical method are its time-consuming nature and the fact that studies have demonstrated that applying an analytical approach to assessment is no guarantee of an objective or reliable assessment (Eyckmans et al. 2009; Eyckmans et al. 2016). Not only is there the problem of disagreement between assessors on the typology or weight of a mistake; the analytical method does not allow to control the degree of difficulty of a ST (Waddington 2001; Anckaert et al. 2008; Eyckmans et al. 2009). In the same vein, deciding on the typology or weight of a culturally inaccurate or poor translation choice could be cumbersome and this would undermine the assessment's reliability.

Both the holistic and the analytical approaches are criterion-referenced assessment methods, which means that the assessors base their scores on pre-established criteria. These criteria – whether exemplified in a scoring protocol in the analytical approach or presumed by the evaluator in the holistic approach – are essentially subjective. The subjective nature of the assessment of translation competence is inevitable because of the nature of human judgement, and arguably desirable, but the problem is that this subjectivity makes the assessment susceptible to reliability errors.

As a way of dealing with the inherent subjectivity of criterion-referenced approaches, norm-referenced assessment has been developed in the realm of language testing. In norm-referenced approaches an individual's performance is determined in relation to the performance of others on the same measure. The primary advantage of norm-referenced tests is that their scores are based on item analysis. Calculating item difficulty and item discrimination not only provides the test developer with indispensable empirical data about how individual items and whole tests are performing in real test situations; it also allows test reliability to be calculated directly, which means that the inevitable margin of error that is the result of human judgement can be quantified and controlled.

3.3.2 The Calibration of Dichotomous Items method

To our knowledge, the only norm-referenced method that has been proposed for the assessment of translations is the Calibration of Dichotomous Items (CDI) method (Eyckmans et al. 2009). In this method the well-known 'item' concept of traditional language-testing theory is transferred to the domain of translation assessment. In a pre-test phase the performance of a representative sample of the student population is used in order to identify text segments that have so-called 'discriminating power'. Every element of the text that contributes to the measurement of differences in translation ability acquires the 'item' status. Only these items inform the scores in the actual translation test. As in language testing, the norm-referenced method presupposes a dichotomous approach: a translated text segment is either acceptable or not (i.e. correct or not), hence the name 'CDI method'. There is no weighing of mistakes (or bonuses) against other alternatives. This does not imply that there is only one appropriate translation for a text segment. Rather, one or more evaluators decide whether alternatives are acceptable or not for each translated segment. The different steps that lead to the calibration of items and tests – pre-testing, establishing discrimination power and estimating the test reliability– allow standardized tests of translation to be constructed across languages (see Eyckmans et al. 2009).

In view of the fact that cultural competence in translation manifests itself at different levels (morphological, syntactic, lexical, discoursal features of texts), and that the sub-components of translation ability are more or less inextricably linked in actual performances, the CDI method seems well equipped to account for the dimension of cultural competence in a translation performance. Similar to that in the holistic and analytical approach, the CDI assessor's task will be to move flexibly from considerations of a linguistic nature to considerations of cultural transfer in order to determine which translation choices are appropriate (and therefore acceptable). However, the advantage of the CDI method is that this necessary element of human appraisal is enveloped in a psychometrically sound methodology that enables the reliability of each translation test to be checked, thus bestowing a much-desired level of objectivity on the assessment of translation competence. Among the total number of items with discriminatory power derived from the CDI method during the pre-test phase of the assessment, the test developer can identify those that involve cultural competence. In this categorization process, it is up to the test developer to decide whether to use a broad or a narrow definition of cultural competence (for example, whether to include instances of unidiomatic language usage in the category of cultural competence). This means that when the actual test is administered, the test developer not only knows how many items fall under the construct 'cultural competence', but he or she can also calculate their contribution to the global test score. Because of the implementation of the 'item-concept' from language testing, cultural competence can be measured in proportion to the other challenges set by the text (since not all text types contain cultural references to the same extent for example).

Thanks to the norm-referenced approach, it becomes possible to determine the degree to which a particular text taps into cultural competence. If desired, the items that measure facets of cultural competence can be further categorized. To follow Nord's (1988) four main types of translation problem, for instance, pragmatic translation mistakes (e.g. culture-bound terms, references to time and place, proper names) can be distinguished from intercultural translation mistakes (e.g. measuring conventions, text-typological conventions), interlingual translation mistakes (e.g. differences in the use of vocabulary and syntax), and text-specific translation problems (e.g. alliteration, puns, rhetorical features and metaphors).

The challenges with respect to cultural knowledge that a text represents also depend on the SLs and TLs at hand. Cultural knowledge or typical phrases that pose difficulties for translators of a certain linguistic and cultural background may be child's play for translators of another linguistic and cultural heritage. Therefore, the actual extent to which the construct of cultural competence intervenes in the translation assessment of any text (or language combination) is hard to predict and can be ascertained only retrospectively. We illustrate this by means of an example: a text that contains cultural references might yield a different distribution of (cultural) items with discriminating power, depending on the characteristics of the group of translation students. Items that involve the translation of terms such as 'tax poll' or 'cream tea' in a translation of an English ST might prove discriminating in an English–French translation but not in an English–Dutch translation. It is precisely the interaction between a particular group of translation students with a particular text that will determine which text segments contribute to the measurement of translation competence. In fact, the only way to differentiate between the different sub-competences in an actual translation is by logging the translation solutions and translation errors that result from the translation from SL to TL by a representative population and to calibrate them as items. When these items are known, the test developer or translator can categorize them according whichever taxonomy they prefer in order to arrive at a profile of the text and the sub-competences it taps into for a particular population of translation students.

In short, the contribution of the CDI method lies in the empirical investigation of competence: through the identification of items that discriminate between weak, mediocre and strong student translators, it becomes possible to assemble a list of translation errors (i.e. items) that is representative of the types of challenge that a particular translation presents for translators of a specific mother tongue. As a next step, this list of items or translation errors/bonuses can be analysed: each mistake or bonus can be traced back to the sub-competence (or combinations of sub-competences) it presumes and can be related to the underlying translation models (PACTE, EMT, TRANSCERT).

A disadvantage of the CDI method is that it is inclusive of every possible sub-competence of translation ability only in so far as the interaction of a particular text with a particular population gives rise to the demonstration of this sub-competence. But in this respect it is no different from the holistic or analytical approach. However, the fact that flaws inherent in the text choice (e.g. a lack of calibrated items because of a mismatch between the students' translation competence and the level of difficulty of the text) will be exposed by the item analysis can be considered an important asset of the method.

4. Conclusion

In the first part of this chapter, the construct of cultural competence within TS was characterized as a rightful concern for translation scholars whose proposed models of translation competence all share the view that translation requires making contextually and culturally adequate lexical and syntactic choices. After describing three authoritative models of translation competence, the close link between linguistic and cultural competence was investigated. It was argued that, next to culturemes, multiword combinations can be considered as indices of socio-cultural competence, and that phraseological knowledge therefore needs to be included in definitions of the construct cultural competence. Student translators should realize that, since language expresses and embodies cultural reality, a language contains a wide array of cultural deposits in vocabulary, grammar and forms of address. Translation courses would benefit from a strong focus on various aspects of source and target cultures in order to increase students' awareness of the prevalence of culture in several aspects of the texts at both a conceptual and a linguistic level.

In the second part of this chapter, the range of sub-competences of translation competence as a whole that have been put forward in the literature were listed, and it was observed that they are almost never measured separately in current translation assessment practice. With reference to the measurement of cultural competence, few assessment tools have been developed and even fewer have been reported in translation journals. Of the proposed methods and approaches, none relates the assessment of translation performance to the described competence models in a principled way. It was argued that although cultural competence can be measured in a decontextualized way (by tapping into the cultural knowledge of translators by means of tests or by gauging their propensity for dealing with cultural differences), it seems more ecologically valid to assess cultural competence as part of text translation.

Holistic as well as analytic approaches can be used in order to assess the dimension of cultural competence when it is incorporated in a global textual analysis of the translation product. However, a norm-referenced approach seems ideally suited to putting cultural competence on a par with all other sub-competences of translation ability. In the proposed CDI method, the assessment of the sub-component 'cultural competence' will be based on a consideration of the performance on the entire text. This is important because in actual performances sub-components of translation ability are more or less inextricable, and the quality of a translation originates in the interaction of a particular text with a particular translator. Moreover, the use of the CDI method will make it possible to gauge the relative weight of cultural aspects in any given text for translators with any particular L1 background.

References

Anckaert, Philippe, Eyckmans, June & Segers, Winibert. 2008. Pour une évaluation normative de la compétence de traduction. *International Journal of Applied Linguistics* 155: 53–76.

Angelelli, Claudia. 2009. Using a rubric to assess translation ability. Defining the construct. In Claudia Angelelli & Holly Jacobson (eds) *Testing and assessment in translation and interpreting*. Amsterdam/Philadelphia: John Benjamins, 13–47.

Arango-Keith, Fanny & Koby, Geoffrey S. 2003. Translator training evaluation and the needs of industry quality training. In Brian James Bear & Geoffrey S Koby (eds) *Beyond the ivory tower: Rethinking translation pedagogy*. Amsterdam/Philadelphia: John Benjamins, 117–135.

Bachman, Lyle F. 1990. *Fundamental considerations in language testing*. Oxford: Oxford University Press.

Bahumaid, Showqi. 2010. Investigating cultural competence in English–Arabic translator training programs. *Meta* 55(3): 569–588.

Bassnett, Susan. 1991. *Translation studies* (Rev ed). London/New York: Routledge.

Beeby, Allison. 2000. Choosing an empirical-experimental model for investigating translation competence: the PACTE model. In Maeve Olohan (ed) *Intercultural faultlines. Research models in Translation Studies I: Textual and cognitive aspects.* Manchester: St Jerome, 43–55.

Bell, Roger T. 1991. *Translation and translating.* London: Longman.

Budin, Gerhard, Krajcso, Zita & Lommel, Arle. 2013. The TransCert project: Ensuring that transnational translator certification meets stakeholder needs. *Translation and Interpreting* 5(1): 143–155.

Butler, Christopher S. 2005. Formulaic language: An overview with particular reference to the cross-linguistic perspective. In Christopher S Butler (ed) *The dynamics of language use.* Amsterdam/Philadelphia: John Benjamins, 221–242.

Campbell, Stuart J. 1991. Towards a model of translation competence. *Meta* 36(2): 329–343.

Colson, Jean-Pierre. 2008. Cross-linguistic phraseological studies: An overview. In Sylviane Granger & Fanny Meunier (eds) *Phraseology. An interdisciplinary perspective.* Amsterdam/Philadelphia: John Benjamins, 117–135.

Dinçkan, Yesim. 2010. Culture-bound collocations in bestsellers: A study of their translations from English into Turkish. *Meta* 55(3): 456–473.

Durrant, Philip & Schmitt, Norbert. 2009. To what extent do native and non-native writers make use of collocations? *International Review of Applied Linguistics* 47: 157–177.

EMT expert group. 2009. *Competences for professional translators and experts in multilingual and multimedia communication.* <https://ec.europa.eu/info/sites/info/files/emt_competences_translators_en.pdf > (accessed 18 September 2017).

Erman, Britt & Warren, Beatrice. 2000. The idiom principle and the open choice principle. *Text* 20: 87–120.

European Certification and Qualification Association (ECQA). <http://www.ecqa.org> (accessed 18 September 2017).

Even-Zohar, Itamar. 1979. Polysystem theory. *Poetics Today* 1: 1–2.

Eyckmans, June, Anckaert, Philippe & Segers, Winibert. 2009. The perks of norm-referenced translation evaluation. In Claudia Angelelli & Holly Jacobson (eds) *Testing and assessment in translation and interpreting.* Amsterdam/Philadelphia: John Benjamins, 73–93.

Eyckmans, June, Segers, Winibert & Anckaert, Philippe. 2012. Translation assessment methodology and the prospects of European collaboration. In Dina Tsagari & Czepes Ildiko (eds) *Collaboration in language testing and assessment.* Frankfurt am Main: Peter Lang, 171–184.

Eyckmans, June, Anckaert, Philippe & Segers, Winibert. 2016. Translation and interpretation skills. In Dina Tsagari & Jayanti Banerjee (eds) *Handbook of second language assessment.* Boston/Berlin: Walter de Gruyter, 219–235.

Fantini, Alvino E. 2009. Assessing intercultural competence. Issues and tools. In Darla K Deardorff (ed) *The Sage handbook of intercultural competence.* London: Sage Publications, 457–476.

Foster, Pauline. 2001. Rules and routines: A consideration of their role in task-based language production of native and non-native speakers. In Martin Bygate (ed) *Researching pedagogic tasks: Second language learning, teaching, and testing.* London: Longman, 75–93.

Garant, Mikel. 2009. A case for holistic translation assessment. *AFinLA-e Soveltavan kielitieteentutkimuksia* 1: 5–17.

González Davies, Maria & Scott-Tennent, Christopher. 2005. A problem-solving and student-centred approach to the translation of cultural references. *Meta* 50(1): 160–179.

Göpferich, Susanne & Jääskelainen, Riitta. 2009. Process research into the development of translation competence: Where are we, and where do we need to go? *Across Languages and Cultures* 10(2): 169–191.

Granger, Sylviane. 1998. Prefabricated patterns in advanced EFL writing: collocations and formulae. In Anthony Paul Cowie (ed) *Phraseology: Theory, analysis and applications.* Oxford: Oxford University Press, 145–160.

Hewson, Lance & Martin, Jacky. 1991. *Redefining translation. The variational approach.* London/New York: Routledge.

House, Juliana. 2006. Text and context in translation. *Journal of Pragmatics* 38: 338–358.

ISO 17100. 2015. Translation Services-Requirements for Translation Services. Technical Committee ISO/TC37, 2015.

Katan, David. 2004. *Translating cultures: An introduction for translators, interpreters and mediators.* Manchester: St Jerome.

Kiraly, Donald C. 1995. *Pathways to translation. Pedagogy and process.* Kent: Kent State University Press.

Kroeber, Alfred L & Kluckhohn, Clyde. 1952. *Cultures: A critical review of concepts and definitions.* Cambridge, MA: Harvard University Press.

Laufer, Batia & Girsai, Nany. 2008. Form-focused instruction in second language vocabulary learning: A case for contrastive analysis and translation. *Applied Linguistics* 29: 694–716.

Li, Jie & Schmitt, Norbert. 2010. The development of collocation use in academic texts by advanced L2 learners: A multiple case study approach. In David Wood (ed) *Perspectives on formulaic language: acquisition and communication.* New York: Continuum, 22–46.

Malmkjær, Kirsten. 2009. What is translation competence? *Revue française de linguistique appliquée* 14(1): 121–134.

Meyer, Meinert. 1991. Developing transcultural competence: Case studies of advanced language learners. In Dieter Buttjes & Michael Byram (eds) *Mediating languages and cultures. Towards an intercultural theory of foreign language education.* Clevedon: Multilingual Matters, 136–158.

Millar, Neil. 2010. The processing of malformed formulaic language. *Applied Linguistics* 32: 129–148.

Nesselhauf, Nadia. 2005. *Collocations in a learner corpus.* Amsterdam/Philadelphia:

John Benjamins.

Neubert, Albrecht. 2000. Competence in language, in languages, and in translation. In Christina Schäffner & Joan Adab Beverly (eds) *Developing translation competence*. Amsterdam/Philadelphia: John Benjamins, 3–18.

Newmark, Peter. 1981. *Approaches to translation*. New York: Prentice Hall.

Nida, Eugene A. 1964. *Toward a Science of Translating*. Leiden: Brill.

Nida, Eugene A & Taber, Charles R. 1969. *The Theory and Practice of Translation*. Leiden: Brill.

Nida, Eugene A. 1994. Translation: possible and impossible. *Turjuman* 3(2): 147–163.

Nord, Christiane. 1988. *Textanalyse und Übersetzen*. Heidelberg: Groos.

Olalla-Soler, Christian. 2015. An experimental study into the acquisition of cultural competence in translator training: Research design and methodological issues. *Translation & Interpreting* 7(1): 86–110.

PACTE. 2000. Acquiring translation competence: hypotheses and methodological problems in a research project. In Allison Beeby, Doris Ensinger & Marisa Presas (eds) *Investigating translation*. Amsterdam/Philadelphia: John Benjamins, 99–106.

PACTE. 2005. Investigating translation competence: Conceptual and methodological issues. *Meta* 50(2): 609–619.

Park, Kyung-Eun, Shin, Keun-Hye & Kim, Ki-Sun. 2015. Research on limitations of indirect literary translation and aspects of cultural vocabulary translation. *Neohelicon* 42(2): 603–621.

Pawley, Andrew & Syder, Frances. 1983. Two puzzles for linguistic theory: Nativelike selection and nativelike fluency. In Jack C Richards & Richard W Schmidt (eds) *Language and communication*. London: Longman, 191–226.

Peraldi, Sandrine. 2014. TransCert: Trans-European voluntary certification for translators. *Bulletin du CRATIL* 13. <http://www.lebulletin ducratil.fr/ index.php/fr/transcert-trans-european-voluntary-certification-for-translators - sandrine-peraldi> (accessed 18 September 2017).

Pym, Anthony. 1991. A definition of translational competence, applied to the teaching of translation. In Miladen Jovanovic (ed) *Translation: A creative profession. Proceedings of the 12th World Congress of FIT*. Belgrade: Prevodilac, 541–546.

Schäffner, Christina & Beverly, Joan Adab (eds). 2000. *Developing translation competence*. Amsterdam/Philadelphia: John Benjamins.

Schmitt, Norbert (ed). 2004. *Formulaic sequences: Acquisition, processing and use*. Amsterdam/Philadelphia: John Benjamins.

Shreve, Gregory M. 1997. Cognition and the evolution of translation competence. In Joseph H Danks, Geoffrey M Shreve, Stephan B Fountain & Michael McBeath (eds) *Cognitive processes in translation and interpreting*. Thousand Oaks: Sage Publications, 120–136.

Skandera, Paul. 2007. *Phraseology and Culture in English*. Berlin/New York: Mouton de Gruyter.

Snell-Hornby, Mary. 1988. *Translation studies: An integrated approach.* Amsterdam/Philadelphia: John Benjamins.

Stubbs, Michael. 2001. *Words and phrases: Corpus studies of lexical semantics.* Oxford, Malden, MA: Blackwell.

Vermeer, Hans J. 1983. Translation theory and linguistics. In Pauli Roinila, Riyva Orfanos & Sonja Tirkkonen-Condit (eds) *Näkökohtia käänämisen tutkimuksesta.* Joensuu: University of Joensuu, 1–10.

Waddington, Christopher. 2001. Different methods of evaluating student translations: The question of validity. *Meta* 46(2): 311–325.

Waddington, Christopher. 2004. Should student translations be assessed holistically or through error analysis? *Lebende Sprachen* 49(1): 28–35.

Wierzbicka, Anna. 2001. Australian culture and Australian English: A response to William Ramsom. *Australian Journal of Linguistics* 21(2): 195–214.

Williams, Raymond. 1976. *Keywords: a vocabulary of culture and society.* London: Fontana.

Wray, Alison. 2002. *Formulaic language and the lexicon.* Cambridge: Cambridge University Press.

Yamashita, Junko & Jiang, Nan. 2010. L1 influence on the acquisition of L2 collocations: Japanese ESL users and EFL learners acquiring English collocations. *TESOL Quarterly* 44(4): 647–668.

ALEXANDRA ROSIERS

Ghent University

How Does a Study-Abroad Experience Contribute to the Intercultural Competence of Student Translators?

Abstract

The importance of intercultural competence as a key skill for translators has been stressed by several influential models of translation competence (e.g. PACTE 2005; EMT expert group 2009). Successful translators today are required to communicate successfully among different linguistic-cultural communities (Kiraly 2000). Translator training should therefore incorporate the development of intercultural competence. One strategy is to encourage students to take part in an Erasmus exchange programme. In some translation and interpreting programmes, this semester abroad is even mandatory. In this chapter, I report on a study using the Multicultural Personality Questionnaire (MPQ-SF; Van der Zee et al. 2013) to gauge student translators' level of intercultural competence before and after an Erasmus exchange programme. Within this socio-psychological approach to measuring an individual's intercultural competence (or 'multicultural effectiveness', as it is called in the model), five personality dimensions are identified: cultural empathy, social initiative, flexibility, open-mindedness and emotional stability. Apart from reporting on the contribution of a study-abroad experience to the development of translator students' intercultural competence, didactic implications of the findings for the teaching of translator competence are also explored.

Keywords: intercultural competence, multicultural effectiveness, student translators, study abroad

1. Introduction

In order to become a proficient translator, students need to develop a wide range of competences. Although the most obvious and essential skill is language competence, in itself it is insufficient for an individual to become an accomplished translator. Besides heuristic and technical skills, one of the crucial competences is cultural knowledge. This is where many student translators struggle, even at an advanced stage of their translator training:

interpreting and translating cultural-specific items remains one of their major challenges.

Cultural references and 'culturemes'[1] might pose problems for student translators at different levels. First, these student translators might not recognize a particular cultural reference as such, which could result in their rendering a vague or incorrect translation. Another potential problem is that the student translator recognizes the cultural reference but does not know how to correctly transfer it to the target language (TL). This obstacle might be caused by insufficient source-culture knowledge when the cultural reference is recognized but not fully understood; it could also be the result of a lack of target-culture knowledge, for instance when the student translator understands the meaning of the cultural reference but is unable to provide an appropriate equivalent in the TL. Both might lead to a vague translation or the omission of the item. In order to produce an accurate target text (TT), a broad knowledge of their own and the foreign culture is of course indispensable to translators: only then can effective communication take place. As Olk (2009) states, translators need to try to explain one culture in terms of the other. In this respect, the translator takes on the role of cultural mediator.

Katan (2009: 89–90) visualizes this process of cultural mediation in a 'logical levels table' in which each level or frame is accompanied by the contexts of culture and the situations that need to be considered. More specifically, the table (see Appendix I) lists the potential differences in the text and the potential differences between cultures. The frames include environment, behaviour, strategies, values/beliefs, identity and role, and mission in society. These levels and their potential pitfalls for intercultural communication illustrate how vast the remit of cultural differences is.

One could argue that the more translators know about the ways of the world, the better translators they become. Castellano (1988, quoted in Baker 1991: 4) argues that one becomes effective as a translator only at 30 and one starts to be in one's prime only at 50. She maintains that the ideal trajectory in the meantime is to gain as much life and cultural experience as possible before embarking on translator training. Regrettably, for many aspiring translators this is not a realistic option. As radical as Castellano's

[1] Culturemes are defined as 'formalized, socially and juridically embedded phenomena existing in a particular form or function in one particular culture' (see Vermeer 1983; Nord 1997).

point of view might seem, though, it does demonstrate just how challenging the task for student translators is. They need to acquire as much cultural knowledge as they can in a limited amount of time.

Fortunately, translation training programmes tend to be well aware of the importance of cultural knowledge and intercultural competence, that is, the ability to communicate effectively with people from other cultures. Consequently, within most translation curricula one will find a range of courses that pay attention to cultural elements. Students are familiarized with cultural customs, political and judicial systems, institutions and so forth. During translation classes these themes are put into context and students are made aware of the necessary transitions from source culture to target culture. In recent years, however, more and more emphasis has been placed on a different, possibly more effective way of acquiring intercultural competence: the study-abroad experience. Given that international mobility for all higher-education programmes has been promoted and financed by the European Union (EU) since 1987, the trend of spending a term abroad is noticeable far beyond the field of translation training. According to the Bologna Declaration, a minimum of 20 per cent of higher-education students should have participated in a study-abroad programme by 2020 (Simons et al. 2013: 1). The Erasmus exchange programme is one of the best-known study-abroad programmes within the EU. Although these programmes are seen as the ideal platform for students to acquire all the skills necessary to function in a globalized world (Simons et al. 2013), few quantitative studies have used pre–post measures to gauge the actual impact of a study-abroad experience or international sojourn on students' intercultural competence (ICC), as mentioned by Rexeisen et al. (2008).

In this chapter, I examine the influence of a mandatory exchange programme[2] on the development of ICC among student translators. At the Department of Translation, Interpreting and Communication at Ghent University, all the students spend the first term of their third BA year abroad. Their ICC is measured before and after the study-abroad period by way of a socio-psychological approach. More specifically, a self-report questionnaire – the Multicultural Personality Questionnaire Short Form (MPQ-SF) (Van der Zee et al. 2013) is used to gauge the effect of the study-abroad experience.

[2] The mandatory study-abroad period is considered a catalyst for the use of acquired knowledge about the language area, the cultural background, the language in itself and intercultural communication in general.

The following sections first provide an overview of the three main translation competence models and how ICC is incorporated in those models. Next, the socio-psychological approach to measuring ICC is presented. It includes a literature review of relevant studies using the MPQ-SF. Subsequently, the methodology of the case study is explained, followed by the results. I then discuss the most important findings of this case study and I focus on the didactic implications for training translation competence.

2. Translation competence models

From the early origins of TS, scholars and practitioners alike have acknowledged that being a competent translator goes beyond mere – albeit essential – linguistic requirements. Translation competence entails a large skillset that is not necessarily mastered by all bilinguals (PACTE 2005). Nowadays, translation competence is seen as a synthesis of sub-competences, all of which contribute to the goal of being able to produce an accurate translation. Although many scholars have described translation competence (Neubert 2000; Schäffner 2000) in terms of a number of required skills, only a handful of models have been proposed. One of those models is that of the Procès d'Adquisició de la Competència Traductora i Avaluació (PACTE) Group.[3] This research group defines translation competence as "an underlying system of knowledge and skills needed to be able to translate" (PACTE 2000: 100) and their model (2003; 2005; 2007) identifies five sub-competences alongside a number of psycho-physiological components, which are illustrated in Figure 1.

[3] One of the main interests of this research group is empirical and experimental-based research into translation competence.

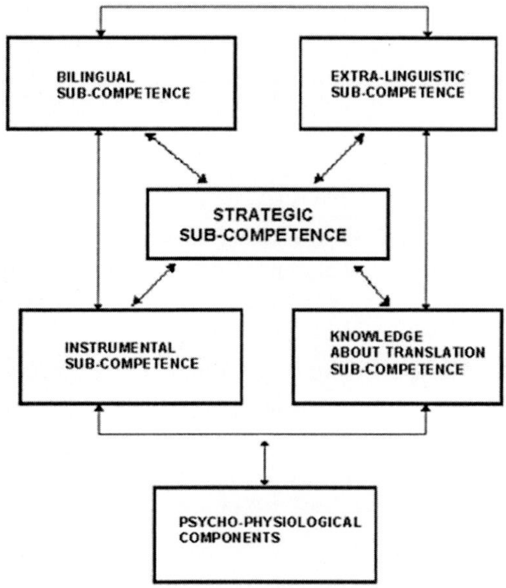

Figure 1: Translation Competence Model
(PACTE Group 2003; 2005: 610; 2007: 331)

The five sub-competences are considered to be interrelated and each sub-competence refers to a specific underlying skillset that the translator needs to master:

- The *bilingual* sub-competence includes pragmatic, socio-linguistic, textual and lexical–grammatical knowledge in each language.
- The *extra-linguistic* sub-competence consists of encyclopaedic, thematic and bicultural knowledge, which is used here as an alternative term for ICC.
- The *translation* knowledge sub-competence represents knowledge of translation processes, methods and procedures.
- The *instrumental* sub-competence refers to heuristic skills and knowledge of information technology.
- The *strategic* sub-competence, which is considered the most important, is responsible for solving problems and safeguarding the efficiency of processes.
- Finally, the *psycho-physiological components* refer to cognitive, behavioural and psychomotor mechanisms (PACTE 2005).

The PACTE model served as a source of inspiration for Göpferich's (2007: 21) model of translation competence. Her model (see Figure 2) differentiates between six sub-competences:

1. communicative competence;
2. domain competence;
3. tools and research competence;
4. strategic competence (all four of which correspond to the PACTE's group bilingual sub-competence, extra-linguistic sub-competence, instrumental sub-competence, and strategic sub-competence respectively);
5. translation routine activation competence in Göpferich's (2007) model encompasses the knowledge and the abilities to automate certain translation processes;
6. the final element, psychomotor competence, refers to the psychomotor abilities required for reading and writing.

In this model, the intercultural element is incorporated in communicative competence, which comprises knowledge about situation-specific conventions in the respective cultures.

This is slightly different from the PACTE model, which places ICC within the extra-linguistic sub-competence (i.e. bicultural knowledge). In other words, some scholars consider ICC to be integrated in language knowledge whereas others regard it as outside of the linguistic skillset.

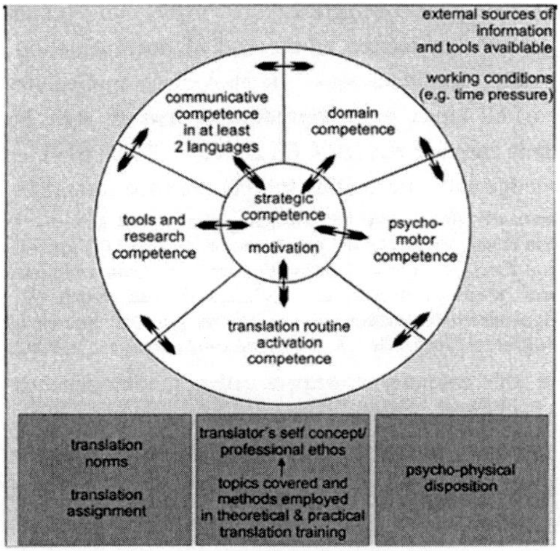

Figure 2: Göpferich's (2007: 21) Translation Competence Model

Besides the PACTE model and Göpferich's model, another authoritative model on translation competence is that of the EMT[4] expert group (2009). As can be seen in Figure 3, this model is made up of five interdependent sub-competences revolving around the sixth central competence: translation service provision. This competence refers to business-like skills such as customer management. The EMT model is particularly interesting for the purposes of our study since it explicitly includes intercultural competence.

[4] The group is mainly concerned with improving the quality of translation training in the EU (European Commission).

Figure 3: EMT Model of Translation Competence
(EMT expert group 2009: 4)

The EMT expert group (2009) provides a detailed description of what they consider to be the necessary competences for translators. In the context of this chapter, I elaborate on the skills underlying ICC. These skills are divided into sociolinguistic and textual dimensions:

- In the sociolinguistic dimension, the main focus is on the recognition of culture-specific elements such as rules of interaction, language variation and register.
- The textual dimension portrays these competences as the practical skills needed to produce an accurate translation. These skills range from broad textual insight such as being able to analyse the macro-structure of a document to very specific skills such as being able to understand presuppositions and allusions in a document or being able to compare cultural elements in a text.

This two-dimensional construct exemplifies how ICC trickles through different levels of the translation task, from understanding source texts (ST) to producing TTs.

3. ICC in translation training

The inclusion of ICC in each of these three models on translation competence – albeit less explicitly in the first two models – and the exhaustive description in the EMT model clearly indicate that ICC forms an inherent part of translation competence. Consequently, student translators are expected to become attuned to cultural differences. According to Bennett (1998), intercultural sensitivity is developed through different stages, ultimately – and in a best-case scenario – resulting in a bicultural personality. In translator training programmes, this sensitivity is mainly stimulated through an instruction-based approach. A bird's-eye view of Master's programmes across Europe suggests that the inclusion of cultural elements and realia in the student translator's curriculum is deemed important. In addition, classes on Cultural History, Literature, Economics and Politics – that is, area studies or *Landeskunde* – increase students' knowledge of a TL's community and culture.

An approach to raising cultural awareness that could be considered much more hands-on is a study-abroad experience or international sojourn. This alternative method of familiarizing students with the customs and characteristics of another culture is gaining in popularity, not only with students but also with educational institutions. Although it demands a large commitment from students, in return it provides ample room for personal growth. Indeed, as the Erasmus Impact Study mentions, the experience is said to bolster students' intercultural competence and to effect a fundamental personal change (European Commission 2014: 62). A number of studies seem to confirm this hypothesis (Brown 2009) and show that even short-term programmes can have a positive impact on intercultural development (Engle & Engle 2004; Anderson et al. 2006). Yet, more quantitative studies using pre–post measures to gauge changes in ICC are called for.

With respect to measuring ICC, a wide array of assessment tools exists in the field of personality and communication research (for an overview, see Fantini 2006). These assessment tools are traditionally self-report questionnaires. For this present study, I opted for the MPQ-SF (Van der Zee et al. 2013), because it is tailored towards specific traits that contribute to ICC – or 'multicultural effectiveness', as it is termed in the model. The questionnaire was originally developed as a selection tool for predicting the level of adjustment to a new cultural environment in expatriates, regardless of how long they stay in that new environment. It targets five personality dimensions that are discussed in the following section.

4. Multicultural effectiveness

Multicultural effectiveness implies that you are likely to adjust well to a new cultural environment and that you are able to deal with people from different cultural backgrounds in a way that enables you to maintain a feeling of wellbeing (Van der Zee & Van Oudenhoven 2000). This adaptability consists of five underlying personality dimensions: cultural empathy, social initiative, emotional stability, flexibility and open-mindedness. These are described below:

- *Cultural empathy* refers to "the ability to empathize with the feelings, thoughts, and behaviours of members from different cultural groups" (ibid.: 294).
- The *social initiative* dimension is defined as "a tendency to approach social situations in an active way and to take initiatives" (Van Oudenhoven & Van der Zee 2002: 681). This dimension is closely related to the extraversion personality trait.
- *Emotional stability* is defined in the MPQ model as "the tendency to remain calm in stressful situations versus a tendency to show strong emotional reactions under stressful circumstances" (Van der Zee & Van Oudenhoven 2000: 294). It can therefore be regarded as a stress-buffering trait.
- The *flexibility* dimension refers to "a capability to adjust oneself cognitively and behaviourally to new situations" (ibid.: 305).
- Finally, *open-mindedness* implies "an open and unprejudiced attitude towards different groups and towards different cultural norms and values" (ibid.: 296).

Combined, these five dimensions predict the degree of adjustment and individual experiences in multicultural settings. Over the past decade, the questionnaire has been used repeatedly with international employees and students. The next section provides an overview of relevant studies using the MPQ.

As the original intention of the MPQ was to predict how well people would cope within a new cultural environment, most studies have investigated the predictive validity of the tool among international employees or students. Quite a few studies have demonstrated that the MPQ's five personality dimensions are indeed predictive of adjustment to a multicultural environment (see Ponterotto & Fietzer 2014). To my knowledge, only two studies have used the MPQ as a tool to assess the effect of an international sojourn on students' multicultural effectiveness. Stronkhorst (2005) evaluated changes in students' MPQ scores after an internship or a study programme abroad. The author found that the 33 students who participated in an international three- to four-month internship in horticulture and agriculture obtained higher scores on the cultural empathy and open-mindedness dimensions after their return. In the study-abroad group consisting of 48 students who had enrolled on an international BA degree programme preparing them for international careers in the fields of communication, public administration, marketing or export, only the scores of the flexibility dimension had increased. Stronkhorst (2005) argues that the time these students had spent abroad (i.e. 3–4 months) might have been too short a period to induce major changes in their personality.

Recently, Schartner (2016) conducted a large-scale longitudinal study with 223 international postgraduate students who spent nine months at a British university. She reported a number of surprising results. First, a significant drop in the scores for cultural empathy and open-mindedness was observed. Schartner explains this unexpected result in the light of high student expectations at the onset of the programme, which might have left the students more vulnerable to disappointment, resulting in lower post-exchange scores for cultural empathy and open-mindedness (10). Furthermore, there was an increase in emotional stability, which again was unexpected, because the change to a new environment is generally regarded to be a very stressful period. Schartner seeks an explanation for this in the timing of the pre-test, which was administered two weeks into the exchange programme. As the first weeks of an international sojourn are considered to be particularly stressful (Young & Schartner 2014), the students might have reported very low emotional stability at that time, which then dissipated as they grew more accustomed to their new situation. No change was reported in the students' flexibility and social initiative.

Both Stronkhorst's and Schartner's studies consisted of heterogeneous participant groups in terms of study programme and country of origin. This seems particularly relevant in Schartner's study as her participants were incoming students originating from five different continents, even if a large proportion of them came from Asia. In contrast, the present study focuses on a homogenous group of students in terms of age, nationality and educational background, all the participants having been enrolled on the same translation training programme. This study aims to relate the personality traits as described in the MPQ to the specific skills required of translators within the umbrella term of ICC.

If we return to the EMT model of translation competence and, more specifically, to the skills underlying ICC, they can be traced back to a few key personality traits such as empathy, flexibility and open-mindedness. Several of the competences subsumed under ICC in the model seem to be related to the ability to empathize with the behaviours – verbal and non-verbal – of the TL community. This so-called 'cultural empathy' is implied in all three competences within the sociolinguistic dimension of EMT's ICC. These three competences are:

- the ability to recognise function and meaning in different language variations;
- the understanding of a community's rules for interaction, both verbally and non-verbally, and
- the ability to adopt a situation-appropriate register (EMT expert group 2009: 6).

This need for cultural empathy can also be found at a textual level as translators are required to recognize and identify cultural-specific elements and references as well as understand the less explicit elements of a text such as allusions and stereotypes (ibid.: 6). Within this textual dimension of ICC, other necessary traits can also be discerned. For example, in order to recognize comprehension problems and produce adequate strategies for these problems, translators need problem-solving skills. A characteristic of good problem-solvers is their tendency to have an open-minded personality (Harlim & Belski 2013). This leads us to presume that open-minded translators might be better equipped to solve translation problems. In addition, culturally competent translators need to be flexible in dealing with different cultures and styles of interaction, particularly as they are expected to "bring together and compare cultural elements and methods of composition" (EMT expert group 2009: 6). This present study establishes whether the development of these personality traits and the consequent boost in ICC that this development implies is actually enhanced by a study-abroad experience.

5. The study

5.1 Research questions

In the light of the conflicting research results discussed earlier in the literature review, I consider this contribution to be an exploratory study. The main research questions are:

- How does a study-abroad experience contribute to student translators' multicultural effectiveness as measured by the total MPQ score?
- How does a study-abroad experience contribute to student translators' cultural empathy, social initiative, emotional stability, open-mindedness and flexibility as measured by the MPQ's subscales?

5.2 Participants

The participants (n = 35) are students enrolled at the Department of Translation, Interpreting and Communication of Ghent University in Belgium. On condition that they have obtained sufficient European Credit Transfer and Accumulation System (ECTS) credits, students are expected to take part in a mandatory Erasmus exchange programme in their third BA year in Applied Language Studies. This BA degree prepares students for one of three Master's (Translation, Interpreting or Multilingual Communication) and has a strong focus on translation competences, with translation classes from and into the foreign languages in each of the BA years. All the students take classes in Dutch (their mother tongue) and two foreign languages. They can combine French, English or German with Spanish, Italian, Russian, Turkish, French, English or German. For their study-abroad term, students have to select a university in a country where one of the languages they study is the native tongue. Depending on the destination, they leave in September or October and return in December, January or February. The participants in this study are predominantly female, there being only four male students out of a total of 35 participants, which is a fair representation of the male-to-female ratio in the BA degree programme in Applied Language Studies at Ghent University. The students' ages from the outset of the study ranged between 19 and 22.

5.3 Procedure

In mid-September, an initial number of 130 students leaving on an international sojourn were sent an email inviting them to participate in this study. They were asked to fill in the MPQ via a web-based address. Although the participants were not able to fill in the questionnaire anonymously, as pre-exchange results needed to be linked to post-exchange results, they were informed that the information they provided would be treated confidentially and would be made anonymous after analysis. They were also informed that it would take approximately five to ten minutes to fill in the questionnaire. A total of 40 students responded and completed the on-line questionnaire. These 40 students were contacted again in February, when all the students had returned to their home university in Ghent, and were asked to fill in the questionnaire once again. Out of these 40 students, 35 returned the completed questionnaire.

5.4 Instruments

As mentioned earlier, Van der Zee and Van Oudenhoven (2000; 2001) developed the MPQ as a selection tool for international employees. The original instrument consists of 91 items that gauge five personality dimensions which together are shown to reflect a person's ability to adjust to a new cultural environment, which they term 'multicultural effectiveness'. In the present study, a reduced form of the MPQ was used that had been developed by Van der Zee et al. in 2013 in order to increase the instrument's utility as a research tool. The MPQ-SF measures the same five personality dimensions (cultural empathy, social initiative, open-mindedness, flexibility and emotional stability), correlates highly with the original version of the MPQ and has sufficient psychometric properties (Van der Zee et al. 2013). However, the MPQ-SF consists of only 40 items, which considerably reduces the time needed to fill in the questionnaire. Each dimension or scale comprises eight items. Respondents indicate whether or not the items are applicable to them on a five-point Likert scale ranging from 'totally not applicable' (1) to 'completely applicable' (5). Scale scores are obtained by adding up the values of the corresponding items. The total MPQ score is the sum of the five scale scores. The on-line questionnaire form (see Appendix II) requires participants to provide an answer for each statement, as a result of which no missing values could occur, and all scale scores as well as the total score could be computed.

5.5 Results

All the statistical analyses were performed using SPSS software version 21 (SPSS Inc, Chicago, IL). The normality of the data was confirmed using descriptive statistics. A paired samples t-test was conducted to compare the students' scores on the five MPQ dimensions before (T1) and after (T2) their study-abroad experience. Table 1 provides the descriptive group statistics. The results of the paired samples t-test are presented in Table 2.

	Time	Minimum	Maximum	Mean	Std. Deviation
CE	1	20	38	31.77	3.851
	2	21	38	31.77	4.538
F	1	10	32	19.86	5.918
	2	10	37	20.83	6.004
SI	1	14	35	25.00	6.198
	2	13	36	25.37	5.688
O	1	18	32	25.49	3.649
	2	18	36	26.71	3.339
ES	1	11	31	21.51	4.925
	2	12	31	22.31	5.318
Total	1	100	152	123.63	14.520
	2	98	168	127.00	15.639

Note: CE = Cultural Empathy, F = Flexibility, SI = Social Initiative, O = Open-mindedness, ES = Emotional Stability; 1 = pre, 2 = post

Table 1: Participants' MPQ-SF scale scores before and after the SA experience (n = 35)

The paired samples t-test shows no significant difference in cultural empathy (t(34) = .000, p = 1.000; *d* = 0) before and after the study-abroad experience. The t-test did not show a significant difference in social initiative (t(34) = –.804, p = .427; *d* = 0.06) between T1 and T2 either. The emotional stability level also remains stable (t(34) = –1.447, p = .157, *d* = 0.16). As regards flexibility, there is a significant increase at T2 compared to T1 (t(34) = –2.205, p = .034), although the effect size is rather small *(d* = 0.16). The level of open-mindedness also increases significantly (t(34) = –2.479, p = .018; *d* = 0.35). Finally, the t-test shows a significant increase in the total score on the MPQ after a study-abroad experience (t(34) = –3.175, p = .003; *d* = 0.23).

	Mean	Std. Deviation	Std. Error Mean	95% Confidence Interval of the Difference		T	df	Sig. (2-tailed)
				Lower	Upper			
CE	.000	2.275	.385	-.782	.782	.000	34	1.000
F	-.971	2.606	.441	-1.867	-.076	-2.205	34	.034
SI	-.371	2.734	.452	-1.311	.568	-.804	34	.427
O	-1.229	2.931	.496	-2.236	-.222	-2.479	34	.018
ES	-.800	3.270	.553	-1.923	.323	-1.447	34	.157
Total	-3.371	6.283	1.062	-5.530	-1.213	-3.175	34	.003

Note: CE = Cultural Empathy, F = Flexibility, SI = Social Initiative, O = Open-mindedness, ES = Emotional Stability

Table 2: Changes in personality after the S experience

6. Discussion

The comparison between student translators' personality traits before and after a study-abroad experience revealed a number of significant changes. The students' overall level of multicultural effectiveness increased considerably. According to Van der Zee & Van Oudenhoven (2000; 2001), this means that these students have boosted their ability to adjust to other cultures and to feel at home in these cultures. As the total MPQ score is the aggregate score of the five underlying dimensions, this increase in multicultural effectiveness is caused by increased figures on one or more of the personality subscales.

First of all, the student translators' scores show that they became more open-minded during their stay abroad. It makes intuitive sense that the experience of living among people from different cultural communities will result in a more open and unprejudiced attitude towards different cultural norms and values. This finding is in keeping with previous research on the effects of international sojourns (Brown 2009). It also corroborates Dewaele and Van Oudenhoven's (2009) study in which London teenagers who were born abroad displayed a greater open-mindedness, as measured by the MPQ, than teenagers who were born in the United Kingdom.

Secondly, a higher level of flexibility was reported after the study-abroad experience. This is consistent with Stronkhorst's (2005) study, where exchange students reported higher levels of flexibility after a stay abroad of 3–4 months. Residing in a foreign country often means adapting to different ways of living. Students need to be flexible if they want to become well-adjusted members of this new community and feel at ease in their new environment. It should be noted that the new community is not limited to the host community; it also refers to the Erasmus community in which students reside, which generally comprises many different nationalities.

Despite a slight increase in the mean score of the social initiative scale, the difference did not prove to be significant. Although it is often expected that spending a term abroad will encourage students to become more extroverted (Bender, Wright & Lopatto 2009), previous research using the MPQ did not establish this. In this respect, this result underpins the findings of Stronkhorst (2005) and Schartner (2016), who both found social initiative to have remained unchanged after a study-abroad period. Social initiative is closely related to extroversion, a higher-order personality trait, which is considered to be a fairly stable trait across the lifespan (Hampson & Goldberg 2006). This could account for the lack of change in this and previous studies. Similarly, the level of emotional stability in student translators was not affected by the study-abroad experience. Emotional stability is regarded a stress-buffering trait and there is some evidence for its relative stability (Li 2006). Again, the stability of this scale seems to be in keeping with general psychological research.

Finally, no change in the scores for cultural empathy was observed. A likely explanation for this finding is the high pre-test score of the participants. Their mean score of 31.77 on a maximum score of 40 is substantially higher than the scores for the other dimensions (see table 1). This high pre-test score leaves little room for improvement during the study-abroad experience. It is reasonable to assume that translation classes and other modules with a prominent focus on cultural aspects had already contributed to the high level of cultural empathy in these students.

7. Limitations and future research

At a methodological level, this study is subject to some limitations. First, the number of participants (n = 35) is relatively low, which makes it difficult to generalize the findings. Secondly, there might be a large variability in the amount of contact students actually had with members of the TL community. Much depends on a number of individual circumstances, such as students' housing; after all, the students' contact with the foreign-language community will vary greatly. The extend of this contact will depend on whether they live in an international student house with other students from the same home university or whether they live in an environment surrounded by members from the new cultural community, for instance a host family. Also, most students went to Western European countries that may not be culturally all that different from their home community. It is plausible that a study-abroad experience in a country that is culturally very remote from one's own culture could result in other personality changes. Furthermore, the exact timing of the testing could not be controlled for. When students were contacted in mid-September, some had already arrived in the country of destination, whereas others had not yet left their home country. The same constraint applies to the post-test, which was administered in February while some students had already returned home in December. It is difficult to estimate to what extent certain effects of the study-abroad experience might have faded or changed two months after the students' return. A final limitation of the study is the lack of a control group. Because all the students are required to participate in the study-abroad experience, we could not compare their changes in ICC to a matched group of students who did not engage in an international sojourn.

Despite these limitations, this study can be a valuable contribution to the field of ICC as well as to TS as it goes beyond the bounds of TS. Moreover, additional studies investigating ICC in a pre–post design are necessary. Particularly interesting in this research design is that the students did not volunteer to take part in the exchange programme. On the contrary, the study-abroad experience is a compulsory module in the regular curriculum of these student translators. Several studies have shown that students who participate voluntarily in a study-abroad experience obtain higher scores even prior to the exchange than those who do not wish to go on an international sojourn (Simons et al. 2013; Leong 2007). This might have led to a rosier picture in previous studies with regard to the advantages of study-abroad experiences, because students might have a pre-existing high level of intercultural sensitivity or competence. The fact that the students in this study were not able to choose whether to study abroad or not provides a much fairer representation of the student population. But, having said this, we have to acknowledge that students enrolled on a language course who know beforehand that an international exchange is included in the programme are likely to be positively predisposed to such an immersion opportunity. However, we do believe the homogeneity of the student population in terms of age, gender, nationality and educational background contributes to the validity of this study.

A question that remains unanswered, though, is whether these changes in ICC are long-lasting. Further research should aim to establish whether the acquired level of ICC remains stable six months or one year after the study-abroad experience. With reference to translation competence, the relation between the MPQ scales and actual translation performance remains to be investigated. Although an increase in multicultural effectiveness is a favourable outcome in itself, the ultimate goal is to improve students' translation competence. A follow-up study should verify whether students with increased multicultural effectiveness obtain higher scores for translation tasks in general and for the translation of culture-specific items in particular.

8. Conclusion

Based on the findings of this study, the inclusion of a mandatory study-abroad period seems to be a beneficial addition to the student translators' curriculum as a complementary way of raising intercultural awareness in students. More specifically, the study-abroad experience seems to increase students' flexibility and open-mindedness. A recent model of translation competence by Kiraly and Piotrowska (2014) offers the potential to include a study-abroad experience in the translation curriculum. They propose a dynamic approach to translator competence that includes the dimension of time. The main premise is that learning is a holistic, unlimited and lifelong process that should include practice at different levels. Within the TS curriculum, Kiraly and Piotrowska place great emphasis on the application of basic skills to realistic situations. These range from project work to internship and workplace experience, which evolve at the same pace as the learner's level of expertise. In the same vein, the study-abroad experience could be included in such a model at an early stage of translator training. The study-abroad experience can be viewed as the application of cultural skills to realistic settings. These cultural skills were first acquired through instruction, which could make translator students the 'perfect' candidates for a study-abroad experience. In fact, recent research has shown that intercultural instruction in combination with the experience of living abroad could be the ideal basis for developing ICC in international students (Young & Schartner 2014). As such, student translators seem to be perfectly equipped to reap all the benefits a study-abroad experience has to offer.

However, if the inclusion of a study-abroad experience is beyond the means of the student or the training institution, there are other avenues to pursue. Students from different countries could join forces and work together on translations or revisions via chat rooms or email correspondence. This form of collaborative learning could form the basis for meaningful encounters between students of different cultural backgrounds and it could broaden their cultural horizons. Closer to home, the impact of native-speaker lecturers – or lecturers who have considerable experience of living abroad – should not be underestimated. For many students this is the first and most immediate connection with the target-language culture, and therefore these lecturers could contribute greatly to students' ICC both in and outside the classroom as they provide a continuous stream of authentic target-culture input.

References

Anderson, Philip, Lawton, Leigh, Rexeisen, Richard & Hubbard, Ann. 2006. Short-term study abroad and intercultural sensitivity: A pilot study. *International Journal of Intercultural Relations* 30(4): 457–469.

Baker, Mona. 1991. *In other words. A coursebook on translation.* London/New York: Routledge.

Bender, Carol, Wright, David & Lopatto, David. 2009. Students' self-reported changes in intercultural knowledge and competence associated with three undergraduate science experiences. *Frontiers: The Interdisciplinary Journal of Study Abroad* 18: 307–322.

Bennett, Milton J. 1998. Intercultural communication: A current perspective. In Milton J Bennett (ed) *Basic concepts of intercultural communication: Selected readings.* Yarmouth, ME: Intercultural Press, 1–34.

Brown, Lorraine. 2009. The transformative power of the international sojourn: An ethnographic study of the international student experience. *Annals of Tourism Research* 36(3): 502–521.

Castellano, Lanna. 1988. Get rich – but slow. In Catriona Picken (ed) *ITI Conference 2: Translators and interpreters mean business.* London: Aslib, 132–135.

Dewaele, Jean-Marc & Van Oudenhoven, Jan Pieter. 2009. The effect of multilingualism/multiculturalism on personality: No gain without pain for third culture kids? *International Journal of Multilingualism* 6(4): 443–459.

EMT expert group. 2009. Competences for professional translators, experts in multilingual and multimedia communication, Brussels, European Commission. <https://ec.europa.eu/info/sites/info/files/emt_competences_translators_en.pdf f> (accessed 18 September 2017).

Engle, Lilli & Engle, John. 2004. Assessing language acquisition and intercultural sensitivity development in relation to study abroad program design. *Frontiers: The Interdisciplinary Journal of Study Abroad* X (Fall): 219–236.

European Commission. Nd. European Master's in translation. <https://ec.europa.eu/info/european-masters-translation-emt_en> (acces-sed 18 September 2017).

European Commission. 2014. The Erasmus impact study. Effect of mobility on the skills and employability of students and the internationalisation of higher education institutions. <http://ec.europa.eu/dgs/education_culture/repository/education/library/study/2014/erasmus-impact_en.pdf> (acces-sed 18 September 2017)

Fantini, Alvino. 2006. Assessment tools of intercultural communicative competence. <http://digitalcollections.sit.edu/worldlearning_publications/1/> (accessed 18 September 2017).

Göpferich, Susanne. 2007. Towards a model of translation competence and its acquisition: the longitudinal study TransComp. In Susanne Göpferich, Arnt Lykke Jakobsen & Inger M Mees (eds) *Behind the mind: Method, models and results in translation process research.* Copenhagen: Samfundslitteratur, 11–38.

Hampson, Sarah E & Goldberg, Lewis R. 2006. A first large-cohort study of personality-trait stability over the 40 years between elementary school and midlife. *Journal of Personality and Social Psychology* 91(4): 763–779.

Harlim, Jennifer & Belski, Iouri. 2013. Long-term innovative problem-solving skills: Redefining problem solving. *International Journal of Engineering Education* 29(2): 280–290.

Katan, David. 2009. Translation as intercultural communication. In Jeremy Munday (ed) *The Routledge companion to Translation Studies.* London/New York: Routledge, 74–92.

Kiraly, Don. 2000. *A social constructivist approach to translator education: Empowerment from theory to practice.* Manchester: St Jerome.

Kiraly, Don & Piotrowska, Maria. 2014. Towards an emergent curriculum development model for the European graduate placement scheme. In Pixel [sic] (ed) *Conference proceedings: The future of education.* Padova: libreriauniversitaria.it, 374–378.

Leong, Chan-Hoong. 2007. Predictive validity of the Multicultural Personality Questionnaire: A longitudinal study on the socio-psychological adaptation of Asian undergraduates who took part in a study-abroad program. *International Journal of Intercultural Relations* 31(5): 545–559.

Li, Ming-hui. 2006. Actively cope with stressful situations: Is active coping a trait or a match between traits and stressful situations? *Vistas Online.* <http://www.counseling.org/docs/default-source/vistas/actively-cope-with-stressful-situations-is-active-coping-a-trait-or-a-match-between-traits-and-stressful-situations.pdf?sfvrsn=10> (accessed 18 September 2017).

Neubert, Albrecht. 2000. Competences in language, in languages and in translation. In Christina Schäffner & Beverly Adab (eds) *Developing translation competence.* Amsterdam/Philadelphia: John Benjamins, 3–18.

Nord, Christiane. 1997. *Translating as a Purposeful Activity: Functionalist Approaches Explained.* Manchester: St Jerome.

Olk, Harald. 2009. Translation, cultural knowledge and intercultural competence. *Journal of Intercultural Communication* 20. <http://www.immi.se/intercultural/nr20/olk.htm> (accessed 18 September 2017).

PACTE group. Nd. Grup Procès d'Adquisició de la Competència Traductora i Avaluació. <http://grupsderecerca.uab.cat/pacte/en> (accessed 18 September 2017).

PACTE group. 2000. Acquiring translation competence: Hypotheses and methodological problems in a research project. In Allison Beeby, Dorsi Ensinger & Marisa Presas (eds) *Investigating translation.* Amsterdam/Philadelphia: John Benjamins, 99–106.

PACTE group. 2003. Building a translation competence model. In Fabio Alves (ed) *Triangulating translation: Perspectives in process oriented research.* Amsterdam/Philadelphia: John Benjamins, 43–66.

PACTE group. 2005. Investigating translation competence: Conceptual and methodological issues. *Meta* 50(2): 609–619.

PACTE group. 2007. Une recherche empirique expérimentale sur la compétence de traduction. In Daniel Gouadec (ed) *Quelle qualification pour les traducteurs?* Paris: La Maison du Dictionnaire, 95–116.

Ponterotto, Joseph & Fietzer, Alexander. 2014. Multiculturalism and adjustment. In Verónica Benet-Martinez & Ying-Yi Hong (eds) *The Oxford handbook of multicultural identity.* Oxford: Oxford University Press, 300–331.

Rexeisen, Richard J, Anderson, Philip H, Lawton, Leigh & Hubbard, Ann C. 2008. Study abroad and intercultural development: A longitudinal study. *The Interdisciplinary Journal of Study Abroad* 4: 1–20.

Schäffner, Christina. 2000. Running before walking? Designing a translation programme at undergraduate level. In Christian Schäffner & Beverly Adab (eds) *Developing translation competence.* Amsterdam/Philadelphia: John Benjamins, 143–156.

Schartner, Alina. 2016. The effect of study abroad on intercultural competence: A longitudinal case study of international postgraduate students at a British university. *Journal of Multilingual and Multicultural Development* 37(4): 402–418.

Simons, Joke, Korevaar, Koen, Hindrix, Karine & Joris, Michael. 2013. Naar het buitenland: een ervaring voor elke student of het resultaat van een vooraf-gaande selectie?! In Joke Simons (ed) *Handboek interculturele competentie*. Brussels: Politeia: 1–20.

Stronkhorst, Robert. 2005. Learning outcomes of international mobility at two Dutch institutions of higher education. *Journal of Studies in International Education* 9(4): 292–315.

Van der Zee, Karen & Van Oudenhoven, Jan Pieter. 2000. The Multicultural Personality Questionnaire: A multidimensional instrument of multicultural effectiveness. *European Journal of Personality* 14: 291–309.

Van der Zee, Karen & Van Oudenhoven, Jan Pieter. 2001. The Multicultural Personality Questionnaire: Reliability and validity of self- and other ratings of multicultural effectiveness. *Journal of Research in Personality* 35(3): 278–288.

Van der Zee, Karen, Van Oudenhoven, Jan Pieter, Ponterotto, Joseph G & Fietzer, Alexander. 2013. Multicultural Personality Questionnaire: Development of a short form. *Journal of Personality Assessment* 95: 118–124.

Van Oudenhoven, Jan Pieter & Van der Zee, Karen. 2002. Predicting multicultural effectiveness of international students: The Multicultural Personality Questionnaire. *International Journal of Intercultural Relations* 26: 679–694.

Vermeer, Hans J. 1983. Translation theory and linguistics. In Pauli Roinila, Riyva Orfanos & Sonja Tirkkonen-Condit (eds) *Näkökohtia käänämisen tutkimuksesta*. Joensuu: University of Joensuu, 1–10.

Young, Tony J & Schartner, Alina. 2014. The effects of cross-cultural communication education on international students' adjustment and adaptation. *Journal of Multilingual and Multicultural Development* 35(6): 547–562.

Appendix I: Logical Levels Table (Katan 2009)

LEVEL	What is going on?	Potential differences to be accounted for in the text	Potential differences to be accounted for between cultures
Environment	Where and when is this 'going on'? In what context of situation?	Lexicogrammatical resources, genre, intertextual links, specialized language	Physical, political, social environment: period, people, setting, artefacts; culturemes, encyclopaedic knowledge, allusions, culture bumps
Behaviour	What is it that is 'going on'? What is to be translated?	Semantics: visible text, locution, cohesion	Visible action/descriptions: (non) verbal behaviour, proxemics
Strategies	How are these things 'going on'? How is it to be translated?	Pragmatics: illocutionary intent/force, register, organization of discourse, house rules, individual style, coherence	Communication preferences: development of ideas. Spoken/written styles, habits, customs; norms, appropriacy, rules; linguaculture
Values/Beliefs	Why are these things 'going on'? What is the purpose of the translation	Intentions: message, hidden message, assumptions, presuppositions	The hierarchy of preferred value-orientations: Beliefs about identity and about what is 'right', 'standard' or 'normal
Identity	Who is involved in this 'going on'? - Original author - Reader(ships) - Commissioner - Translator as copier/manipulator	Actors in the text: personalities, animated subjects	National, ethnic, gender, religious, class, role; individual personality and cultural provenance(s)
Role, mission in society	Is this 'going on' coherent with my role/mission and the relevant social forces? How do I need to act with regard to the social forces?	Text as agent of change or status quo: esteem, ethics (of actors), long-term perlocutionary effects	The social forces. Power issues: hegemonies, ideologies, moral issues, professional issues

Appendix II: The Multicultural Personality Questionnaire – Short Form (van der Zee et al. 2013)

MPQ Short Form-40

To what extent do the following statements apply to you?

(Please indicate the answer that is most applicable to you)

		totally not applicable	hardly applicable	moderately applicable	largely applicable	completely applicable
1	Sympathizes with others	1	2	3	4	5
2	Tries out various approaches	1	2	3	4	5
3	Finds it difficult to make contacts	1	2	3	4	5
4	Is reserved	1	2	3	4	5
5	Likes routine	1	2	3	4	5
6	Sets others at ease	1	2	3	4	5
7	Takes the lead	1	2	3	4	5
8	Is often the driving force behind things	1	2	3	4	5
9	Is looking for new ways to attain his/her goal	1	2	3	4	5
10	Makes contacts easily	1	2	3	4	5
11	Keeps calm when things don't go well	1	2	3	4	5
12	Has a feeling for what is appropriate in a specific culture	1	2	3	4	5
13	Seeks contact with people from a different background	1	2	3	4	5
14	Has fixed habits	1	2	3	4	5
15	Likes to imagine solutions for problems	1	2	3	4	5
16	Is insecure	1	2	3	4	5
17	Wants to know exactly what will happen	1	2	3	4	5

		Totally not applicable	hardly applicable	moderately applicable	largely applicable	Completely applicable
18	Enjoys other people's stories	1	2	3	4	5
19	Starts a new life easily	1	2	3	4	5
20	Is under pressure	1	2	3	4	5
21	Gets upset easily	1	2	3	4	5
22	Leaves the initiative to others to make contacts	1	2	3	4	5
23	Pays attention to the emotions of others	1	2	3	4	5
24	Looks for regularity in life	1	2	3	4	5
25	Is nervous	1	2	3	4	5
26	Functions best in a familiar setting	1	2	3	4	5
27	Is a good listener	1	2	3	4	5
28	Works according to plan	1	2	3	4	5
29	Is inclined to speak out	1	2	3	4	5
30	Has a broad range of interests	1	2	3	4	5
31	Is apt to feel lonely	1	2	3	4	5
32	Enjoys getting to know others profoundly	1	2	3	4	5
33	Takes initiatives	1	2	3	4	5
34	Is not easily hurt	1	2	3	4	5
35	Works mostly according to a strict scheme	1	2	3	4	5
36	Notices when someone is in trouble	1	2	3	4	5
37	Senses when others get irritated	1	2	3	4	5
38	Worries	1	2	3	4	5
39	Works according to strict rules	1	2	3	4	5
40	Is a trendsetter in societal developments	1	2	3	4	5

List of Contributors

Julie Deconinck is Assistant Professor at the Department of Linguistics and Literary Studies of the Vrije Universiteit Brussel (VUB). She teaches a variety of English language and translation courses to students in the Applied Linguistics programme of the VUB. Her research interests include L2 vocabulary learning, language teaching, translation pedagogy, and, more recently, the social and cultural aspects of language learning and multilingualism in general.

June Eyckmans is Associate Professor at the Department of Translation, Interpreting and Communication of Ghent University where she teaches courses on Applied Linguistics. Her research interests centre on cognitive linguistic approaches to foreign language learning and on translation and interpreting studies, in particular the methodology of interpreting and translation assessment. She publishes on these subjects in internationally refereed journals and she currently supervises research projects on individual differences in translation studies, phraseology, study abroad, and L2 vocabulary acquisition. She sits on the board of Anéla, the Dutch Association of Applied Linguistics.

Philippe Humblé is Professor of Spanish Translation and Intercultural Communication at the Department of Linguistics and Literary Studies of the Vrije Universiteit Brussel (VUB). He studied Romance Philology at the KULeuven and holds a doctoral degree in bilingual lexicography (Universidade Federal de Santa Catarina/University of Birmingham). At the Universidade Federal de Santa Catarina (Brazil), he taught Spanish language and literature, bilingual lexicography, and the use of corpora for twenty-five years. He has published on translation studies, corpora studies, and intercultural relations in translation.

Ana Ibáñez Moreno is Associate Professor at the Faculty of Philology of the Spanish National University of Distance Education, UNED (Spain). She holds a PhD in English Linguistics. Her current research mainly focuses on the teaching and learning of foreign languages. She is an active member of the UNED-based research group ATLAS (Applying Technology to LAnguageS), and she is currently working with other colleagues on the development of a MALL (mobile assisted language learning) application based on audio description (AD) tasks.

Natalia Kaloh Vid is Associate Professor at the Department of Translation Studies, Faculty of Arts, University of Maribor, Slovenia. She holds a PhD in Translation Studies about the influence of ideology on literary translations, and a PhD in contemporary Russian literature. She has also published extensively on literary translations, the didactics of translation, re-translations, translations of culturally-specific elements, and translations of children's literature. She is the author of the books *Ideological Translations of Robert Burns's Poetry in Russia and in the Soviet Union* (2011) and *Sovietisms in English Translations of M. Bulgakov's The Master and Margarita* (2016).

Geoffrey S Koby is Professor of German and Translation Studies at Kent State University, where he lectures on translation quality assessment, translation theory, and professional commercial, legal, and financial translation. He is founding past president of the American Translation and Interpreting Studies Association (ATISA). He co-edited the 2016 *Monti* volume *Economic, Financial and Business Translation: from Theory to Training and Professional Practice* with Daniel Gallego Hernández and Verónica Román Mínguez, and is finalizing the *Linguistica Antverpiensia* volume *Translator Quality: Empirical Approaches to Assessment and Evaluation.* His main research interests are translation quality assessment and evaluation, as well as translation pedagogy.

Vlasta Kučiš is Associate Professor at the Department of Translation Studies, Faculty of Arts, University of Maribor, Slovenia. Her doctoral thesis focused on the social, political and ideological influences exerted on translators and translating as a profession. Her fields of research are translation and communication studies, intercultural communication, translation theory, and specialized translation. She is also the head of the international CEEPUS TRANS-network (TRANScultural Communication and TRANSlation), as well an organizer of several TRANS-summer academies and international conferences. She has experience in intercultural communication and foreign language adult education and is currently a member of the international scientific research group TransLaw and Babel's editorial board.

José Lambert is Emeritus Professor at KULeuven. He studied Romance Philology at KULeuven, and holds a PhD (1972) in Comparative Literature from that same university. He was a Visiting Professor at the University of Pennsylvania, New York University, University of Alberta, Facultés Notre-Dame de la Paix at Namur, among many others, before teaching in Brazil, at the Universidade Federal de Santa Catarina (2011-2015) and the Universidade Federal do Ceará (2015-). For over 40 years, he has played a key role in the institutionalization of Translation Studies, on which he has published widely. He is the co-founder (with Gideon Toury) of *Target, International Journal of Translation Studies.*

Natalia Naydenova is Associate Professor at the Philological Department of the Peoples' Friendship University of Russia, Moscow. Her research interests include language and identity as well as translation theory and translation teaching methods in a number of fields, from postcolonial literature to banking and finance. She is the author of the *Dictionary of Banking and Financial Terms: Russian – English – French – Spanish.* She has also worked as a translator and interpreter for several of the largest banks in Russia, and co-edited the volume *Littérature africaine et identité: un hommage à Chinua Achebe* (2013).

Kanavillil Rajagopalan is Professor Emeritus of Linguistics at the State University at Campinas (UNICAMP), Brazil, and a Senior Researcher at the National Council for Scientific and Technological Development (CNPq). He is currently involved in the postgraduate programmes of the

State University of the South-East of Bahia (UESB) and the Federal University of Tocantins (UFT), both in Brazil. He is one of the editors of the journal *WORD*. His main academic interests include philosophy of language, linguistic pragmatics, applied linguistics, English language teaching, and translation theory.

Alexandra Rosiers is a PhD student in Translation Studies at Ghent University. Her doctoral research focuses on a number of individual difference variables among translators, interpreters, and multilingual communicators. More specifically, she aims to establish whether personality differences (e.g. extraversion, flexibility and empathy) and cognitive differences (e.g. working memory and attention control) occur between translators, interpreters and multilingual communicators, both in professional and student populations. She is a member of the research group MULTIPLES at the department of Translation, Interpreting and Communication at Ghent University.

Arvi Sepp is Professor of German Literature at the University of Antwerp and Professor of German and Translation Studies at the Vrije Universiteit Brussel. His research interests centre on the translation of migration literature, twentieth-century German (Jewish) literature, autobiographical writing, and popular culture. The relation between ideology and aesthetics in German literature equally counts among his most important research foci. He is co-director of the Brussels-Ghent Centre for Literature in Translation/Centrum voor Literatuur in Vertaling (CLIV).

Helene Stengers is Assistant Professor of Spanish, Translation and Interpreting at the Vrije Universiteit Brussel. Her research interests lie in interpreting studies, applied comparative linguistics, cognitive linguistics, phraseology and foreign language acquisition – with a view to optimizing foreign language pedagogy as well as interpreter and translator training. She is the current coordinator of the Brussels Institute for Applied Linguistics (BIAL).

Elżbieta Tabakowska is Professor Emeritus at the Jagiellonian University of Kraków, Poland, and specializes in cognitive linguistics and translation studies. She founded the UNESCO Chair for Translation Studies and Intercultural Communication at the Jagiellonian University, and headed it between 2002 and 2012. As a practising interpreter and translator, she authored numerous published translations. Her own publications include seven monographs and over a hundred and fifty articles, published in Poland and abroad. Between 2007 – 2010 she was a member of a group of European Union experts appointed to develop standards for M.A. programmes in Translation Studies.

Anna Vermeulen is Associate Professor at the Department of Translation, Interpreting and Communication of the Faculty of Arts and Philosophy at Ghent University (Belgium). She holds a PhD in Spanish linguistics. Currently, her main focus of research is on the teaching of audiovisual translation. She is an active member of the Ghent-based research group GOLLD (Ghent on Language Learning and Didactics).

Jan Walravens is Professor of Translation and Culture in the Faculty of Letters, Translation and Communication of the Université Libre de Bruxelles. In addition, he works as an adviser for the Education Department of the City of Brussels (Centre for Methodology and Applied Pedagogy). As his research activities were initially focused on the teaching of Dutch as a foreign language, he remains actively engaged in reflective work on foreign and second language teaching. The main thrust of his academic work now concerns the comparative study of cultural identities and translation. He has served on several advisory boards for language and culture.

Catherine Way is Associate Professor of Translation at the University of Granada and leader of the AVANTI research group. She has co-edited several books, including the Proceedings of the 6th EST Conference. She is a member of the Editorial Boards of *Puentes* and *The Interpreter and Translator Trainer* (previously editor), and a member of the Advisory Boards of *Fachsprache*, *International Journal of Legal Discourse* and the series *Aprende a traducer,* amongst others. Her main research interests are legal translation, translator training, and action research. She has acted as an expert on legal translator training for the EU in the TRAFUT programme.

Judith Woodsworth is Professor of Translation Studies in the Department of French Studies at Concordia University. She has translated two novels, *Still Lives*, by Pierre Nepveu, and *Hutchison Street*, by Montreal novelist Abla Farhoud, to be released in March 2018. Most noted for *Translators through History* (with Jean Delisle), her monograph *Telling the Story of Translation: Writers Who Translate* was published in 2017 by Bloomsbury, and her edited volume *The Fictions of Translation* is forthcoming from Benjamins. She was founding president of the Canadian Association for Translation Studies. Her research has focused on French literature, literary translation, as well as translation theory and history.

Subject Index

accuracy 146, 152, 165, 178
acquisition 164, 214, 219
adaptation 58, 81, 188, 215
advertisement 81, 83, 92, 94, 194
ambiguity 16, 23, 197, 203
analytical 41, 55, 119, 169, 224–226, 228
ARDELE 135, 142–143, 146, 151, 153
assessment 26, 131, 159, 170, 179, 185, 202, 214, 220–221, 224–227, 229, 243
assignment 116, 119, 121, 123, 129, 131, 145, 203, 204, 210
ATA 185–187, 190–191, 194–195, 199–205, 209, 211
attitudes 18, 80, 82, 100, 160, 218, 223
audience 27, 81, 123, 138–139, 142, 145, 150, 152, 172, 191, 193
audiodescription 149–150, 152–168
awareness 15, 29, 61, 100–102, 104, 110, 136, 138, 146, 148, 152–153, 159–160, 163–164, 178, 186, 190, 215, 223, 228, 243, 253
behaviour 45, 82, 84, 110, 142, 165, 171, 178, 215, 218, 222, 236
business 18, 21, 32, 34–35, 58, 84, 100–106, 108, 111–112, 241
category 59, 66–67, 178, 187, 192, 196–197, 202–203, 226
CDI 225–226, 228–229
CEFR 136–137, 143
certification 185–187, 194, 199, 217, 221
CIC 163–165, 175–177, 179
cognition 31, 65–68
cognitive 47, 74, 83–84, 161, 223, 240
collaborative 166, 177, 254
conceptual 18–19, 24–25, 54, 59, 82, 166, 175, 188, 199, 228
corpus 29, 45, 153, 205, 220
creative writing 115, 123
creativity 23, 74, 81, 112, 123, 172
criteria 21, 81, 109, 186, 224, 225
Critical Discourse Analysis (CDA) 80, 82–85, 166–167, 175–176, 179

cross-cultural 39, 40, 55, 58, 67, 81, 99–102, 109–112, 116, 146–147, 188, 214–216
cross-cultural activity 39
cross-cultural awareness 110
cross-cultural competence 67, 100, 112, 188
cultural empathy 244–249, 251
cultural translation 56, 80, 95, 223
cultural turn 69, 99, 115, 160, 214
curriculum 21, 28, 243, 252–253
Descriptive Translation Studies (DTS) 16, 18, 20, 31, 33–35, 44–45, 47
dictionary 108, 121, 167, 170, 186, 190, 198
discourse 20, 21, 24–25, 30, 39–42, 57, 81, 83–84, 86, 100, 102, 105, 108, 137, 160–161, 166–169, 198, 218
discursive 57, 68, 105, 168–169
domestication 47, 58, 120, 122
European Credit Transfer and Accumulation System (ECTS) 143, 247
education 15, 20, 22–23, 32, 35, 41, 58, 70–71, 110, 136, 142, 237
educational 221, 243, 245, 253
effectiveness 223, 243–245, 247–248, 250, 253
empathy 159, 164–165, 175, 244–246, 251
equivalence 29, 57, 104, 106, 214
Erasmus 142–143, 237, 243, 247, 251
ethnocentric 216
ethnolinguistics 66
European Certification and Qualification Association 216–217
European Union 33, 218, 237
examination 179, 185–188, 190–191, 194–195, 197, 199, 202–205, 211, 217, 224
exercise 74, 84, 116–117, 120, 122–123, 131, 147, 223
experimental 144, 148, 238
expert 67, 216–217, 241–242, 246
explicit 17, 40, 43, 68, 85, 88, 126, 147, 152, 172, 215, 246
finance 101–104, 106, 112
flexibility 223, 244–249, 251, 253
FLL 136, 146
FLT 136, –137, 146
foreignization 47, 58, 120–121, 122
framework 20, 43, 46–48, 66, 85, 119, 143, 164, 170, 172–173, 179, 202, 216–217
gender 67, 69, 215, 253

genre 80
globalization 22, 26, 31, 33, 58–62, 73, 94
grader 186, 195–198, 202–203
grammar 47, 67–69, 73–74, 100, 106, 139, 228
heuristic 47, 222–223, 235, 239
holistic 224–226, 228, 253
homogeneity 19, 23, 253
hybridity 26, 116, 132
identity 33, 40, 43, 59, 68, 136, 138, 152, 215, 236
ideology 80–83, 95, 215
idiomatic 109, 139, 214, 218–219
immigrant 56, 125, 126
institutionalization 21, 23, 25, 29, 34
intercultural competence 67, 73, 136–137, 142, 159–160, 163, 188, 216, 237, 241, 243
Intercultural Studies 22, 39
interculturalism 116, 131
interlingual 54, 56, 62, 73, 85, 151, 227
international sojourn 237, 243, 245, 248, 252
internationalization 19, 21, 28, 29
internet 14, 19, 23–25, 166, 191, 195, 204–205
interpreting 25, 32–33, 41, 86, 117, 160, 172, 221, 236
ISO 139, 213, 216–217
ITU 139
legal 103, 121, 141, 162, 166, 167, 169, 171–173, 189, 194, 202
lexicon 47, 87, 218
literal 90, 116, 121, 146, 220
literary translation 14, 116–120, 131
manipulation 20, 44, 83
measurement 221–223, 226–227, 229
media 84, 95, 140
mediation 56, 66, 99–100, 236
mediator 65, 95, 99, 214, 236
medical 31–32
mentality 71, 86, 92
methodology 84, 103, 167, 174, 179, 186, 191, 222, 226, 238
mistranslation 74, 187, 193, 196–198, 202
misunderstanding 43, 187, 192–194, 202–203
mobility 24, 161, 164, 166, 237
module 101, 106, 112, 143, 252
motivation 144
Multicultural Personality Questionnaire (MPQ) 237–238, 243–244, 246–251, 253
multiculturalism 26, 116, 215
multilingual 116, 137, 217
multilingualism 20, 34

narrative 85, 123–124, 128, 142
networks 15, 20, 23, 35
norm 30, 100, 214, 225, 227, 229
normative 16, 32, 35, 44, 82
objectivity 140–141, 164–165, 226
omission 85, 187, 190, 198, 203, 220–221, 236
open-mindedness 223–249, 251, 253
PACTE 213, 217, 222, 224, 228, 238–241
paraphrase 199, 220
pattern 82, 173, 204, 218
performance 170, 189, 220, 222, 224–226, 229, 253
personality 85, 130, 136, 223, 243–244, 246, 248, 250–252
phraseology 218–220
practice 14–15, 26, 29, 41–42, 54–55, 57, 59–61, 66, 68, 86, 117, 119–120, 122, 128, 138, 140, 167, 169–170, 175, 191, 214, 221, 224, 229, 253
pragmatics 17, 81
praxis 40–42, 44–45, 120
professional translation 14, 185
proficiency 67, 69, 102, 143–144, 152, 190, 204
questionnaire 144–145, 151, 237, 243–244, 248
realia 66–68, 74, 243
reliability 195, 221, 225–226
rewriting 81, 131
rubric 67, 177–178
sensitivity 153, 215, 243, 253
skill 136, 186, 214, 218, 223, 235
Skopos theory 47, 83
sociolinguistics 68, 160, 217, 242, 246
sociology of translation 16
source text 57, 109, 123, 165, 190, 214, 216, 224
speaker 70, 72, 105–106, 138, 143, 146, 172, 192, 254
standardized 185, 191, 208, 226
storytelling 85, 116–117, 119–120, 122–123, 129
student translator 224, 236, 243
study abroad 253
stylistic 101, 104, 106, 108, 217
sub-competence 172, 214, 228, 239, 240
subjectivity 46, 141, 225
target text 47–48, 57, 116, 120, 161, 165, 190, 214, 216, 236
technical translation 121, 189
technology 41, 117, 162, 189, 200, 239
terminology 19–20, 25, 27, 100, 102–103, 117, 131, 162, 167, 169, 186, 189, 191–194, 197, 200, 202, 218

test 48, 107, 109–110, 112, 145, 221–223, 225– 227, 245, 249, 251–252
trainees 45, 159, 161–171, 173–179
training 15, 17–19, 21–23, 27–35, 39, 44–49, 68–69, 73, 80, 100–103, 106, 110, 116, 138, 153, 159, 160–167, 170–173, 175, 179, 188, 204, 217, 219, 221, 224, 236–238, 241–243, 246, 254
transcultural 83, 137, 215–216, 218
Trans-European Voluntary Certification for Translators 216
TRANSCERT 228
transfer 15, 55, 57, 87, 94, 104, 118, 214, 226, 236
translatability 29, 54, 214
translation ability 214, 217, 220, 226, 228–229
translation competence 46, 67–69, 213, 216–217, 220–222, 225–229, 238, 240–242, 246, 253
translation course 106, 116–119, 123, 131
translation market 14, 35
translation strategies 47, 122, 175, 215
Translation Studies (TS) 14–29, 31–35, 39–44, 65, 74, 79–80, 82, 84, 99, 115, 119, 136, 160, 161, 167, 170, 213–214, 216, 221–223, 228, 238, 252–253
translation training programme 246
translator competence 253
Translator Studies 31
translator training 46–47, 49, 159, 161, 164, 173
transposition 30, 66, 192
untranslatability 69, 74, 214
usage 123, 187, 190, 196–197, 203, 226
validity 221, 224, 244, 253
values 60, 75, 82, 84, 86, 88–89, 95, 116, 163, 217–218, 223, 236, 244, 248, 250
variation 90, 187, 205, 217, 242
voice 48–49, 105, 109, 125, 131, 139

Name Index

A

Al-Kharabsheh, Aladdin 189
Álvarez, Román 55, 83
Ammann, Margret 17, 19–20, 32

B

Bahumaid, Showqi 188–190, 202, 204, 219, 222–223
Baker, Mona 46, 67, 82, 236
Bargiella-Chiappini, Francesca 100
Bartmiński, Jerzy 66
Bassnett, Susan 14, 80, 99, 115, 160, 215
Bellos, David 122
Benecke, Bernd 138–139
Bennett, Milton J. 161, 243
Berry, Michael 42–44
Bhabha, Homi K. 3, 44, 59
Boone, Mary E. 171–172
Boye, Sarah 2–3
Brislin, Richard 40–41, 110
Byram, Michael 137, 160

C

Calzada Pérez, María 82–84
Cano, Ana Gregorio 163–164
Carbonell, Ovidio 56
Castellano, Lanna 236
Cooper, Frederick 61
Cronin, Michael 46
Cynrim, Andrea 161–165, 175–177, 179

D

Darbelnet, Jean 16, 30, 34
Dam-Jensen, Helle 167
Deleuze, Gilles 56
Dewaele, Jean-Marc 250
Dinçkan, Yesim 219–220
Dudley-Evans, Tony 100

E

Elsass, Peter 61
Even-Zohar, Itamar 14, 18, 30, 44, 215
Eysteinsson, Astradur 59–60

F

Fairclough, Norman 84, 167, 169
Fawcett, Paul 79
Fels, Deborah 135, 140
Flanagan, John 110
Frame, Alex 45

G

Gallagher, Hugh 58
Gambier, Yves 28–29, 67
Gee, James Paul 137
Gile, Daniel 13, 46–47
González Davies, Maria 45–46, 170
Göpferich, Susanne 217, 240–241
Grosch, Harald 161,
Guattari, Félix 56

H

Hague, Daryl R. 165–166
Hassel, Ursula 138
Hastrup, Kirsten 61
Hepp, Andreas 2
Heringer, Jürgen 80
Hermans, Theo 14, 44
Hietaranta, Perrti 188–189, 205
Hofstede, Geert 104, 111
Holliday, Adrian 137, 140, 152
Holmes, James S. 13–26, 28–29, 31
House, Juliana 160–161, 219
Hua, Zhu 99
Hyks, Veronica 139, 141

J

Jakobson, Roman 24, 30

K

Katan, David 2, 160, 187–188, 219–220, 236
Kiraly, Don 100, 166, 216, 235, 253
Klemensiewicz, Jerzy 70
Kramsch, Claire 3

L

Lantolf, James 138
Lauring, Jakob 100
Laviosa, Sara 45
Leenen, Wolf Rainer 161
Lefevere, André 14, 80–82, 99, 115, 160
Leistyna, Pepi 41,
Levý, Jiřý 17, 24, 170
Lipska, Ewa 66

M

Major, André 121
Malmkjær, Kirsten 46, 217
Meyer, Meinert 3, 216
Mounin, Georges 16, 30
Schmitt, Peter A. 189
Schmitt, Norbert 219

N

Newmark, Peter 32, 214
Nida, Eugene 15–17, 30, 80, 161, 214–215
Nord, Christiane 80–81, 83, 216, 227, 236

O

Ochs, Elinor 188–189
Olalla-Soler, Christian 223
Olk, Harald 236
Orero, Pilar 135, 138, 140–141
Ortiz, Fernando 60

P

Pavlenko, Aneta 138
Piekkari, Rebecca 32, 34
Pilch, Jerzy 69, 71–72
Piotrowska, Maria 253
Prunč, Erich 81–82
Pujol, Joaquim 135, 141
Pym, Anthony 13, 30, 45, 222

R

Reiß, Katharina 83
Robinson, Douglas 57, 171
Rosman, Abraham 55
Rubel, Paula 55

S

Sanz Moreno, Raquel 142
Schäffner, Christina 80, 83, 217, 222, 238
Schartner, Alina 245, 251, 254
Scott-Tennent, Christopher 170, 215
Séguinot, Candace 170, 188
Shlesinger, Miriam 45
Silverstein, Michael 54
Simeoni, Daniel 45
Simon, Sherry 59, 116, 118, 131
Snell-Hornby, Mary 13–14, 22, 40–41, 80, 214–215
Snowden, David J. 171–172
Spivak, Gayatri Chakravorty 59
St John, Maggie Jo 100
Stronkhorst, Robert 245, 251

T

Thomas, Alexander 161
Toury, Gideon 13–20, 23, 29, 44, 170, 190, 263
Tymoczko, Maria 3, 56, 81

U

Udo, John Patrick 135, 140

V

Van den Dop, Tamar 143
Van der Mark, Ingrid L. 164–165
Van der Zee, Karen 235, 237, 243–244, 248, 250
Van Dijk, Teun A. 79, 83–85
Van Oudenhoven, Jan Pieter 244, 248, 250
Venuti, Lawrence 28, 54, 57–58
Vermeer, Hans J. 79–80, 83, 220
Vidal, María Carmen-África 55, 83
Vinay, Jean-Paul 16, 30, 34
Vreeke, Gert J. 164–165
Vygotski, Lev 138

W

Warren, Austin 17
Weissbort, Daniel 59–60
Wellek, René 17
Wierzbicka, Anna 66, 69, 71, 104, 218
Wilss, Wolfram 44, 170
Witte, Heidrun 161

Z

Zhu, Honglin 164

Repräsentation – Transformation
representation – transformation
représentation – transformation
Translating across Cultures and Societies
hrsg. von Ao. Univ. Prof. Dr. Michaela Wolf (Universität Graz)

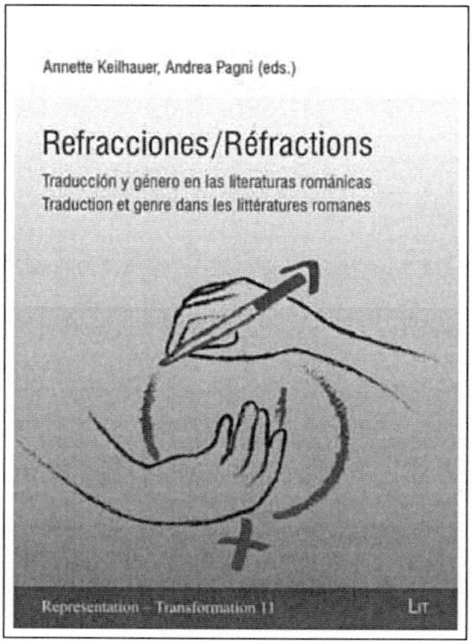

Annette Keilhauer; Andrea Pagni (Eds./Hg.)
Refracciones. Réfractions
Traducción y género en las literaturas románicas. Traduction et genre dans les littératures romanes
Este libro ofrece un aporte innovador a la reflexión sobre la incidencia del género en los procesos traductivos en distintos momentos de la historia de la traducción literaria en Francia, España y las Américas. El concepto de "refracción" remite a la interacción del género con otros factores sociales y culturales a lo largo del proceso de traducción. Desde la historia cultural, la traductología, los estudios literarios y la lingüística se focalizan las condiciones históricas de la actividad traductora, las estrategias editoriales y el acto mismo de la traducción literaria en su interacción con el género.
Bd. 11, 2017, 250 S., 29,90 €, br., ISBN 978-3-643-50696-2

Abdel-Wahab Khalifa (Ed.)
Translators Have Their Say?
To address the idea of agency in translation is to highlight the interplay of power and ideology: what gets translated or not and why a text is translated is mainly a matter of exercising power or reflecting authority. The contributions of this volume aim to serve as an attempt to understand the complex nature of agency in terms of its relation to agents of translation; the role of translatorial agents and the way they exercise their agency in (de)constructing narratives of power and identity; and the influence of translatorial agency on the various processes of translation and hence on the final translation product as well.
Translation and the Power of Agency
Bd. 10, 2014, 208 S., 29,90 €, br., ISBN 978-3-643-90551-2

LIT Verlag Berlin – Münster – Wien – Zürich – London
Auslieferung Deutschland / Österreich / Schweiz: siehe Impressumsseite

Philipp Hofeneder
Die mehrsprachige Ukraine
Übersetzungspolitik in der Sowjetunion von 1917 bis 1991
Bd. 9, 2013, 216 S., 24,90 €, br., ISBN 978-3-643-50544-6

Heike van Lawick; Brigitte E. Jirku (Hg.)
Übersetzen als Performanz
Translation und Translationswissenschaft in performativem Licht
Bd. 8, 2012, 320 S., 29,90 €, br., ISBN 978-3-643-50451-7

Beatrice Fischer; Matilde Nisbeth Jensen (Eds.)
Translation and the reconfiguration of power relations
Revisiting role and context of translation and interpreting
Bd. 7, 2012, 296 S., 29,90 €, br., ISBN 978-3-643-90283-2

Claudia Kainz; Erich Prunč; Rafael Schögler (Eds.)
Modelling the Field of Community Interpreting
Questions of methodology in research and training
Bd. 6, 2011, 344 S., 24,90 €, br., ISBN 978-3-643-50177-6

Norbert Bachleitner; Michaela Wolf (Hg.)
Streifzüge im translatorischen Feld
Zur Soziologie der literarischen Übersetzung im deutschsprachigen Raum
Bd. 5, 2010, 376 S., 34,90 €, br., ISBN 978-3-643-50245-2

Denise Merkle; Carol O'Sullivan; Luc van Doorslaer; Michaela Wolf (Eds.)
The Power of the Pen
Translation and censorship in 19th century Europe
Bd. 4, 2010, 304 S., 24,90 €, br., ISBN 978-3-643-50176-9

Gisella M. Vorderobermeier; Michaela Wolf (Hg.)
„Meine Sprache grenzt mich ab ... "
Transkulturalität und kulturelle Übersetzung im Kontext von Migration
Bd. 3, 2008, 312 S., 24,90 €, br., ISBN 978-3-8258-1294-2

Rudolf Pölzer
Kein Land des Übersetzens?
Studie zum österreichischen Übersetzungsmarkt 2000 – 2004
Bd. 2, 2007, 216 S., 19,90 €, br., ISBN 978-3-8258-9553-2

Michaela Wolf (ed.)
Übersetzen – Translating – Traduire
Towards a "Social Turn"?
Bd. 1, 2006, 368 S., 24,90 €, br., ISBN 3-8258-9552-1

LIT Verlag Berlin – Münster – Wien – Zürich – London
Auslieferung Deutschland / Österreich / Schweiz: siehe Impressumsseite